Public Broadcasting

and the

Public Interest

MEDIA, COMMUNICATION, AND CULTURE IN AMERICA

Michael C. Keith and Donald A. Fishman, Series Editors

WAVES OF RANCOR
Tuning in the Radical Right
Robert L. Hilliard and Michael C. Keith

SCREENED OUT
How the Media Control Us and What We Can Do About It
Carla Brooks Johnston

DISCONNECTED AMERICA
The Consequences of Mass Media in a Narcissistic World
Ed Shane

QUEER AIRWAVES
The Story of Gay and Lesbian Broadcasting
Phylis Johnson and Michael C. Keith

INVISIBLE STARS
A Social History of Women in American Broadcasting
Donna L. Halper

PUBLIC BROADCASTING AND THE PUBLIC INTEREST
*Michael P. McCauley, Eric E. Peterson, B. Lee Artz, and
DeeDee Halleck*

Public Broadcasting

and the

Public Interest

Michael P. McCauley,
Eric E. Peterson,
B. Lee Artz,
and DeeDee Halleck
Editors

M.E. Sharpe
Armonk, New York
London, England

Library of Congress Cataloging-in-Publication Data

Public broadcasting and the public interest / edited by Michael P. McCauley . . . [et al.].
    p. cm. — (Media, communication, and culture in America)
    Conference papers.
    Includes bibliographical references and index.
    ISBN 0-7656-0990-8 (alk. paper)
    1. Public broadcasting—United States. 2. Broadcasting policy—United States. 3. Public
interest—United States. 4. Political participation—United States. 5. Democracy—United
States. I. McCauley, Michael P., 1958– II. Series.

HE8700.8 .P824 2003
384.54′0973—dc21
                                                   2002070712

Contents

List of Tables and Figures

Tables

Figures

Series Foreword

Public radio and television are the premier broadcast services in America and have been for three decades. In an age when the majority of commercial radio stations program pop music and inane babble, and commercial television outlets air mind-numbing "sick-coms" and reality shows about dysfunctional households, public broadcasting has consistently offered intelligent and compelling features. It has kept the electronic media from drowning in the morass of fast-food audio and video spewed from the nearly 12,000 spot-driven signals on the radio and television bands. While commercial radio and television have had their share of shining moments in the post–World War II era, it has been public broadcasting that has upheld, and in many cases exceeded, the standards attained during radio's much heralded heyday of the 1930s and 1940s and television's golden age of the 1950s and 1960s, when creativity and innovation were allowed more than an occasional excursion into the ether. As the blanding of the commercial radio dial accelerates today due to rampant station consolidations and downsizings—the result of the elimination of ownership caps in 1996—the service that public radio provides its loyal audience becomes an even more precious commodity. This new book by Michael P. McCauley, Eric E. Peterson, B. Lee Artz, and DeeDee Halleck, an appropriate and valuable addition to the series, seeks to examine the unique role of electronic media in American society and culture. Moreover, it addresses issues central to public broadcasting's continued existence as a public trustee in an age when the government funding it relies on is rapidly diminishing and other new and evolving listening and viewing technologies, such as the Internet and direct broadcast satellite, compete with the traditional airwaves. In these insightful chapters, public broadcasting is carefully and thoughtfully examined and in the process its value as a communication medium is challenged, ratified, and confirmed yet again.

Michael Keith
Boston College

Foreword

Critics have been writing obituaries for U.S. public service broadcasting nearly from the moment of its inception. This is understandable. Public broadcasting as established in the United States was neither vibrant nor encompassing, but merely an obsequious appendage of what remained an overwhelmingly dominant corporate-commercial broadcasting system. With occasional exceptions, U.S. public broadcasting does not serve more than a small fraction of the community; does not provide space for a truly independent journalism nor, indeed, for an independent audiovisual culture more generally; and, in an era of carefully segmented audiences and targeted media, is ever more committed to reorganizing itself as merely another channel of the commercial sponsor system.

Why should we care?

Media systems are indispensable components of cognition and opinion-formation under contemporary conditions. The establishment of an accessible, accountable, and critical media system indeed remains a fundamental prerequisite of meaningful democratic decision-making. Article 19 of the Universal Declaration of Human Rights confirmed this fundamental freedom long ago: "Everyone has the right to freedom of opinion and expression; this right includes freedom to hold opinions without interference and to seek, receive and impart information and ideas through any media." Were this edict to be taken seriously, Americans would know far more than they do about their country's often perilous and unjust role in world affairs. Equally, they would be able to relate their own local experiences of injustice and inequality to those of others. That indeed is why we need—urgently—to create a true public service broadcasting.

The Internet is not going to solve this problem. Increasingly, the top-down development of a corporate-commercial Internet only compounds this democratic blockage.

The present volume, on the other hand, allows us to take a truly significant step in the right direction. It connects us to deep, careful thought as to what public broadcasting might be—and what, based on the historical record, it should not try to be. Difficult problems of finance, mission, and orientation are engaged by academic analysts and community media activists, both from the United States and beyond. Answers to such vital questions may not be expected to arrive on a platter; it is the process of discussion and debate itself that is fundamental. *Public Broadcasting and the Public Interest* is not another obituary, but rather the beginning labor in an urgently necessary project: the reclaiming and social redefinition of our media system.

Dan Schiller
Professor of Communications
Library and Information Science, and Media Studies
University of Illinois at Urbana-Champaign

Acknowledgments

The idea for this book began in the early fall of 1997, when Mike McCauley gave a public lecture at the University of Maine about the perceived "mainstreaming" of public radio content in the United States. Following the talk, four people came to the front of the room, each of them saying that "we really need to do a conference about this!" These four, Eric Peterson, Mike Howard, Amy Fried, and Nathan Godfried, joined McCauley on the planning committee for "Public Broadcasting and the Public Interest," the June 2000 conference for which this volume is named. Each of these people worked hard to attract paper submissions and featured speakers, and Eric Peterson deserves special thanks for handling seemingly hundreds of little problems that cropped up along the way.

Financial support for the conference came, first of all, in the form of a generous gift from the Florence and John Schumann Foundation and its president, Bill Moyers—a man who is deeply committed to bringing out the best in public broadcasting. Other support came from the Department of Communication and Journalism, the College of Liberal Arts and Sciences, and the Canadian American Center at the University of Maine; special thanks go to Dean Rebecca Eilers, who backed the project enthusiastically from the start. The Peace and Justice Center of Eastern Maine helped us bring Bob McChesney, Amy Goodman, and Jerry Starr on board as featured presenters, and in-kind services were provided by the Unitarian Universalist Society of Bangor and WERU-FM in East Orland, Maine. The Office of Communication, United Church of Christ was instrumental in helping us arrange an important presentation about microradio, and Sean Treglia and Michael Delli Carpini of the public policy program at the Pew Charitable Trusts provided another generous gift of funding late in the game.

Conference participants who effectively became members of the planning committee include Lee Artz, Ralph Engelman, Bill Hoynes, and Jerry Starr. Ralph Engelman receives special thanks for his tireless efforts in putting together an excellent panel on the various crises that then plagued the Pacifica radio network. Logistical support in Orono and Bangor was provided by Bruce Stinson, Dave Bagley, and the staffs of University of Maine Conference Services and Information Technologies; other assistance came from Mark McCafferty, Kristen Hurd, Sachiko Takase, Nancy Smith, Keir Peterson, Gordon Young, and Patricia Turcic. The entire editorial team owes a debt of gratitude to Judy McCauley-Groth and Sally McKinnon for arranging and hosting two large social gatherings that helped conference participants get to know one another much better. Indeed, Judy—who had other important things to do with her time—sometimes acted as a taxi service between the University of Maine campus and various places of lodging in Bangor!

The editors thank Michael Keith, Donald Fishman, Andrew Gyory, Henrietta Toth, and Esther Clark for their interest in publishing this volume and in making our experience with M.E. Sharpe a most pleasant one. Finally, the biggest kudos of all go to the more than sixty conference participants who either submitted and delivered papers, moderated sessions, or delivered keynote and plenary addresses. Virtually everyone left the conference with a smile on their face, having experienced a deep immersion in collective thought with some of the leading experts on public broadcasting in the United States, Canada, and other countries. This enthusiasm helped sustain the editors as they selected the best papers for presentation in this volume, and we hope the pages that follow will help readers feel the same level of engagement with the ideas and proposals contained therein.

Introduction

Michael P. McCauley, Eric E. Peterson, B. Lee Artz, and DeeDee Halleck

Rumors about the death of public service broadcasting (PSB) over the past few decades have been, quite thankfully, a bit premature. The British Broadcasting Corporation (BBC), America's Public Broadcasting System (PBS), and National Public Radio (NPR) and dozens of other noncommercial networks around the world are alive and kicking in spite of encroachment from commercial broadcasters and, not coincidentally, a great deal of related political pressure. These first two pressures are certainly exacerbated by the fact that most countries are poised on the brink of an explosion of channels, as new spectrum-efficient forms of digital broadcasting take hold.

Despite vital signs that are stable for now, many observers feel the prospects for the continued survival of PSB could well lessen with each passing year, unless something is done to better mediate the pressures of the marketplace. In his timely reader on global PSB, Marc Raboy (1997, 2) offers a succinct statement of the central question these broadcasters can expect to face: "What social and cultural goals attributed to broadcasting require a specially mandated, noncommercially driven organization [that is] publicly owned, publicly funded to the extent necessary, and publicly accountable?" To this, we may add two more questions: Is there a feasible way for public service broadcasters to accommodate the global advance of commercial media or to accept the notion that their organizations are now necessarily embedded within the context of commercialization? If so, how shall we conceptualize new media, including the Internet, in ways that maintain public service values?

When posing these questions, it is important to acknowledge that the existential dilemma public service broadcasters now face is but one subset of a larger dilemma faced by people in virtually every country, working in every imaginable field of endeavor. McChesney (1999, 78) notes that new digital communications technologies make it possible for firms in just about any industry to become players in global markets. From a purely selfish point of view, this practice offers a lucrative and cost-effective means of growing a business. The governments of nations with capitalist economies, operating in concert with the World Trade Organization, World Bank, and International Monetary Fund, support many efforts to boost the fortunes of transnational corporations. While the impulse to "go global" is legitimate beyond question for ambitious corporate executives, we may note that the globalization of capitalism brings riches to some but not to millions of others—Russia and Argentina being two dramatic cases in point. The Enron scandal in the United States illustrates this naked ambition for profit, unencumbered by the fact that the corporation's talent for hiding financial liabilities resulted in gains that were, at best, ill gotten. Company officials and their friends in government and industry—the ones who are reasonably safe from the long arm of the law—padded their bank accounts in various ways. Legions of devoted lower-level employees and ordinary investors outside the company took a heavy financial beating.

The world has yet to experience a crisis of similar magnitude from the pursuit of profit in the media industries, but lurking beneath the cover pages of corporate balance sheets are a number of important, if often opaque consequences. Since passage of the U.S. Telecommunications Act of 1996, most of the old limits on the number of broadcasting stations any one corporation could own have vanished. The resulting media landscape is one in which commercial megafirms have gobbled up smaller operations with unbelievable gusto (Campbell 2002; Croteau and Hoynes 2001; Starr 2000). Indeed, some liken this activity to a frenzied burst of commodities trading. The financial efficiency of these maneuvers, at least for the short term, is undeniable. For example, when a media giant buys six or seven radio stations in the same locality, the next thing that almost invariably happens is an immediate downsizing of on-air staff, especially news personnel and other announcers who work outside the normal hours of peak listening. These new station groups deliver outstanding service to the purveyors of consumer goods: they offer "one-stop shopping" for airtime and permit advertisers to reach six or seven tightly conceived niche audiences in the process. So far, so good, right? Unfortunately, these business decisions force listeners to pay an unexpected price. With a significantly reduced cadre of on-air personnel, the managers of commercial radio stations throughout the country typically feel free to increase the number of commercial messages they run each hour. Indeed, one new digital editing technology allows commercial programmers to speed up the voice of a deejay, newscaster, or talk show host while also finding and deleting any pauses or pockets of "dead air." By using this technology, station operators can theoretically trim actual program content by up to six minutes per hour—all in the pursuit of an extra few minutes for advertising (Rosenwein 2002; Kuczynski 2001).

The total amount of time that Americans spend listening to radio shrank by 12 percent from 1990 to 2000, partly because of the perception of heavier doses of commercials (Kuczynski 2001). This fact does not yet seem to concern the executives that run major radio groups. So long as reductions in audience size fail to result in lower advertising rates, these practices are likely to continue. And the impulse to wield the sword of managerial efficiency is not confined to radio companies. For years, Ben Bagdikian, author of *The Media Monopoly* (2000), has conducted a simple accounting of the number of firms that control the U.S. media—radio, TV, film, print publications, and other forms of mass communication. In 1983, the year his first edition was published, Bagdikian found that fifty corporations controlled the bulk of U.S. media; by 2000, that number had dropped to six. Although these media empires are likely to continue their global quest for smaller firms, further consolidation at the top seems to have given way to joint ventures with a handful of other international and regional giants—further concentrating production and distribution in the hands of the few.

It is one thing to note the unequal distribution of wealth that results from media consolidation and globalization, but these strategies also have important consequences for political systems that aspire to democracy. Increasingly, global media conglomerates offer easy-to-digest content that encourages ordinary citizens to make their way through an ever-changing array of human cultures by striving to avoid anxiety and, more importantly, any feelings or beliefs that would erode the impulse to buy consumer products. Reflecting on this phenomenon, Blumler and Hoffmann-Riem (1992, 206) wonder whether people who live in many contemporary societies will continue to settle for these media "snacks" instead of the more substantial haute cuisine that has often been provided by PSB. This analogy is, perhaps, best applied to the sphere of political communication.

> In democracies where measures of trends across recent election campaigns are available, the balance of admittedly mixed evidence suggests that, in multichannel conditions of commercialized competition for the attention of less politically engaged audiences, media coverage of politics is diminishing in amount, as well as becoming more "mediated," more focused on power tactics at the expense of issue substance, and more negative. (Blumler and Gurevitch 2001, 2)

In a world increasingly constituted by global media, people who choose not to exercise the information-gathering responsibilities of true citizens have every opportunity to find lots of predigested political pseudocontent and to experience it as a highly atomized branch of journalism we might call "news about me." If I don't like what I read in the *New York Times*, or see on PBS's *News Hour*, no problem! I can easily go to one of hundreds of specialized Internet sites or cable channels and find just the sort of content that supports my own cultural and political beliefs.

The process of consuming media products in this manner can be reassuring for people whose chief wish is never to grow or change, but the long-term political consequences of this behavior for the body politic are not good. We live in a global culture in which the ideal of hyperindividuality offered to us by the mass media is often mistaken for actual freedom in both political thought and cultural practice. This is a dangerous idea since it tends to reduce the efficacy of reasonably well-functioning media systems in rooting out political corruption and corporate malfeasance, when necessary, and in providing meaningful opportunities for human creativity in science, art, and other social and cultural spheres. Advertising-driven media also default in their responsibility to help ordinary citizens trust that the political system can actually be made to work for them, instead of on them. Hence, the value of adequately funded public service broadcasters whose operations are sufficiently insulated from undue corporate or political pressure. After all, if public broadcasters do not assume the mantle of educators, artists, journalists, and political watchdogs, which other broadcasters will?

Again, the global spread of commercial media puts strong obstacles in the way of people who attempt to forsake media "snacks" in favor of food that is nutritious and, in the long run, life-sustaining. This situation brings us to the central challenge of public service broadcasters today—how to reach significant groups of people who seem to be content with light, entertaining news and cultural fare and, instead, provide them with content that is attractive, thought-provoking, and more deserving of the citizens of a democracy. The challenge for noncommercial radio and television systems, and for those who would use the Internet for egalitarian purposes, is to become relevant to wider swaths of the overall population without compromising core principles of service in the public interest.

Theorizing the Public Interest in Broadcasting

The modern media of telecommunications can be of great value to people who insist on participating fully in the quest for a democratic society and polity.[1] Specifically, we may speak of three policy imperatives through which the media can narrow the gap between those who are variously advantaged, and disadvantaged, by the workings of their nation's political economy:

- Efforts to ensure that information about the political agenda, appropriate in level and form and accurately reflecting the best knowledge available, is easily and universally accessible to all citizens;
- Efforts to help citizens participate in a relevant way in political discussion;
- Efforts to ensure that citizens may exert influence on the selection of subjects on which mediated information is available. (adapted from Dahl 1989, 338–339)

These imperatives suggest a conceptualization of media audiences that Ien Ang calls *audience-as-public:*

The audience-as-public consists not of consumers, but of citizens who must be reformed, educated, informed as well as entertained—in short, "served"—presumably to enable them to better perform their democratic rights and duties. Within this context, broadcasting has nothing to do with the consumerist hedonism of [U.S. commercial broadcasting]. (1991, 28–29)

Though useful in a normative sense, the audience-as-public conception fails to account for the ways in which the news media have typically been structured in the United States. Ang's second conception of *audience-as-market* comes much closer to prevailing practice. In this view, the transfer of meaningful information to citizens is of secondary importance; the overriding goal is to make consumers aware of products or services and to pique their attention with highly entertaining programs. A particular bit of communication is considered effective as soon as audience members give their attention to it, regardless of civic impact (Ang 1991, 29; McQuail 1987).

We submit that this distinction between audience-as-public (citizens) and audience-as-market (consumers) is crucial to understanding the development and future transformation of public service broadcasting. In the paragraphs that follow, we offer three conceptions of normative media performance—a guide, if you will, to the strategies that broadcasters can use in making their systems more relevant (or not) to the cultivation of the noblest civic values.

The Public Service Approach

This model of media performance is fundamentally a broadcasting model, one that came into being in the first two decades of the twentieth century. The British government, which created the British Broadcasting Company in 1922, was its principal architect. When British engineers, lawmakers, and civil servants looked for information on broadcasting systems, they turned, naturally, to the emerging radio industry in the United States. But they promptly rejected the U.S. model of broadcasting for two reasons: the audio chaos that ensued from lax regulation of the electromagnetic spectrum and a fear of "commercialized" programs on the part of Britain's opinion-forming classes (Hearst 1992; Curran and Seaton 1991; Briggs 1985). These tastes and perceptions soon led to the development of public service radio, a form of broadcasting explicitly designed to serve the public good rather than private gain.

Advocates of the public service approach view "the public" as a superordinate entity composed of many social and cultural subgroups; they also feel the free market has failed to deliver the benefits that some of these subgroups have come to rightfully expect. Yet members of this public do not always make decisions that serve the greater good. Hence, the notion of guardianship—that government agencies must help decide what the greater good is and then find ways to protect it (McQuail 1987; Dahl 1989). The public service approach holds that all potential audience members should have access to media content, at least in terms of reception. Content should meet minimum standards of informational quality, such as impartiality, ideological balance, and avoidance of grossly bad taste. Further, the media have a special responsibility to help marginal groups communicate effectively with other sectors of the superordinate public (Blumler 1992; Gurevitch and Blumler 1990; Blumler, Brynin, and Nossiter 1986).

The public service broadcasters of Western Europe, with their ethic of comprehensive service, offer a good example of this approach. Unlike the U.S. situation, in which the public/commercial split implies a division of programming focus, European public broadcasters give their audiences a wide array of programming—"from *Dallas* . . . to Pavarotti," as one observer puts it. These broadcasting systems are pluralistic in terms of programs made, audiences served, and responsiveness to various social subgroups. As organs of their respective states, they are also politicized; each tends to safeguard the genres of news, current affairs, and political programming. Finally, public service broadcasters generally embody the value of anticommercialism, the notion that market forces should be kept at bay (Blumler 1992).

The public service approach is not without problems. For one thing, broadcasters that use it sometimes give off a strong scent of paternalism:

> public service broadcasting is explicitly conceived as an interventionist institutional practice: it should presumably contribute to the construction of "quality" citizens rather than merely catering to, and therefore reinforcing and reproducing, the already existing needs and wants of consumers.

> Succinctly, in classic public service philosophy the project of broadcasting is an "art of effects" aimed at reforming the audience. (Ang 1991, 102–103)

The BBC and other public service broadcasting systems operate, to some extent, on a foundation of guardianship and paternalism. This begs the question of "who guards the guardian?" Indeed, the BBC has never been immune to influence from the British government, the military, and the market: it learned how to censor antigovernment news during the general strike of 1926; how to transmit the government's propaganda and "attitude management" messages during World War II; and, eventually, how to secure bigger audiences through the provision of light entertainment programs (Seaton 1991).

Readers who are most familiar with U.S. public radio and television will note that the brand of public service broadcasting described above is different from the kind offered by NPR, PBS, and the Corporation for Public Broadcasting. Precise details about these differences are spelled out adequately in the chapters that follow; suffice it to say that a history of funding through license fees and sizable government appropriations is one of the major factors that distinguishes the British model of PSB from the one found in America. Federal support now makes up a relatively small portion of the funding mix for U.S. public broadcasting. This limited support is good, in a sense, as it effectively removes the specter of past threats from Washington to send the industry to the poorhouse, should it fail to tread lightly in the area of controversial social programming. On the other hand, NPR and PBS have learned to program for the tastes of individual donors and corporate sponsors who, for the most part, are based in the middle- to upper-middle-class sectors of society. Relative independence from the federal government was first a boon for public broadcasters, but that achievement has also forced noncommercial radio and TV managers to learn the tools of niche marketing. In this instance, finding the right niche has meant the crafting of program schedules to serve a relatively small audience that is well educated, well compensated, and mostly white.

The Commercial Approach

Most theorists of media and democracy agree that the public service broadcasting approach offers a better pathway to a healthy polis than the operating model used by commercial broadcasters. The commercial approach that now prevails in the United States has a long history in other parts of the Western world. It is now widely regarded as the main legitimating principle for print media (and, increasingly, for broadcast media) in liberal democracies. Fundamentally, it holds that an individual should be free to publish what he or she likes, because free and public expression is the best way to arrive at the truth. The rhetoric of the commercial approach holds that consumers have a great deal of control over radio and TV programming. Broadcasters maximize their profitability by offering programs they believe most consumers will desire; therefore, the broadcasters who attract the most listeners or viewers are those who best satisfy the public interest. In theory, the commercial approach also holds that our news media should serve as useful sources of information about happenings in the world outside the home nation and as watchdogs against corruption or tyranny in government (Croteau and Hoynes 1994; Fowler and Brenner 1982; U.S. Federal 1984).

It would be difficult for a reasonable person to disagree with these statements, yet efforts to put them into practice have met with considerable difficulty. This difficulty has much to do with the institutional forms that press organizations have assumed in the Western world. Specifically, press freedom has become identified with property rights or, specifically, the right to own and use means of publication free from government interference. The consequences of this view have been noted frequently by critical communication scholars. First of all, we may note that the oligopolies that dominate Western media actually reduce audience choice and consumer control (McQuail 1987; Hoynes 1994; Croteau and Hoynes 1994). Commercial media companies offer quantitative audience ratings as proof of their attentiveness to certain audience segments, yet, as Blumler, Brynin, and Nossiter (1986, 357, 358) tell us, ratings say nothing about the *intensity* of an audience's attraction to certain programs. These authors also point out that the audiences of commercial broadcasters cannot actually demand a program; they "can only accept or reject a program after it has been shown." Indeed, some leading proponents of the commercial approach claim that audiences have little or no constitutional right of access to broadcast messages. The primary rights, they argue, lie with broadcasters whose interests in media properties must remain unfettered by demands for any particular kind of content (Fowler and Brenner 1982; Kelley and Donway 1990).

Another criticism of commercial broadcasting is that the rising capitalization of the industry restricts entry into the market. Critical media scholars also tend to dismiss the notion that commercial media typically serve as watchdogs for the public or as primary purveyors of information useful to all citizens (Curran 1991; Croteau and Hoynes 1994). In the commercial approach, the public is conceived as a mass audience, "an aggregate of potential consumers with a known social-economic profile at which a medium or message is directed" (McQuail 1987, 221). This approach offers an economistic pathway to the fulfillment of democratic values; theoretically, it allows no room for regulators or other government authorities to influence the shape of media content.

In terms of diversity, the commercial approach holds that content should reflect the interests of society's mainstream. Further, content diversity should be judged across all media; in other words, it is all right for any one station to offer a narrow range of programs, so long as other kinds of content are available elsewhere. One important premise that undergirds this approach, but seldom appears in conversations about it, is the notion that commercial media depend on the maintenance of a strong consumer ethic. In this view, audiences fulfill their roles in the democratic process of communication by continuing to purchase the consumer goods featured in print and broadcast advertisements (Czitrom 1982; Hurwitz 1988).

The Public Sphere Approach

Scholars who fear the global commercialization of media typically seek to preserve traditional public service values in the broadcasting systems of their own countries, while also moving beyond the model offered by the BBC, in some respects. Some of these scholars have developed a body of normative broadcasting theory that has been applied to real-world organizations only in small fits and starts. The importance of this general approach lies in the potential for public communication to serve as a model of societal integration, one that would value citizenship over consumerism. We can trace the contours of this approach to the early career of Jurgen Habermas, a political philosopher who, in the mid-1950s, became part of the famous Institute of Social Research in Frankfurt, Germany. Habermas was fascinated with "the pathology of modernity" and astonished by the way that businesses in Western countries seemed able to cultivate consumer demand.

In his first major book, Habermas outlined the notion of a "bourgeois public sphere" in eighteenth-century Europe, a sense of public space that developed with the advent of entrepreneurial capitalism. Meeting in coffeehouses, political clubs, and salons, the earliest entrepreneurs discussed newspapers and books, engaged in political debate, and criticized the authority of the state (Habermas 1962/1989, 22–31).[2] Unfortunately, this public sphere did not last very long. State censorship and other factors diminished free public debate in the late nineteenth century. Interest in book culture and politics declined, and the physical space of the public sphere also deteriorated with the advent of private transportation in the twentieth century and the resulting development of suburbs and shopping malls. The function of public opinion formation gradually passed from the realm of coffeehouse discussions and into the offices of opinion managers. Indeed, Habermas contends that public relations has become a major force in the creation of legitimacy for the institutions of capitalist societies. He says this transformation has produced a public realm in which organizations and governments create "spectacles" for largely passive audiences, along with the illusion that the general public is made up of skeptical citizens who freely form their own opinions (Habermas 1962/1989, 193–195).

The nation whose media system now embodies the greatest number of public sphere values is the Netherlands. McQuail (1992a) ties these values to the overall context of social pillarization in that country during the late nineteenth and early twentieth centuries. Pillarization is the vertical stratification of social structures around communities of interest, including church groups, political parties, trade unions, schools, and women's organizations. This system "divided the population along the lines of *value systems*" and "promoted peaceful co-existence and cooperation between the diverse pillars," thus neutralizing "the disruptive effects of class conflict and class struggle" (Ang 1991, 122). Ideally, the Dutch broadcasting system is open to all social groups that can demonstrate a sufficient degree of popular support (McQuail 1992b). Some contemporary Dutch broadcasters have come to resemble commercial media outlets, according to Ang (1991, 122). In her view, however, "powerful remnants of the pillarized tradition still live on" in the Netherlands, especially at the institutional level.

In the United States, the public sphere tradition is best embodied by Pacifica Radio—the broadcast arm of a larger foundation established in 1946 by pacifist Lewis Hill and his colleagues (Lasar 2000; Engelman 1995). The charter of the Pacifica Foundation lays out the mandate:

> To engage in any activity that shall contribute to a lasting understanding between nations, races, creeds and colors; to gather and disseminate information on the causes of conflict between any and all of such groups; and through any and all means available to this society to promote the study of political and economic problems, and the causes of religious, philosophical and racial antagonisms. (quoted in Trufelman 1979, 28)

The Pacifica network, one of the pillars of American community broadcasting, was designed as an alternative to the commercialism of mainstream radio and to the most timid and conservative sectors of educational radio. Moving beyond public "service" broadcasting, Pacifica represents broadcasting *by the public*— at least as represented by community groups and social movements. As William Barlow puts it, Pacifica stations and other community broadcasters "use the airways to promote community dialogue and to present audio evidence in support of movements for progressive social change. They seek to democratize non-commercial radio in the U.S." (1988, 101).[3]

In theoretical terms, the public sphere approach supports a collection of minipublics that must be maintained and protected in the face of efforts to assimilate them into any superordinate group. In this conception of democracy, the media (and other public institutions) dissolve as many distinctions as possible between society's economically advantaged members and those who are disadvantaged in that regard. Advocates of the public sphere approach believe that all individuals should be able to both send and receive media messages. They contend that any simple provision of multicultural programming will not suffice; rather, they argue that the media should provide methods through which shifting combinations of small-scale subcultural interests can express themselves (McQuail 1987; see also Dahl 1989).

The public sphere approach is most distinctive in the way its proponents seek to achieve normative goals. It calls for a negotiation of social order between competing interests—a negotiation facilitated by the media. Advocates of this approach also favor some form of social ownership, so that certain media outlets can be kept free of commercial or market influences. Another key element is the explicit use of the political communication process to stimulate citizen participation. This change might occur through public participation in the agenda-building process within newsrooms; it could also happen if ordinary citizens were better able to produce media content themselves (Hoynes 1994).

The most resolute model of the public sphere approach is articulated by those who advocate democratic, participatory communication. They include Pacifica Radio and community radio broadcasters in the United States, community radio (CORADEP) during the Sandinista years in Nicaragua (Artz 1994), and affiliates of the Association of World Community Radio Broadcasters (AMARC). These organizations embody calls for direct public participation in the production of programming—citizens speaking in their own voices and on their own shows, in all of their diversity. Yet beyond the Pacifica network and community radio in the United States, broadcasting in the Netherlands, and the German broadcasting system—with its decentralized structure and autonomous broadcasting policies for various regions—public broadcasting that follows the public sphere model is limited. For most of the Western world, this approach remains more an ideal than a reality (McQuail 1992b; Hoffmann-Riem 1992).

Solutions, Anyone?

Given the encroachments that commercial media, and the entirety of commercial culture, have made upon the field of public service broadcasting, how should those interested in ensuring a better future proceed? How can we maintain the public service values that now inhere in noncommercial media and extend them into a newly constituted public sphere of electronic communication—in a way that maintains a sharp distinction with respect to commercial broadcasting? And how can we ensure that the values people most cherish about PSB and other participatory media models are also applied to significant portions of the Internet? These are the questions that motivate the authors of the chapters that follow. These authors have all sparked, at one time or another, to the concerns and beliefs that formed the basis of a conference titled "Public Broadcasting and the Public Interest" in the summer of 2000: that examinations of public broadcasting should be broadly cross-disciplinary and cross-cultural, and that any significant investigations of the field should balance the participation of academics, media practitioners, and activists. We believe this book is proof positive of the willingness of those who care most about public broadcasting to engage one another in thoughtful dialogue about the industry's future.

The prescriptions for change found throughout the book vary widely, but tend to follow four major themes. Several authors insist that future conceptions of "public" broadcasting must make room for the participation of multiple publics, not just the relatively privileged class of people that have traditionally been courted by the managers of noncommercial stations. Some describe the frustratingly slow process of creating virtual communities of interest on the Internet, yet most of them hold out hope that parts of the new digital landscape will be cultivated with public service values in mind. A few authors contemplate—over the protests of others—the possibility that some public broadcasters can find ways to enter limited commercial endeavors, so long as the proceeds are used to support their original normative missions. Finally, some of our contributors hold the view that those who benefit most from the gift of free frequency allocations—commercial broadcasters—will someday be made to pay a portion of their profits into trust funds that would support noncommercial media for decades to come.

Robert McChesney (1999, 1998) has often repeated the sobering truth that if today's broadcasting media are ever to serve the interests of multiple, diverse publics, their transformation will necessarily be a part of a much wider movement to demand progressive change on the societal level. For some would-be media activists, the task of "changing the world" seems daunting. However, the authors whose work appears in this volume encourage media activists to continue to take steps (small or otherwise) toward the end goal of progressive social change. Small is definitely beautiful when it comes to projects like these, which include the forging of partnerships between public broadcasters and local civic groups, the mastering of new broadcasting technologies to better serve disenfranchised audiences, and new linkages between practitioners of community radio and public access television.

Technologies now exist for the delivery of listener-driven programs via small-scale, community-oriented media—the type of content one could never expect from commercial media. And efforts to reform the finances of public service broadcasting are critically important for the maintenance of spaces on the radio and TV dial where the sale of consumer products is not the ultimate goal. In sum, those people who treasure public service broadcasting enough to fight for its long-term health must keep moving forward, simply putting one foot in front of the other and taking care not to be overawed by the entire gamut of necessary reforms. The more that individuals and small groups of people are able to do this, the more likely it is that public service broadcasting, other, more participatory media, and Webcasting will be at the service of those who consider themselves citizens, rather than consumers. It is our humble hope that this book will inspire people to take media reform more seriously and to begin working in earnest toward systems of noncommercial broadcasting that truly represent the interests of all citizens.

Notes

1. The following analysis is adapted, with permission, from a lengthier theoretical treatment in M. McCauley, "National Public Radio: Maintaining Mission in the Marketplace," in *Citizenship and Participation in the Information Age*, ed. M. Pendakur and R. Harris (Toronto: Garamond Press, 2002).

2. Criticisms of the public sphere concept have been many and varied. The most telling of these critiques notes that the bourgeois public sphere Habermas writes about is quite exclusionary when it comes to the interests of women and other traditionally subordinate groups. Still, Habermas, his intellectual allies, and many of his critics maintain the value of the public sphere ideal as a normative guidepost for communication in a democratic society (see Fraser 1992; Habermas 1992; Garnham 1992; Garnham 1995; Keane 1995; Meehan 1995).

3. The Pacifica vision has never been free of internal problems; indeed, struggles between factions that hold competing visions for the network nearly killed it on the eve of the new millennium. For more details, see Matthew Lasar's chapter in the first section of this book.

References

Ang, I. 1991. *Desperately Seeking the Audience.* London: Routledge.

Artz, B. 1994. "Communication and Power: Popular Radio in Nicaragua." *Journal of Radio Studies* 2: 205–228.

Bagdikian, B. 2000. *The Media Monopoly.* 6th ed. Boston: Beacon Press.

Barlow, W. 1988. "Community Radio in the U.S.: The Struggle for a Democratic Medium." *Media, Culture and Society* 10: 101.

Blumler, J. 1992. "Public Service Broadcasting Before the Commercial Deluge." In *Television and the Public Interest: Vulnerable Values in West European Broadcasting*, ed. J. Blumler. London: Sage, 7–21.

Blumler, J., and M. Gurevitch. 2001. "The New Media and Our Political Communication Discontents: Democratizing Cyberspace." *Information Communication & Society* 4, no. 1: 1–13.

Blumler, J., and W. Hoffmann-Riem. 1992. "New Roles for Public Service Television." In *Television and the Public Interest: Vulnerable Values in West European Broadcasting*, ed. J. Blumler. London: Sage, 202–217.

Blumler, J., M. Brynin, and T. Nossiter. 1986. "Broadcasting Finance and Programme Quality: An International Review." *European Journal of Communication* 1: 343–364.

Briggs, A. 1985. *The BBC: The First Fifty Years*. New York: Oxford University Press.

Campbell, R. 2002. *Media and Culture: An Introduction to Mass Communication*. 3d ed. Boston: Bedford/St. Martin's.

Croteau, D., and W. Hoynes. 1994. *By Invitation Only: How the Media Limit Political Debate*. Monroe, ME: Common Courage Press.

———. 2001. *The Business of Media: Corporate Media and the Public Interest*. Thousand Oaks, CA: Pine Forge Press.

Curran, J. 1991. "Mass Media and Democracy: A Reappraisal." In *Mass Media and Society*, ed. J. Curran and M. Gurevitch. London: Arnold, 82–117.

Curran, J., and J. Seaton, eds. 1991. *Power Without Responsibility: The Press and Broadcasting in Britain*. 4th ed. London: Routledge.

Czitrom, D. 1982. *Media and the American Mind: From Morse to McLuhan*. Chapel Hill: University of North Carolina Press.

Dahl, R. 1989. *Democracy and Its Critics*. New Haven, CT: Yale University Press.

Engelman, R. 1995. *Public Radio and Television in America: A Political History*. Thousand Oaks, CA: Sage.

Fowler, M., and D. Brenner. 1982. "A Marketplace Approach to Broadcast Regulation." *Texas Law Review* 60, no. 2: 207–257.

Fraser, N. 1992. "Rethinking the Public Sphere: A Contribution to the Critique of Actually Existing Democracy." In *Habermas and the Public Sphere*, ed. C. Calhoun. Cambridge, MA: MIT Press, 109–142.

Garnham, Nicholas. 1992. "The Media and the Public Sphere." In *Habermas and the Public Sphere*, ed. C. Calhoun. Cambridge, MA: MIT Press, 359–376.

Gurevitch, M., and J. Blumler. 1990. "Political Communication Systems and Democratic Values." In *Democracy and the Mass Media*, ed. J. Lichtenberg. Cambridge: Cambridge University Press, 269–289.

Habermas, J. 1962/1989. *The Structural Transformation of the Public Sphere*. Cambridge, MA: MIT Press.

———. 1992. "Further Reflections on the Public Sphere." In *Habermas and the Public Sphere*, ed. C. Calhoun. Cambridge, MA: MIT Press, 421–461.

Hearst, S. 1992. "Broadcasting Regulation in Britain." In *Television and the Public Interest: Vulnerable Values in West European Broadcasting*, ed. J. Blumler. London: Sage, 61–78.

Hoffmann-Riem, W. 1992. "Protecting Vulnerable Values in the German Broadcasting Order." In *Television and the Public Interest: Vulnerable Values in West European Broadcasting*, ed. J. Blumler. London: Sage, 43–60.

Hoynes, W. 1994. *Public Television for Sale: Media, the Market, and the Public Sphere*. Boulder, CO: Westview Press.

Hurwitz, D. 1988. "Market Research and the Study of the U.S. Radio Audience." *Communication* 10: 223–241.

Keane, John. 1995. "Structural Transformations of the Public Sphere." *Communication Review* 1, no. 1: 1–22.

Kelley, D., and R. Donway. 1990. "Liberalism and Free Speech." In *Democracy and Mass Media*, ed. J. Lichtenberg. Cambridge: Cambridge University Press, 66–101.

Kuczynski, A. 2001. "Radio Squeezes Empty Air Space for Profit." *New York Times*, January 6, 2000, A1. Reprinted with permission of author in *Living in the Information Age: A New Media Reader*, ed. E. Bucy. Belmont, CA: Wadsworth, 72–75.

Lasar, M. 2000. *Pacifica Radio: The Rise of an Alternative Network.* Updated ed. Philadelphia: Temple University Press.

McChesney, R. 1998. "The Political Economy of Global Communication." In *Capitalism and the Information Age: The Political Economy of the Global Communication Revolution*, ed. R. McChesney, E. Wood, and J. Foster. New York: Monthly Review Press, 1–26.

———. 1999. *Rich Media, Poor Democracy: Communication Politics in Dubious Times.* Urbana: University of Illinois Press.

McQuail, D. 1987. *Mass Communication Theory: An Introduction.* London: Sage.

———. 1992a. "The Netherlands: Safeguarding Freedom and Diversity under Multi-channel Conditions." In *Television and the Public Interest: Vulnerable Values in West European Broadcasting*, ed. J. Blumler. London: Sage, 96–111.

———. 1992b. *Media Performance: Mass Communication and the Public Interest.* London: Sage.

Meehan, J. 1995. "Introduction." In *Feminists Read Habermas: Gendering the Subject of Discourse*, ed. J. Meehan. New York: Routledge.

Raboy, M., ed. 1997. *Public Broadcasting for the 21st Century.* Luton, U.K.: University of Luton Press.

Rosenwein, R. 2002. "Trafficking in News." *Brill's Content*, July/August 1999, 95–97. Reprinted with permission of author in *Readings in Mass Communication: Media Literacy and Culture*, ed. K. Massey, 2d ed. Boston: McGraw-Hill, 179–184.

Seaton, J. 1991. "Part II: Broadcasting History." In *Power Without Responsibility: The Press and Broadcasting in Britain*, ed. J. Curran and J. Seaton, 4th ed. London: Routledge, 131–211.

Starr, J. 2000. *Air Wars: The Fight to Reclaim Public Broadcasting.* Boston: Beacon Press.

Trufelman, L. 1979. "The Missing Chapter: Pacifica Radio." *Public Telecommunications Review* 7, no. 5: 27–33.

U.S. Federal Communications Commission. 1984. "Notice of Inquiry and Proposed Rulemaking in the Matter of Deregulation of Radio." 73 FCC 2d 457, September 27, 1984. In *Documents of American Broadcasting*, ed. F.J. Kahn, 4th ed. Englewood Cliffs, NJ: Prentice Hall, 368–385.

Part I

Defining the Public Media Terrain

1

Introduction

B. Lee Artz

The Public and Its Definition

The debate over the future of public broadcasting in the United States and elsewhere is complicated by the questionable legitimacy of the term "public." Identifying the will of the public and how it will be represented has always been a central challenge for societies aspiring or claiming to be democratic. In order to decide broadcasting practices in a multicultural democratic society, coming to grips with what we mean by the public is absolutely essential because at heart of the controversy is a disagreement over what the public is, what it wants, and how media technology should be used. Although not all of the chapters here directly address these questions, most recognize the background of analytical difficulty and political controversy surrounding any definition of the public.

In media reports and social commentary, "public" often appears as a singular noun as well as a singular symbolic and political entity, synonymous with "the people"—another elusive, amorphous term of questionable analytical value. In its most relevant usage as an adjective—used frequently in the chapters that follow—"public" stands in contradistinction to "private," with public indicating a service accessible to all or a space open to all, whereas private signals some manner of privileged exclusivity in intent or purpose and limited access. Yet, beyond clarifying accessibility to a site or resource, the term "public" has little purchase as a definer of actual people, providing obfuscation for political propagandists and a lack of clarity for public media advocates and practitioners. In the United States, for instance, the will of the public is often presumed to be singularly represented by orchestrated opinion polls, consumer purchases, or bipartisan elections, which regularly involve less than 25 percent of the "public." For public broadcasters, National Public Radio (NPR), and the Public Broadcasting System (PBS), the "public" refers to an assiduously constructed demographic of audience donors—largely white, urban professionals . . . not too young and not too liberal—a demographic unrepresentative of the broadcast signal area's actual public, which is largely young, working-class, and ethnically diverse. Observations about the validity of the term and concept of "public" are by no means profound, but are nonetheless quite frequently ignored or dismissed. We all seem to know what we are talking about, but therein lies the problem: the terrain on which we walk is familiar, but still unknown.

The public, of course, is not singular in its constitution. The public is amorphous, diverse, a collection of entities with multiple, often conflicting interests, experiences, tastes, and concerns. Indeed, we might better speak of multiple publics because the public (in the United States and elsewhere) is a complicated patchwork of ethnicity, gender, age, religion, culture, and other social conditions and experiences. Certainly the U.S. public lives within an identifiable dominant culture of Christianity, capitalism, baseball, and other recognizably shared practices and perspectives, but each public still has multiple variations. One marker that might give some legitimacy to the term "public" is social class, because the overwhelming majority of people—of whatever ethnicity, gender, age, religious belief, or pastime preference—work for a wage, own little more than personal property, depend on public institutions, and aspire to a secure, comfortable life. Ironically, this broad commonality justifying some use of the word "public" is the one corporate advertisers, politicians, and the media most often seek to avoid. Conceptualizing a generalized, classless public discounts differences within the actual public, disguising the shared social, cultural, and economic inequalities within that public. Of course, this classless public is anything but according to the vision promoted by programmers, producers, advertisers, and public media fund-raisers who collectively articulate a distinction of taste drawn from professional middle-class sensibilities, concerns, and buying habits—all passed off as representative of the "public." While the public appears as an amalgam of demographic markets and consumers to commercial and public broadcasters, the public appears to political aspirants as little more than a voiceless mass in need of charismatic representatives who might speak on behalf of its interests.

The new legions of corporate deregulators and privatizers have further undermined what little representational validity the concept of "public" once had by arguing that the public (as a collection of consumers) is best served by private institutions (as sellers of commodities). From Sacramento to New

York, public officials eagerly sell the naming rights of public parks and buildings to corporate "signers." From elementary schools to public universities, administrators offer exclusive retailing deals to soft-drink manufacturers, telecommunications and content providers, and sportswear giants. The corporate malling of retail space has become wholesale corporate mauling of public space—each commercial encroachment erodes the accessible space for public discourse for all of the multiple constituents of the public. Such privatization also undermines the publicly enacted social and cultural practices, including the expectation and execution of public discourse and debate. Abolishing public space and commodifying communication serves the public only if the public signifies a collection of consumer-spectators—like so many potatoes in a sack waiting to be delivered to the appropriate advertiser, including, on occasion, PBS, as William Hoynes details in his contribution to this volume.

Briefly stated, the problem of defining the public and providing a means for its participation in the affairs of humanity remains crucial to the democratic vitality of any society and must be continually addressed. Yet a more urgent problem confronts us: sites for public discussion and debate are fast disappearing as the almost total deregulation of media and other industries has unleashed a rampage of privatization and commercialization of public space everywhere. Initial and incomplete answers regarding the character and activity of the public must suffice to guide us while we defend the right and opportunity of all publics to participate in decision-making and meaning-making, including full access to media production and distribution.

The Public and Its Media

A corollary to the problem of defining the public appears in the various characterizations of public media, public service media, or public access media. Early North American public broadcasting advocates espoused a vision of educational, noncommercial public service broadcasting, indicating their shared understanding that mass communication could be used to educate the public. This public service model represents the views of the public articulated by Walter Lippmann, John Dewey, and other public intellectuals of the time: the public needed education, leadership, socialization. Well-intentioned, this public service model nonetheless leaves the public largely on the receiving end of broadcasting, subject to the goodwill and intentions of public servants. This is perhaps the most interesting omission in the rhetoric of public broadcasters and their critics, including communication researchers who usually insist that communication means interaction. Even current media use of technology (which cultural theorist Raymond Williams insisted be called broadcasting, not mass communication) allows for increased access to production and transmission by public groups, especially given the increase in spectrum availability, low-power FM broadcasting, and satellite and cable innovations.

Undoubtedly, this observation on absent public-community agents in production, programming, and transmission is recognized by each of the contributors to this text, although not all foreground public access and participation, and several appear to accept the premises of public "service" broadcasting codified in the 1967 Carnegie Commission report. Nonetheless, mere aid-without-development undermines participation and creates dependencies, while the availability of media reception without access to media production stunts citizen participation and democracy.

Presenting the Arguments

In his University of Maine conference keynote address, "Public Broadcasting: Past, Present, and Future," reprinted here, Robert McChesney echoes the public service model perspective in his account of the history of public broadcasting in the United States. Referring to public service media in other countries, McChesney offers the examples of *All in the Family* and popular sports programming as the kind of public service broadcasting that could coexist with commercial broadcasting if government institutions were more responsive to public service perspectives. Of course, questions remain about the efficacy of a public media system that leaves programming decisions in the hands of public service administrators, rather than the citizens themselves. As McChesney notes, it isn't broadcasting personnel, but rather the institutional structure that handicaps public broadcasting.

Perhaps more importantly, McChesney unpacks the shifting arguments against all forms of public media—from shortage of spectrum to multiplicity of channels, from the public media's elite audience to their lack of popular appeal, from the information superhighway to the declining need for public media in the digital age. He points out that all media technology and its social use depend on political policy. McChesney's call for an organized social movement for public media is underscored by what happens when media policies are decided according to government and corporate interests. The 1934 Federal Communications Commission (FCC) turned the airwaves over to commercial broadcasters; the 1996 Telecommunications Act further deregulates broadcasting and awards all new spectrum to commercial media. Today, U.S.-led free market globalization pushes the privatization, commercialization, entertainment media agenda, short-circuiting the potential for public service broadcasting and public access to media production in general.

The disturbing details of media globalization are addressed by Vincent Mosco in his essay, "Brand New World? Globalization, Cyberspace, and the Politics of Convergence." Mosco's thorough dissection of the myths of cyberspace and globalization lays bare the threat to public media in the digital age. Even as the Internet and other forms of telecommunication face no public service responsibility, media mythmakers trumpet that cyberspace will expand democracy and public discourse in the realm of modems and fiber optics. Why fret about the declining public sphere when a "virtual" public is conveniently located just a click away? Ironically, the discourse about a virtual public approximates the substance of media conceptions of the public today: it is ubiquitous without location, has no decision-making expression other than consumption, and has no collective, independent, political voice. In fact, shifting the terrain of the public to cyberspace does not transform the public and its access to communication so much as it transforms communication into one more commodity available for sale to the atomized component parts of the virtual public. As Mosco notes, this virtual public is safely ensconced far from decision-making on production and resource allocation—which is left to private and government representatives (whose rendering of public service runs toward meeting the needs of the consumer). In short, the commodification of communication wrought by telecommunications convergence encroaches on the public terrain of communication, depoliticizing the public. We might add that commodification of communication also "depublics" politics and communication, restricting public participation in the production of communication and democratic decision-making.

The spreading commodification of everyday life also subverts the functioning of public service broadcasting, as William Hoynes documents in "The PBS Brand and the Merchandising of Public Service." Hoynes identifies the changes that accrue to public service broadcasting in an era of deregulation and privatization. Gone is the call for public broadcasting as a forum for debate. Gone too is the call for public broadcasting as an outlet for diverse community voices. In its place we have public service as a particular "brand" of broadcasting marketed to the media consumer. Accepting the discourse of marketing and advertising, PBS has adopted the branding model of corporate media. From "Arthur" dolls and "Doo-Wop '50s" CDs to mugs, calendars, and program videos, PBS has entered the world of corporate synergy. PBS as a network seeks to "brand" itself as a particular kind of media commodity, characterized by educational programming for children, upscale music and theater performances for the culturally inclined, and nature, travel, and history documentaries for the educated. Hoynes concludes,

> As PBS becomes more integrated into the commercial media system and
> develops a business model that sees public television as an increasingly

commercial enterprise, the foundations of the public service model are deteriorating. Indeed, the branding strategy is an attempt to turn the cultural value of the old PBS into financial value for the new PBS. This exchange is a means of transforming public service, and the trust that accompanies such public service, into a marketable commodity.

Clearer evidence of the outcome of commodification of the media would be difficult to find.

Hoynes does not highlight it thus, but the shortcomings of public service broadcasting are also apparent in PBS's branding campaign. The public may or may not be served, entertained, or educated, but confined to spectatorship, the public is prohibited from producing a truly public media, *for* and *by* the public and its constituent parts. Without any control or influence over production of programming, the public (however constructed) remains a voiceless, amorphous mass, relying on public interest advocacy groups to influence the public service broadcasters. The commercialization of public service broadcasting pushes the public even further away—its preferences and interests can be registered only through purchases of commodities that represent public broadcasting programs.

Robert Avery and Alan Stavitsky further clarify these dichotomous models of public broadcasting in "The FCC and the Public Interest: A Selective Critique of U.S. Telecommunications Policy-Making." Upon reviewing representative documents from the FCC and public broadcasting advocates, Avery and Stavitsky discovered two distinct perspectives. One relies on an "instrumental" view of public broadcasting and favors a marketplace model; in contrast, the "educational" view of public media adopts a trusteeship model. Since the 1980s, deregulation and competition have been the watchwords for those who believe that the public speaks most clearly at the check-out counter, insisting that public interest is best served if public broadcasters offer their wares as commodities in the marketplace of media choices. Public service advocates respond that public interest can be protected only by noncommercial institutions that would ensure diversity of programming, enrich the cultural life of the masses, and reflect the interests of minority groups. As Avery and Stavitsky argue, this is no idle debate: if the FCC and Congress accept the language and perspectives of the marketplace model, public broadcasting will suffer and ultimately die. They conclude that "[i]f public broadcasting is to survive in this country, it must have the freedom to abandon the competitive strategies that have been imposed by the values of the commercial marketplace. . . . What is needed above all is a citizens' movement that can reenergize the role of the public in public broadcasting."

The final chapter in this section reports on the kind of citizen's movement that is necessary to keep the public in public media. Matthew Lasar recounts the raid on Pacifica radio and the organized national movement defending community-access broadcasting in "Pacifica Radio's Crisis of Containment." This story is a fitting conclusion to this section as it provides a glimpse into the political issues at stake and the leading role that democratic media activists must take in media production and in media reform. The key here is participation. Unlike public service broadcasters affiliated with NPR or PBS, Pacifica radio exists not only as a form of listener-sponsored media, but more importantly as *listener-directed* media with local community boards, community programming, and (just recently) a national board elected in part by listeners and producers. Pacifica, despite its recent difficulties and future challenges, may be the best model for public broadcasting—surpassing both the marketplace and trusteeship model—because it places the public where it belongs: behind the microphone, in the producer's seat.

Making the Media Terrain Public

In their totality, the chapters in this section demonstrate that public service and public interest must give way to the public. Ultimately, public broadcasting can serve the public and meet the public interest only if the public, in all of its diversity, speaks for itself. Over mountains, valleys, and rivers to farmhouses, high-rises, and bungalows, the public media terrain will not be truly democratic until the public participates in producing its own media.

2

Public Broadcasting

Past, Present, and Future

Robert W. McChesney

I think there's a general sense that public broadcasting is in turmoil, in crisis, and its future is very unclear.* That's really what I want to talk about, ways to think about our past and our present that might guide us to a future where we'll have a media system broadly, and a broadcasting system specifically, that we can be proud of, that will do the necessary things we need to have done in a democracy.

Conventional wisdom holds that public service broadcasting is justified because of the physical scarcity of the airwaves. That's the reason we don't have public service newspapers or magazines. It's unnecessary there because anybody can start a newspaper or magazine if they want. But since the airwaves were a scarce resource, and there could be only a handful of broadcasters in a given community, it would be unfair to turn those over to private interests to capitalize upon. It was only proper that the government retain some of them and operate a public service system in the interest of the general public. That was the rationale for why we had public service broadcasting develop globally, not just in the United States. Public service broadcasting in this climate became a well-meaning but largely elitist attempt to ram unpopular programming down people's throats. That, too, is the conventional wisdom.

Now, conventional wisdom tells us that with the rise of multichannel television, with the rise of the Internet, with the "end of scarcity," there's no more need for public service broadcasting. After all, even the most minute

---

*This chapter is an edited version of the keynote address delivered at the Public Broadcasting and Public Interest conference, University of Maine, June 17, 2000.

need can be met on the Internet, if not on cable television with 500 channels. So apparently the justification for public service broadcasting is gone.

I think that's wrong. I don't think the historical record supports that conventional wisdom. What I'd like to do is talk about the weaknesses in the conventional wisdom and provide an alternative way to think about the notion of public service broadcasting. I will argue that the need for public service media, to use a broader term, is greater now than it's ever been in our history. Conventional wisdom is absolutely disastrous if taken seriously, and we should definitely oppose it at every turn.

The United States has never had public service broadcasting in the global or historical sense of the term. We call it public service broadcasting, but it isn't. What we mean by public broadcasting historically or globally is full-service broadcasting, with education, entertainment, and public affairs aimed at the entire population of a country. Its attributes are being nonprofit and noncommercial; dealing directly with the public instead of using ratings; having a relationship with the entire population to develop programming, not just the boring educational stuff, not just journalism and public affairs, but entertainment, the whole works. That was what public service broadcasting meant historically. At its very best, it has done exactly that. Canada has examples of it. Britain, Germany, Japan, India, and Scandinavia have some wonderful examples. Still to this day many national systems do, although the glory days are in the rearview mirror for most public broadcasting systems.

We've never had anything close to that in the United States. In the early 1930s there was a war in this country that I chronicled in *Telecommunications, Mass Media, and Democracy* (1993), a battle over the nature of broadcasting in this country. The forces that wanted to establish a public service system in this country were defeated. Their defeat was nailed in the coffin with the 1934 Communications Act. After that it was clear and forever the case, until this day, that commercial interests dominate American broadcasting. They have first claim to it, and any public service interests will come only after the needs of the commercial broadcasters have been satisfied. What that meant in the United States is that when public broadcasting slowly developed here in the late 1930s, 1940s, and 1950s, finally culminating in the 1967 Public Broadcasting Act, what public broadcasters really were commissioned to do, despite all the rhetoric, whatever the words might have said in these statements of intent, was only the programming that commercial interests deemed unprofitable. They could do only the programming that had no "market." What would happen if they'd done programming that profited commercial interests? What if public broadcasters in 1972 put *All in the Family* on the air without ads, like the British Broadcasting Corporation (BBC) would have done? What would have happened? The National Association of

Broadcasters, the trade association for commercial broadcasters, would have immediately gone to Congress and raised holy hell. "This is unfair competition," they would have bellowed. "Shut the infidels down immediately." Given the power of this lobby, Congress no doubt would have acceded; hence no Public Broadcasting System (PBS) executive would have ever considered such a move. It was simply accepted as the nature of things in public broadcasting that you just don't do the stuff for which there is an audience. You only do the stuff no one wants to watch. That dilemma has faced public broadcasters in this country from day one.

Another example of what you couldn't do in this country that was done in Europe, a reason why public broadcasting was wildly popular across Europe, was that you couldn't show sports without ads. This is one of the things that makes public broadcasting a staple in Germany and Scandinavia. Why is it in this country, where we have so-called amateur college sports . . . why aren't more of these events shown on public television stations without ads? The athletes aren't getting paid. That would have done wonders to advance the popularity of public broadcasting in this country. But of course that's strictly off limits because there's plenty of good money to be made, albeit not for those providing the labor. There's an audience there. But, as I said, you can't do that. Instead you get documentaries about pandas.

In other words, this was a dead-end street for public broadcasting. You get to do marginal shows. You can never justify high-level support because you never have a great number of viewers or listeners. There's strong pressure, therefore, to turn to other revenue sources. In this context, what public broadcasters have done in the United States over the past thirty years is very impressive. But it's still very limited. There are clear limitations on exactly what you can do, how far you can expand. Public broadcasting in this country, at its very best, has never come within the smallest shadow of a real public broadcasting system in terms of audience, in terms of impact. The difference is like night and day. Public broadcasters in Germany and Britain get or have gotten in recent years around 40 percent of the audience in prime time, with twenty or thirty channels competing. What do we get here? The very best rating they've ever had, what is it, one percent? Going beyond ratings, just in terms of the impact, we've never come close. Those limitations are built into the system. It has nothing to do with the people managing public broadcasting. Within those constraints they've probably done as well as they could possibly do in terms of developing an audience.

Unprincipled conservative populists are not entirely incorrect in their critique of public broadcasting. (I say unprincipled because they have no coherent principle except, perhaps, the unprincipled defense of wealth and privilege.) They argue that public broadcasting is an elitist enterprise. There is an element of truth to it. What evolves rationally in the United States in public broadcasting in this context, if you can do only the stuff that is not profitable and you're going to depend on listeners and viewers to bankroll you for a large portion of your income, is a clear pressure to pitch your programming to the upper-middle class. That's the rational thing to do. Anything else would be suicidal if you're running a station. So you have a system pitched at those who have disposable income and who give you money during pledge drives. The system has played into that conservative critique.

Does this mean that public service broadcasting, what I call *real* public service broadcasting, cannot coexist with commercial broadcasting, that they are locked in a conflict so that they can't exist in the same system? No, I don't think that's the case. Historically, if you look at other countries, you can see where they have successfully coexisted. Britain is, or was, the classic case in point and the one closest to us. In Britain, the reason why you could have the BBC coexist with commercial stations, I think, is quite clear historically. First, public broadcasting in Europe has been fully funded, unlike in the United States. At the same time, commercial broadcasters were held to high public service standards. They did not have a system where the commercial broadcasters could do whatever they wanted to make money and then the BBC got to pick up the pieces. Instead, the people who were licensed to do commercial broadcasting still had to meet public service standards. There are some scholars who argue that for certain periods of British history the commercial broadcasters did more public service than the BBC did. The quality was that high. That was the key.

What happened in Britain during the Thatcher era was that government intervention encouraged privatization of broadcasting with decreasing public service regulation. As commercial broadcasting in Britain became dominant, the BBC was elbowed out and put in a position not unlike the position the U.S. public broadcasters have been in, although the BBC started from a much higher position at the beginning, a much stronger position than the U.S. public broadcasters.

This is what's been happening globally to public service broadcasting. The key has been government intervention on behalf of commercial broadcasting, which then becomes ascendant in systems around the world—in Germany, India, across Asia, across Europe. Traditional public broadcasters lose their political power and find themselves in a very precarious position, while the commercial broadcasters do just the popular entertainment stuff that is most profitable. With decreased national funding, public broadcasters are then in a tough spot. They have two choices. One, in addition to public affairs and educational programming, they can try to stay "popular" by turning to entertainment to attract larger audiences. But then when they go to their Congress or Parliament to get funding, the commercial lobbies say, "Why are you subsidizing competition? That's not fair." And they've got a point. It really isn't fair. So they lose their subsidy. The other choice is, "OK, we won't compete with you. We'll just do what those U.S. guys are doing. We'll do the educational stuff that no one wants to watch." Then they go back to their Congress or Parliament and say, "Now give us money," and they are told, "Forget it. No one watches you. Why should we bankroll you?" It a dead-end street. It's a hopeless choice. And it is seemingly inevitable that either way you go you end up going commercial. You have no choice if you play by the rules of the market. The only issue is how quickly you go and how you manage it. You have to go commercial. You've got to make that money somewhere.

You see it today with the BBC. Probably the most successful public broadcaster in the world, the BBC has basically made a decision this past decade to accept the global commercial media system as dominant and try to find a place as a lucrative commercial niche within that system. It does so by partnering with commercial media, being a commercial enterprise outside of the United Kingdom, and using its commercial bounty made overseas to subsidize what will remain, it claims, a noncommercial entity within Britain. Whether you can be an empire and a democracy, so to speak, at the same time is a historical question that a lot of people have asked. We'll see. My hunch is that it is unlikely. But the point remains. The BBC is probably the only public broadcaster that even has that as an option. No other public broadcaster can possibly try a strategy of being commercial in one place and noncommercial elsewhere. They don't have the language advantage the BBC does, having an English-speaking market that the BBC can go to in order to sell. So it's a very dark picture for public service broadcasting globally. And increasingly, ironically, and tragically, when you go to Europe now, the consultants are telling the European public broadcasters, "Look at what they're doing in America to figure out how to get out of this. This is the way to go. They've figured it out in America." Are you kidding? What a farce.

The claim of the conventional wisdom is that this situation is inevitable. This situation is due to technology, pure and simple. The 500 TV channels and the billions of Internet Web sites mean there is simply no way public service broadcasting can survive. Public broadcasting was predicated on the scarcity of having only a few channels and a few choices. Now, however, with all these 500 channels, there is no justification for publicly subsidizing a channel that will have a small portion of the market. If you accept the premise, it is difficult to argue with that logic. But the premise is wrong: this situation isn't due to technology any more than it was due to scarcity years before.

In a different political environment and culture, the technology we have now could be used to expand public service broadcasting. This could be the golden age of public service broadcasting. We could have a fleet of community access stations, local stations, national networks. It is the political environment that makes the technology useless today. There's nothing inherent in this technology that demands that we have ten companies owning hundreds of stations and a commercialized Internet with scads of Web sites. I think it's a sign of the intellectual lockjaw of our times that democratic access seems so implausible. Commercialization of technology is just accepted as natural. Having more channels means massive commercialism. It means a few owners owning everything. That's taken as a given. We see it today in how public service broadcasters approach the Internet. They have viewed it more as a commercial mechanism to make money to expand their revenue base rather than as something to be used to expand their public service mission first and foremost. It's a tragic error in my view, but one that makes sense within the paradigm public broadcasters face.

The real culprit in my view is not technology, but neoliberalism. Neoliberalism captures the essence of what's going on globally, and in the United States, better than any other term. Back in the 1930s, and even into the 1960s, there was an aphorism about fascism. They said, "What's the difference between fascism and capitalism? Fascism is capitalism with the gloves off. Fascism is capitalism without democratic rights, without elections, without freedoms." That's actually not true. We now know that fascism is a far more complicated phenomenon than that. There are mass movements, all sorts of bigotry, racism, a whole complex of social contradictions going on other than just capitalism and naked class power. But neoliberalism *is* capitalism with the gloves off—it is capitalism premised on the idea that the rich should rule the world. Whoever makes the most money wins. Deregulate business. Lower taxes. Tame and lessen the power of labor. Turn everything that can possibly be made profitable over to the market, subject to market principles, with a "damn the torpedoes" attitude toward the social consequences. The environmental and social waste the system might produce is called "externalities" and left to the philosophers to discuss. But it's certainly not to be worried about by those in the real world.

Milton Friedman is the guru of neoliberalism. He wrote a book in the early 1960s called *Capitalism and Freedom.* I think it should be required reading for everyone in the United States and the world. This is the book that lays out the philosophy that has guided Thatcher and Reagan, that guides Clinton and Bush, and expresses their view of how the world should be organized. It's worth noting that Friedman, from the beginning of his career until today, has been an enemy of public service broadcasting. He has argued that all communication should be subject exclusively to market principles. The market should run everything, owners and advertisers included.

Under neoliberalism in the United States, public service broadcasting survives, but not on the principles of the market. There's no principled explanation for it now. It survives only due to political strength. You can muscle up a lobby that listens to it and will fight for it. That's the case in the United States, Germany, Britain, and Scandinavia. On principle, it doesn't fit in at all with neoliberalism. One of the great conflicts in Europe today is the European Union (EU) dealing with the fact that public service broadcasting violates all the free market principles they're trying to install as they put in a continent-wide market for the corporations. The media companies are constantly complaining to the European Union, "We have to compete with these guys who are being subsidized. Stop it." The EU agrees. There is a real conflict there. There has been a real tension because it's a square peg in a round neoliberal hole.

So is there a need for public service broadcasting today? Conventional wisdom says no. The neoliberals say no, of course not. My view is that now there is a greater need than ever for public broadcasting. Why is that? It has nothing to do with scarcity of resources or an abundance of technology. It is much more fundamental than that. The founders of public service broadcasting, the real visionaries who wrote about it—people like Joy Elmer Morgan, John Dewey, and Graham Spry in Canada—have made a much more sublime argument. They said that democracy needs a healthy nonprofit, noncommercial media sector. That's the core issue involved here.

A business-run media system in an inegalitarian society will never reflect the interests of the whole population—a corporate media cannot represent the majority of citizens. There will be a clear tension there. You can't have a democracy without having a healthy, democratic media system. It seems banal, almost. It's so elementary. That was much of the basis of the argument for public service broadcasting that was made in the United States and in Canada. That scarcity stuff was something lawyers and politicians cooked up later, to sell public broadcasting to legislators, judges, and bureaucrats. You can't get people off their butts on the scarcity thing. You organize a movement on the vision of democratic media, not all this talk about gigabytes in the spectrum. That's what the Canadians did in the 1920s when they organized to set up the Canadian Broadcasting Corporation (CBC). That is what the Americans tried, but failed to do at the same time.

So while the scarcity argument for public broadcasting may have lost its rationale and luster and the abundant technology argument succumbs to marketplace idiocies, the democratic argument is stronger than ever. If you look at what's happening in the global media system or the U.S. media system today, the need for a nonprofit, noncommercial sector has never been greater.

Let's talk about what the media system looks like in the United States. Today's U.S. media system is basically the property of about two dozen companies. They dominate the lion's share of what people consume as media: cable, television, magazines, books, the works. Of those two dozen, there's an elite first tier of about eight or nine superconglomerates. You know their names: Disney, AOL Time Warner, Viacom, Rupert Murdoch's News Corporation. This top handful of conglomerates owns, among them, all the Hollywood movie studios, all the television networks, over half the cable systems, the majority of the cable channels, four of the five companies that sell 90 percent of the music in the United States. Those top eight or nine have a pretty tight grip on a lot of stuff. These are largely noncompetitive markets dominated by just a handful of companies. So it's impossible for a newcomer to enter these markets.

We are told that this is just the American way. These are hard-working, plucky entrepreneurs who woke up at five in the morning, shined their shoes, scrubbed their teeth, went out there and gave the people what they wanted, grew rich and successful, and that's the way it is in the free world. This has so little to do with our actual media system that it is nonsensical. Our media system is the direct result of government laws, policies, regulations, and subsidies. All but one of the first eight media empires were built on a government subsidy, either a gift of spectrum to have monopoly rights to key channels in all the major markets, or the gift of monopoly rights to cable systems.

In short, the system is created in our name but without our consent. Media policy-making in the United States is incredibly corrupt. The core decisions were, and are, made behind closed doors, with no public participation and minimal media coverage. The ultimate example of this was the 1996 Telecommunications Act, a truly dreadful law that we're suffering the consequences of to this day. This law is of singular importance for shaping our media environment and our communications environment for the next generation or two, yet there was virtually no public participation whatsoever. The "debate" was conducted entirely by huge lobbies duking it out behind closed doors to see who would get the biggest piece of pie. It's like the scene in *Godfather II* where all the U.S. mob families are sitting on top of a Havana hotel cutting up a cake shaped like Cuba. That's what the Telecommunications Act was like. Here's the globe, pal. Who's going to get the biggest chunk? The long-distance companies, the over-the-air broadcasters, the cable companies, or what have you. That's how it was done.

In the media system we get as a result, the concentrated ownership that we're getting more and more of has distinctly negative implications for democracy. Even if I said nothing more, having so few people holding that much power is a fundamental problem. It doesn't matter how good they are or what sort of people they are—it's just wrong in a democracy. Democracy is predicated on the idea that people can communicate, not just choose from nine options that are preselected for them. That's the problem with our media system. And unfortunately, the people who run these media systems, whether good or bad, produce outcomes that are beneficial to their shareholders, to their advertisers, the core constituencies that matter to them, and quite negative outcomes for the rest of us. The journalism is dreadful and the entertainment is often a hypercommercialized morass. We may have diversity in the number of stations, but we have a numbing lack of genuine ideological or cultural diversity, not to speak of creativity. As I said, by democratic standards the need for public broadcasting has never been greater.

Let me give you just one example of the problem we face with the corporate media system. The commercial media play a big part in creating the bogus electoral system we have. This is an unspoken part of the problem of the corporate media system, and one reason why public broadcasting is so important. What the commercial broadcasters have done is cut out broadcast journalism coverage of campaigns, for the most part. Instead they say to candidates, "If you want to be covered, buy an ad." The TV political advertisement has become the lingua franca of American politics and a huge source of revenues and profits for the corporate media. I don't want to go off on political advertising too much. I'll leave you with this comment about it as a form of political communication. Robert Spero, who was the head of advertising for Ogilvie and Mather in the 1980s, used to get upset when people would compare political advertising to advertising for products like beer and mouthwash. He thought product ads had vastly greater integrity. So he took a year off from his job and did a content analysis of every presidential political ad from 1952 to 1976. What he showed was that every single one of those ads, if held to Federal Trade Commission (FTC) standards for advertising, would have been found fraudulent. He has a book that chronicles this. These ads are garbage. There's no other word for it. And the worst part of it is that they cost a fortune, so successful candidates either have to be extremely rich or appeal to those with gobs of money. The cost of the average federal campaign jumps 40 percent every four years. Listen to this statistic: Ninety percent of the individual campaign contributions that are given come from the wealthiest 1 percent of Americans. The majority of that money then goes to these media corporations to buy these ridiculous TV ads. If you want to know why people are demoralized or despondent about American politics, I don't think any other statistic will tell you more about our bankrupt political culture. And the corporate broadcasters are the number-one lobby that opposes campaign finance reform.

This isn't an accident. Having a demoralized, depoliticized culture is not an accident. It's not like Milton Friedman is out there in his think tank grinding his teeth and saying, "We've got the economics right but the politics haven't worked out. We need people voting more and paying more attention." In fact, it's quite the opposite. I urge you, once again, to read Friedman's *Capitalism and Freedom*. It's a 200-page book on the relationship of capitalism to freedom and the good life. I don't think the word "democracy" is in the book anywhere, except maybe once or twice as a passing reference. The way Friedman defines the good life, and a free society, is one in which the market runs everything. There's virtually no place for public life, no public culture. Everyone's energy is put purely into commercial interests. Political debate is limited to minor debates over how big the police department will need to be, in order to protect property and contracts. An aroused citizenry would be a negative, because public policy would be likely to interfere with the sacred market. So a highly depoliticized society is precisely what works best with neoliberalism.

So if one maintains an elementary commitment to participatory democracy, the case for public service broadcasting is stronger than ever. Yet, having said that, at the same time I want to emphasize that we have to rethink it a great deal. The old model is as out-of-date as the singing telegram. The elitist models that have been criticized have been justifiably criticized. I think the sort of work that people in this room are doing—dealing with the tough issues of how you organize an accountable, democratic public broadcasting service—is absolutely essential. It is a difficult problem. One thing we know for sure is that it can't be solved unless it is out in the open and we debate it. It's not going to be settled behind closed doors.

If we make it a priority, I believe we can come up with a better system than the one we have. Other countries have done a much better job, but we have to strive to go beyond that. We have to rethink public service broadcasting not just to be the traditional national broadcaster with programming for the whole country, but also to include local broadcasting to a greater extent and to include community broadcasting, public access, and microradio. We need a national service aimed at the entire population as well as distinct services for minorities and underserved communities and youth. We have to envision public service media as a whole panoply, a whole range of broadcasting.

And we're not just talking about broadcasting. This is another important point. The conventional wisdom says that since all media are converging, thanks to digital communication, there's really no distinction now between broadcasting and movies, or movies and music, or music and newspapers, so we should just toss out public service broadcasting. It's irrelevant. In fact, I think we should *expand* our notion of public service broadcasting to public service media. That's ultimately what it's all about: generating a nonprofit, noncommercial, healthy, pluralistic media system that serves the people of the country. It would not serve Madison Avenue and Wall Street, first and foremost.

So my argument is . . . that what we need to do is struggle for broad media reform, reduce private power, and enhance the nonprofit, noncommercial sector. This fight is emerging at this historical moment, or at least I hope it is. There are many facets to this movement. There's the movement for reformed and enhanced public broadcasting, what I have been speaking about, but it goes beyond that.

Another important area is antitrust law. I think this is an area where we're going to see a lot more work in the next few years. Ultimately, what we need in this country are public hearings to establish ownership policies for media. Provide a level playing field on what you can own and what you can't own, rather than trying to do it piecemeal, one deal at a time. That approach has been a complete fiasco. I think to make antitrust work today, we don't have to abandon the antitrust tradition and come up with a new one; we simply have to return to the original tradition. Antitrust developed in this country as a result of the populist movement. It was a popular uprising that said, "Too much concentrated wealth is inimical to democracy." If one person is worth $80 billion and millions are paupers, you can't have political equality. That was what got people to organize for antitrust. With that logic, I think most antitrust scholars today would say that the first industry that would be challenged would be the media industry. There's too much concentrated power there. The reason why concentrated power is wrong isn't simply the increasing power over cultures and power over markets. It's that it gives these industries so much political power that they are unregulatable. They're bigger than the population. They're almost at that point, if they're not there now. It will take a huge movement to tame these industries. That's the whole motive of antitrust, breaking up concentrated wealth that becomes politically ungovernable.

Going back to my initial points, we need broadcast and cable regulation. Those companies that use the airwaves, that use cable systems, need requirements. We have to have public service requirements for them. Not a number of them, but a few I can think of that would be very good ones. Why not make it a condition of a broadcast license that no broadcaster shows political advertising? Why not? I've run this one by the Kiwanis Club and people stand up and start hooting and hollering. They love it. No one likes those ads. They're garbage. Just get rid of them. OK, some people will say, "Hey, what about a person's First Amendment right to buy an election?" Then I propose the following: let candidates purchase TV and radio political ads, but their opponents on the ballot will receive a free ad of identical length immediately following the paid ad. I suspect that once a candidate can't purchase dominance over the voter's attention, but has to win it on a level playing field, the practice will all but disappear.

Likewise, why not do what they do in Sweden, Greece, and Norway, and say, "No TV advertising to kids under twelve, period?" I can say that to any audience in this country and no one says, "No, I *love* advertising for the kids." The truth is, it is terrible, it is obscene what we're doing to kids. It's unacceptable. And why don't we take all the ads off television news and try to set up some sort of journalism on television that's under the control of journalists, not advertisers? At most of the talks I give, all I have to do is say "local TV news," and people start laughing. It's a punch line. Local television news is so bad in this country that it's a punch line.

Finally, on this list, we need to work aggressively to think about creative, democratic ways to subsidize nonprofit, noncommercial media. This is of paramount importance because, for example, having access to starting a Web site doesn't mean a thing if you don't have the resources to put something good out there. If you are forced to go to purely commercial means to support it, the limitation is built in. We've been supporting corporate media for a hundred years with massive subsidies. Now, I think it is time to support noncorporate media, independent, nonprofit, noncommercial media. One proposal by an economist named Dean Baker is that all Americans should be able to take $200 off their taxes and allocate it to any nonprofit medium of their choice. The Internal Revenue Service (IRS) has a strict code, as anyone knows who's worked in media, on what qualifies as a nonprofit medium. It's hard to sneak one by the IRS. There are no ideological strings attached. The Nazis could get all the money if people wanted it. People could give up to $20 or $30 billion to nonprofit media in our culture without any government strings attached, thereby creating a healthy media sector and a lot of healthy, nonprofit, noncommercial competition.

We have to think creatively about things like this. Communication is too important to leave to the market. Communication is too important to think it will take care of itself. It won't take care of itself. We can see what's happened when media policy is left to the market and to the politicians who are bought and paid for by the corporate media giants. It's been a fiasco.

There are a lot of people working on media issues inside the beltway in Washington, struggling mightily to try to squeeze out a gigabyte here and a gigabyte there, with no public recognition, getting nowhere, and having no support. They're fighting an uphill fight, or even a hopeless fight in that situation. What they really need is popular support. As Saul Alinsky said, more than once, "The only way you can beat organized money is with organized *people.*" You can have all the good arguments in the world, but if you don't have organized people going up against organized money, you're going to lose. If we're going to think seriously about actually changing the media system, it's going to require a lot of popular support. Winning lectures at debating contests at Cambridge or Harvard isn't going to get us anywhere. We have to talk to people, organize them like Jerry Starr is doing at Citizens for Independent Public Broadcasting. Get people to understand the issues and work on them.

We should also look abroad for ideas. I have been studying recently what political parties around the world are doing on these issues. What is clear is that as the global media system evolves, it looks more and more like the one in the United States. What is also clear is that this is becoming more and more of an issue around the world. In Sweden, New Zealand, Australia, India, Brazil, and elsewhere, organizing around media reform is becoming much more of an issue. Preserving and expanding public broadcasting is foremost on the list. The parties that are pushing this, without exception, are the antineoliberal democratic parties, the parties to the left. What they're finding is that it's very popular with all the voters. That's the exciting thing about it. When the left protects public service broadcasting in Australia and New Zealand, the right-wing parties generally can't mess with it because the left has built up popular support. In Sweden, the left got a ban on advertising to children under twelve, and when the conservatives return to power they can't even dream of trying to reinstate advertising to children. People have tasted what it's like not to have advertising for children under twelve. They're never going to go back. So it takes left parties abroad to push this issue, but it's popular with the entire population. I think that's going to be the case here, too. I think if we're ever going to win here, it's going to be the political left that takes the lead on the issue; but support will also come from people spread throughout the population in general. I don't think this is an issue that's limited to people who would be considered on the left or progressive or left-liberal. I think it's an issue that anyone who favors democracy can support.

Amy Goodman says that these notions of liberal and conservative, once you get beyond the statements of pundits, really lose a lot of their meaning nowadays. Those terms don't really mean a whole lot when you go out and talk to people about issues. I do about fifty talks a year to general, nonacademic audiences. I will talk to anyone who will listen to me if my schedule permits, be they conservative, religious, labor unions, Kiwanis Clubs, or nudists. My experience is that while not everyone agrees with you, people *are* really interested in media issues. Jerry Starr talks about public opinion surveys that have been done by PROMO (Project on Media Ownership), a New York-based media research group, and his organization that show remarkable interest in these issues and support for sweeping media reform. The first reaction I get from audiences is usually, "Why haven't we ever heard about this stuff before? Why is it top secret?" They haven't heard about it for a reason. It is not in the interests of corporate media to publicize debates over their existence. It's the last thing you should expect. But there's a real groundswell of interest in it.

One group that is somewhat sympathetic to reform, that used to be diametrically opposed to it, is journalists. For most of the twentieth century and well into the 1980s, journalists were die-hard defenders of the status quo. They hated criticism of the status quo. They were very thin-skinned. When I left journalism in the early 1980s and went to graduate school, I would offer my critique of journalism as serving business and commercial interests and being lousy for democracy. My friends who were still journalists would say, "You don't know what you're talking about. We've got everything under control in the newsroom. Go back to the seminar room. Everything's fine." Now, after fifteen years of consolidation, concentration, and the attack on journalists' autonomy, when I go to talk to my friends who are journalists, or journalists who aren't my friends, and I give them my rap, they say, "Bob, you don't know what you're talking about. You're off in the library and the seminar room . . . it's much *worse* than you think." There has been a sea change in the attitude of a lot of working journalists who became journalists because they really wanted to do good work. They find themselves covering Jon-Benet Ramsey or JFK Jr. What passes for political journalism now in much of our media system is getting a sound bite from one politician, and then crossing the aisle and getting the sound of someone else biting back. That's not journalism. That's stenography. Many journalists know that. Now, the journalists' union supports media reform. They understand the effects of this corporate media consolidation, in terms of destroying the quality of journalism.

A quite rational response to my argument that we need the left in order to lead the struggle for media reform would be to say that it is hopeless, that the left doesn't exist in the United States . . . it's a joke. To the official culture of the corporate media, and from the vantage point of inside the Washington beltway, and to the world of people who travel from airport to airport and from gated community to gated community, progressive social movements seem like a ridiculous notion, completely foreign to the experience they have. But there's something percolating in this country. It's undeniable. I've talked at a lot of colleges. There is a movement afoot. There are people, especially young people, who are really dissatisfied with the way this country is going, dissatisfied with the direction, who are beginning to organize politically about it. I don't know where it's going to go, but I'm going to blow on those flames with every ounce of strength in my body. It happened in Seattle. In the past two years, 200 college campuses have started antisweatshop campaigns. They've won on a lot of campuses. High schools and community colleges are active. It's an extraordinary movement. I've talked at Northern Illinois University—hardly the Berkeley of the Midwest—and at the University of Dayton. Two dozen students at each of them organized around these issues and participated in demonstrations in Washington. Smart kids. They know their stuff. They're smarter than I was at their age.

What's interesting about these groups is that the media are right at the center of their focus. They understand the importance of communication and of media reform. The role of the corporate media is an unacceptable role to the emerging generation of social activists. It has a scissors effect on these kids, the same scissors effect it has on all of us. On the one hand, it's the totally bankrupt commercial life we're constantly fed ("shop till you drop, make as much money as you can, take care of number one") that is basically a morally bankrupt life. On the other hand, we have the sad reality of the gross social injustice and inequality that the system produces . . . that's almost inescapable unless you live entirely in a gated community and on the Internet. It's simply a world that's unacceptable. Those two factors are only getting worse. In the end, the depoliticization that is the product of this sort of media system basically collapses because it can't withstand reality. We're social beings. We aren't meant to just live by ourselves, to put on our blinders until we drop. It's just not right for us. We have to deal with problems socially. I think that's ultimately going to return to the fore, hopefully sooner rather than later. That's my goal, and that should be the goal for all of us.

The smart money would say, "It's hopeless." Not just media reform, but progressive social change at all. This society is entrenched. People are happy. The economy is booming. Nothing can change. But remember, the smart money said that Eastern Europe would never change peacefully. As late as 1985, all the smart people were saying nothing could ever change there. We had to spend billions of dollars because it was entrenched forever. As late as 1988, the smart money was saying you could never have peaceful change in South Africa. The smart money's wrong, usually. Don't listen to the smart money. My view is the opposite. We're in historically uncharted waters right now. I don't think anyone knows where we're going. But I do think if enough people come together to demand democratic media as part of a broader campaign for democracy, anything can happen. We really don't know.

I'll leave you with one of my favorite quotes from Noam Chomsky. He describes the choice that each of us faces. He says, "If you act like there's no possibility of social change for the better, you *guarantee* there will be no social change for the better."

3

Brand New World?

Globalization, Cyberspace, and the Politics of Convergence

Vincent Mosco

In her award-winning book *No Logo*, Naomi Klein (2000) reminds us that we are living in a branded world. Starting from the view that the brand is "the core meaning of the modern corporation," she documents the global spread of brand identities made most successful in such visual brand icons as the Golden Arches of McDonalds and the Nike Swoosh. Brands have spread beyond the specific commercial product like the hamburger or running shoe to encompass places, events, people, activities, and now governments. My hometown of Ottawa has gone through several brands, most recently spending close to a quarter-million dollars to marry its new high-tech image with its attractive surroundings. Sadly, it came up with the brand name Technically Beautiful, to less than resounding support. Now the Canadian national government, perhaps taking a cue from a popular beer commercial celebrating Canadian identity, is promoting the need to brand Canada.

If we can brand countries, why not the world? Indeed, globalization might be better viewed as a brand for the world than as an analytical tool or concept for understanding political and economic processes. It is much too loose and contested to serve usefully as a means to understand the world, but as a brand it provides an expression that is its own explanation. In this respect, globalization exists *sui generis* as the word for what is happening today, not unlike the mantra whose utterance places the chanter among a group of believers who need say no more. Concepts lead to questions. As a brand, globalization leads to only one response: Amen. Brands don't tell stories, advance conversations, support narratives, or propel politics; they end all of these. The iconic brand is the period, better still the exclamation point; it is a rhetorical stop sign. (Or in the case of Coca-Cola—which has branded highway signs across Tanzania—the brand is literally that nation's stop sign.)

Successful brands transcend not only the products that inspired them but the limits of the brand itself. They do so by turning the mantra into the myth. This is significant because myths are different from brands in that they are meant to tell stories, animate conversations, and extend narratives. These qualities are difficult for us to think about because we are trained to test the value of ideas by assessing their truth or falsity. Indeed it is common to define myth as falsehood. But, as Alisdair MacIntyre (1970) reminds us, myths are not about these things; they are not true or false, but living or dead. And the power of myth is based on its ability not to reflect reality, but rather to live on in the face of, or in spite of, what a positivist may judge to be real. A myth is alive if it continues to give meaning to human life, if it continues to represent some important part of the collective mentality of a given age, and if it continues to render socially and intellectually tolerable what would otherwise be experienced as incoherence. In this respect, globalization is one of the master myths of our time. More than just a way of branding the world, it informs the world with a story about how different people come together to transcend their messy differences to create a universal culture. It is a story that, in its more sophisticated forms, inoculates itself by admitting to deficiencies, bumps in the road, unevenness, and genuine divides. But these too will be overcome by the inevitable spread of globalization (roughly a combination of Hegel's unfolding dialectic and Disney's "It's a Small World After All").

Computer communication is central to the myth of globalization because it provides the latest version of what James Carey (1992) once called "the electrical sublime," at once both the banal infrastructure for globalization and the spectacular vision of universal intelligence celebrated in the breezy triumphalism of *Wired Magazine* and the disturbing visions of people like the theologian Teilhard de Chardin (1959), with his image of the *noosphere,* a literal atmosphere of thought mounting in pressure upon a globe whose linked intelligence prepares the way for an evolutionary leap. Cyberspace provides the transcendent spectacle, what Leo Marx once called "the rhetoric of the technological sublime," offering hymns to progress that rise "like froth on a tide of exuberant self-regard sweeping over all misgivings, problems, and contradictions" (1964, 207). It renews what was once promised by the telegraph, telephone, radio, and television, propelling the myth of globalization specifically by offering the literal connection, the missing link that will bring about the end of history, the end of geography, and the end of politics.

Cyberspace anoints globalization with a near apocalyptic quality—the end of history. Not merely the expansion of commerce beyond national boundaries, it becomes, in the work of Frances Fukuyama (1992), Nicholas Negroponte (1995), and Ray Kurzweil (1999), to name just some of the leading thinkers, a radical disjunction in time, opening the way to a new epoch no longer bound by the economic, technological, or even biological limitations that have marked every historical period. For Fukuyama, globalization and liberal democracy mark the end point in an evolutionary process that has taken people through stages of development (e.g., hunting and gathering, agriculture), modes of thinking (mythic, religious, philosophic), and forms of governance (tribal, feudal, communist, fascist). For the director of MIT's Media Lab, Nicholas Negroponte, the end of history comes with the end of an analog world and the arrival of a digital one to which we must accommodate. In matter-of-fact prose, he offers a modern-day prophet's call to say good-bye to the world of atoms, with its coarse, confining materiality, and welcomes the digital world, with its infinitely malleable electrons able to transcend spatial, temporal, and material constraints. The world of atoms is ending, he says; we must learn to be digital. Ray Kurzweil brings the ballast of strong technological credentials to a best-selling book that casts the end of history in biological terms. The radical disjunction means the end of death as we know it, as we rapidly refine the ability to preserve our intelligence in software so that "life expectancy is no longer a viable term in relation to intelligent beings" (Kurzweil 1999, 280). For Kurzweil, one of history's fundamental problems is that we have been dependent on the "longevity of our *hardware*," that physical self that he laments through Yeats as "but a paltry thing, a tattered coat upon a stick." History as we know it ends as we "cross the divide" and "instantiate ourselves into our computational technology" (1999, 128–129).

In addition to crossing the divide in time, cyberspace helps to drive globalization's promise to cross the spatial divide, putting an end to geography as we know it. For Frances Cairncross (1997), this means the "death of distance," as cyberspace, unlike material space, permits us to experience what it means to be anywhere at any time of our choosing. Accepting this view, Kenichi Ohmae (1990, 1995) celebrates a "borderless world" where any attempt to create boundaries is doomed to failure, a world that William Mitchell (1999) calls an "e-topia" of near boundless choices for where and how we live and work. For him, the Net does not just extend geometry: "The Net negates geometry . . . it is fundamentally and profoundly *antispatial*. It is nothing like the Piazza Navona or Copley Square. You cannot say where it is or describe its memorable shape and proportions or tell a stranger how to get there. But you can find things in it without knowing where they are. The Net is ambient—nowhere in particular and everywhere at once" (Mitchell 1999, 8).

Even those like Margaret Wertheim (1999), who takes a less triumphal view, still see cyberspace as profoundly spatially disjunctive, exploding the singularity of the Enlightenment's vision of one empirical space and introducing an experience dimly reminiscent of the medieval era where existential space is inherently dual—comprised then of secular and spiritual space, today of material and cyberspace.

Finally, cyberspace promises to end politics as we know it by undermining bureaucratic constraints on building networked democracies and by sweeping away age-old strategic thinking (Mosco and Foster 2001). In the work of the Tofflers (1995), George Gilder (2000), George Keyworth, and other members of the Progress and Freedom Foundation, the end of politics means more than just using computer communication to create electronic democracy. It also redefines what we have traditionally called politics by grounding power in networks rather than institutions. New economic power rests in looser structures, systems with nodal points whose power derives not from their geographical supremacy but from networked interdependence and flexibility. Real-time and twenty-four-hour networks of information flows overthrow the physical city and the nation-state too, creating new laws to which politics must comply or be threatened with extinction. Proponents go as far as to envision a quantum politics whose indeterminacy mirrors that of the subatomic world. The end of politics also means the end of fear, particularly the age-old fear of military attack, because computer communications enables a defense against it. The need for offensive weapons and strategies of mutually assured destruction disappears as ballistic missile defense systems lift a protective umbrella that shields the world. From the time that Ronald Reagan first called for such a defense, telling Mikhail Gorbachev that he saw the "hand of providence" in it, to George W. Bush's latest reinvention, we hear the language of a new dawn in global security, of world peace, driven by a kind of *machina ex deo* that will transform politics as we have known it throughout history.

There are several ways to respond to these myths of cyberspace and globalization. One way is to simply debunk them. And indeed the history of communication technology, including the telegraph (Standage 1998), telephone (Martin 1991), radio (Douglas 1987), and television (Fisher and Fisher 1996), reveals a pattern. The arrival of each advance is accompanied by the triumphalist expression that it marks a break with history, the death of distance, and an end to the politics of division, if not the arrival of world peace. Sure, each also typically contains a subtext that worries about the impact on the family, privacy, and what passes at the time for authentic communication. But there is no doubt that each wave of communication technology, with its associated systems like electricity, has its time to bask in the glow of the technological sublime before the inevitable routinization sets in and common sense, in the Gramscian sense, catches its breath. Then there returns a view that Raymond Williams gave some conceptual heft: technology is little more than a congealed social relationship. As such, it is capable of good, evil, and, as it literally withdraws into the woodwork of our homes and offices, considerable banality.

It is also useful to address myths by taking them more seriously. If in fact their value is determined not by their empirical truth or falsity but rather by whether they are living or dead, then the question is not "are they true," but rather "what keeps them alive?" Myths are sustained by social practices that involve the leadership of iconic storytellers whose accomplishments in one area give them a platform to promote mythic storytelling. Bill Gates's ability to sustain a business monopoly permits him to mythologize about revolution and transcendence in his books *The Road Ahead* and *Business @ The Speed of Thought*. Of course, the storytelling no longer takes place around a campfire, unless you consider the television to be an electronic hearth, but through a dense, recombinant, and reiterative field of media that amplifies, simplifies, and customizes the tales of Gates, Negroponte, Gilder, the Tofflers, and others for global audiences. These deceptively simple stories of a new age, a new economy, the next new thing, often contain the sophisticated practices perfected by magicians and conjurers over the centuries. These protective covers, including what Barthes (1972) called the process of inoculation, even find a role for the ancient and wily trickster now taking on the shape of the computer hacker.

Revealing the components and processes of modern myth-making does assert that myths matter, but in order to understand why they do, it is important to consider the values and desires they tap into. The cyberspace myth is a story about how ever smaller, faster, cheaper, and better computer and communication technologies help to realize, with little effort, those seemingly impossible dreams of democracy and community with practically no pressure on the natural environment. According to this view, it empowers people largely by realizing the perennial dream of philosophers and librarians: to make possible instant access to the world's store of information without requiring the time, energy, and money to physically go where the information is stored. Moreover, the story continues, computer networks provide relatively inexpensive access, making possible a primary feature of democracy—that the tools necessary for empowerment are equally available to all. Furthermore, this vision of cyberspace fosters community because it enables people to communicate with one another in any part of the world. As a result, existing communities of people are strengthened and whole new "virtual" communities arise from the creation of networks of people who share interests, commitments, and values. In essence, by transcending time, space, and resource constraints, approximating what Karl Marx called "the annihilation of space with time" (1973, 539), cyberspace provides the literal and figurative missing links that bring genuine, sustainable democracy and community to a world in desperate need of both. One can begin to understand what James Carey meant when he said that "nostalgia for the future" is one of our most potent pastorals (1992, 200).

Myths can be understood for what they reveal, but also for what they conceal. In this case, the myth of globalization and cyberspace is a primary example of what Barthes meant when he defined myth as depoliticized speech. As Chantal Mouffe perceptively puts it, "Here, as in many other cases, the mantra of globalization is invoked to justify the status quo and reinforce the power of big transnational corporations. When it is presented as driven exclusively by the information revolution, globalization is deprived of its political dimension and appears as a fate to which we all have to submit" (2000, 119).

What is this political dimension? Globalization can be thought of as the response of business to what several writers, including the conservative political scientist Samuel Huntington, referred to as the crisis of governability of the 1970s (Crozier, Huntington, and Watanuki 1975). That decade brought to a culmination the growing problems of the Fordist model of economic development. That model was based on mass production of standardized products and services by national firms and their heavily unionized workers for markets of mass consumers overseen, regulated, and, in some cases, controlled by national governments. But by the mid-1970s, the model was shredded by the growth of transnational firms based in numerous countries and interested in producing a multiplicity of products often customized for complex and shifting markets of consumers. These firms no longer needed the support of their traditional unionized workforces and sought to transform their dealings with both labor and the national governments that had overseen the relationships between business and labor, and between business and consumers.

Globalization began as an economic transformation from a Fordist to a post-Fordist economy. But that left a crisis in the governance of this new economy; no, not the new economy of the dotcoms, which pundits once thought had rewritten the economic rule book until most of them were crushed by the old rule book. Rather, it is a new economy of global capitalism in which business seeks the freedom to operate where labor is cheap for the skills business needs, where taxes are low, where rules protecting workers and consumers are weak, where the social safety net is feeble, and where environmental protections are tenuous and barely enforced. The resistance of governments, workers, consumers, and other civil society organizations produced for the political right a crisis of governability. The response was political globalization, the transformation of national governments, new regional and international treaties, and governance bodies that would carry out as fully as possible the economic agenda of transnational business. As a result, social welfare states became neoliberal corporate states, even if some carry the "third way" brand. The rest are little more than national versions of the old company town, reborn as the company state. Meanwhile the North American Free Trade Agreement (NAFTA), the European Union (EU), the World Trade Organization (WTO), and other regional and global additions extend corporate governance with little more than a nod (perhaps a bit more in the case of the EU) to social welfare, citizenship, and the natural environment (Mosco and Schiller 2001).

Globalization myths also conceal a great deal about the nature of cyberspace, and here it is useful to focus on the relationship between two processes: digitization and commodification. Digitization refers to the transformation of communication, including words, images, motion pictures, and sounds, into a common language. It provides enormous gains in transmission speed and flexibility over earlier forms of electronic communication, which were largely reliant on analog techniques (Longstaff 2000). Mythmakers leap from here to the view that the world of atoms is morphing into a virtual utopia. This is a serious mistake because it neglects to recognize that digitization takes place in the context of, and greatly expands, the process of commodification, transforming use value to exchange value. The expansion of the commodity form provides the context for *who* leads the process of digitization and *how* it is applied. It is used first and foremost to expand the commodification of information and entertainment: specifically, to enlarge markets in communication products, deepen the commodification of labor involved in the production, distribution, and exchange of communication, and expand markets in the audiences that receive and make use of electronic communication (Mosco 1996). Digitization not only takes place in the context of powerful commercial forces; it serves to advance the overall process of commodification worldwide, along with its specific application to communication. Cyberspace therefore results from the mutual constitution of digitization and commodification.

Digitization expands the commodification of communication content by extending the range of opportunities to measure, monitor, package, and repackage information and entertainment. The packaging of material in the paper and ink form of a newspaper or book has provided a flexible means to commodify communication, offering an adequate form in which to measure the commodity and monitor purchases. Challenges arose in the commodification of communication when what Bernard Miege calls "flow" type communication systems arose, most importantly television (1989). How does one package a television program for sale to a viewer? Initially, commodification was based on an inflexible system of delivering a batch of broadcast channels into the home with viewers paying for the receiver and for a markup in products advertised over the air. This system did not account for differential use of the medium or make any clear connection between viewing and purchasing. It amounted to a Fordist system of delivering generic programming to a mass audience that was marketed to advertisers for a price per thousand viewers. Each step toward the digitization of television has refined the commodification of content, allowing for the flow to be "captured," or, more precisely, for the commodity to be measured, monitored, and packaged in ever more specific or customized ways. Early cable television improved on broadcast systems of commodification by charging per month for a set of channels. As this medium has become digitized, companies can now offer many more channels and package them in many different ways, including selling content on a pay-per-view basis. Material delivered over television, the Internet, or some combination of these and other new wired and wireless systems can now be flexibly packaged and then repackaged for sale in some related form, with the transaction measured and monitored by the same digital system.

In addition to expanding the commodification of communication content, the recursive nature of digital systems expands the commodification of the entire communication process. Digital systems that precisely measure and monitor each information transaction can be used to refine the process of delivering audiences of viewers, listeners, readers, movie goers, and telephone and computer users to advertisers. In essence, companies can package customers in forms that specifically reflect both their actual purchases and their demographic characteristics. For example, packages of eighteen- to twenty-five-year-old men who order martial arts films on pay-per-view television can be sold to companies, which spend more for this information than for information about other audiences because they want to market their products to this specific sector with as little advertising wasted on groups who would not be interested or able to buy. This is a major refinement in the commodification of viewers over the Fordist system of delivering mass audiences, and it has been applied to almost every communication medium today (Mosco 1996).

A similar extension of commodification applies to the labor of communication. The replacement of mechanical with electronic systems eliminated thousands of jobs in the printing industry as electronic typesetting did away with the work of linotype operators. Today, digital systems allow companies to expand this process. Newspaper reporters increasingly serve in the combined roles of editor and page producer. They do not simply report on a story; they put it into a form for transmission to the printed and, increasingly, the electronic page. Companies retain the rights to the multiplicity of repackaged forms and thereby profit from each use. Broadcast journalists carry cameras and edit their own tape for delivery over television or computer networks. The film industry is beginning to deliver digital copies of movies to theaters in multiple locations over communication satellites, thereby eliminating the distribution of celluloid copies for exhibition by projectionists. Software is sold to customers well before it has been debugged on the understanding that they will report errors, download and install patches and other corrections, and figure out how to work around problems. The ability to eliminate labor, combine it to perform a multiplicity of tasks, or shift labor to unpaid consumers further expands the revenue opportunities (Hardt and Brennen 1995; McKercher 2000; Sussman and Lent 1998).

The mutual constitution of digitization and commodification helps to explain the rapid integration of the communication sector and the concentration of corporate power within it.

Specifically, the adoption of a common digital language across the communication industry is breaking down barriers that once separated print, broadcasting, telecommunications, and the information technology or computer data sectors. These divisions have been historically very significant because they contained the legal and institutional marks of the particular period in which they rose to national prominence. The print publishing industry is marked by a legal regime of free expression, limited government involvement, and local, typically family, ownership. Broadcasting and telecommunications came later, rising to prominence alongside the rise of strong nation-state authority and national production regimes. The legal system in Canada, as well as those of the United States and Europe, placed a greater regulatory burden on radio, television, and telephone systems, even going as far as to create publicly controlled institutions in these sectors, in order to accomplish national objectives such as reflecting a national identity and building a national market. National companies were more likely to control commercial broadcasting and telecommunications systems than was the case in print publishing. The information technology or computer data industry took off in the post–World War II era and embodies the trend away from nation-state regulation (except to advance the expansion of businesses) and toward control by multinational firms. There are numerous legal and institutional struggles within this sector, but it began from the premise that, unlike broadcasting and telecommunications, the computer industry would face no public interest or public service responsibilities, no system of subsidized pricing, no commitment to universality of access, and no expectation that national firms would be anything more than one step on the way to multinational control (Schiller 1999; McChesney 1999). And this has become the model for the convergent communication industry.

The combination of digitization and commodification and the growing integration of communication sectors into a consolidated electronic information and entertainment arena explain much of why there has been an unprecedented acceleration in mergers and acquisitions. Communication systems in the United States are now largely shaped by a handful of companies, including Microsoft, AT&T (which also owns the largest cable television firm), General Electric–NBC, Viacom–CBS, Disney–ABC, and AOL Time Warner (which owns Turner Broadcasting). There are others, including non-U.S. firms like Bertelsmann (which owns Random House) and Vivendi, the French telecommunications firm. Indeed, each of these firms has a significant transnational presence through outright ownership, strategic partnerships, and investment. The Canadian arena is even more highly concentrated, with arguably four firms in the most dominant position. These include BCE-CTV–Thomson, Rogers–Maclean Hunter, CanWest Global–Hollinger, and Quebecor–Sun Media–Groupe Vidéotron. The combination of growing concentration and diminishing regulation leads some critics, most recently Cass Sunstein (2001), to fear that cyberspace will be little more than a commercial space with less than adequate room for diversity and the clash of ideas so vital to democracy.

The transformation, however, is far from complete. Canadian communication firms, like their counterparts in the United States and elsewhere, face enormous pressures toward regional and global integration (Mosco and Schiller 2001). To advance transnational corporate communications services in general, and media services in particular, nationally controlled communications institutions would have to be eliminated or at least marginalized, and public service principles would have to be sharply diminished. U.S. corporate and political leaders lobbied during the 1980s and 1990s to advance these sweeping changes within broader efforts to liberalize trade and investment rules. Government initiatives, private economic diplomacy, bilateral negotiations between states, and multilateral organizations such as the World Bank, the International Monetary Fund, and the WTO all played important roles in this process. The Free Trade Agreement (FTA), which brought together Canada and the United States, and NAFTA, which added Mexico, comprised prominent initiatives within this larger movement. Each was perceived as a prelude to a broader push for liberalization of global trade and investment within the organizational context of the General Agreement on Tariffs and Trade (GATT) and the WTO.

But there is good reason to question whether all of this will work so smoothly. Media concentration often does not produce the synergies that companies anticipate and sometimes results in content that fails to attract audiences. Digitization is not a flawless process and numerous technical problems have slowed its development. More importantly, we can observe deeper political contradictions. Neoliberalism is rooted in the retreat of the state from critical areas of social life, including the communication arena, where the state historically was directly involved in the construction of infrastructure, the development of technical standards, the regulation of market access, and the direct provision of services. According to the neoliberal view, such functions are best provided by the private sector with minimal state involvement. Aside from the ideological commitment to this perspective, neoliberalism aims to customize state functions, to tailor them to suit business needs and thereby avoid the problems that the vision of the state as a universal or public space, open to a wide range of contestation, once provided. But the communication arena demonstrates that it is not so easy to accomplish this feat.

One of the most significant of what are typically presented as narrow technical concerns is standardization. Digitization succeeds only to the extent that common technical standards are used to harmonize the processing, distribution, and reception of digital signals. It is one thing to translate audio, video, and data streams into digital packets; it is quite another to ensure their flawless flow through global information grids. In order to accomplish this, a wide range of standards for equipment necessary to encode and decode signals, and for managing the data flows through networks, is essential. Achieving such agreement is normally difficult because competitors are reluctant to cooperate. This requires sharing information, which itself is increasingly valued in its own right and central to success in developing new technical systems.

Capitalism has traditionally dealt with this problem by establishing government agencies or private-public partnerships that serve as independent arbiters of standards. For example, almost a century and a half ago, competing telegraph interests established the International Telecommunications Union (ITU), a global body made up of mainly government organizations and run on a one-nation, one-vote basis to establish global standards for the new technology. Over the years, the ITU expanded its role as each new communication technology came along, specifically, to set standards for the telephone, allocate broadcasting frequencies, and eventually determine the orbital locations of communication satellites. But as the number of nations grew—particularly the number of former colonial societies eager to create standards to expand widespread access and not just the profits of communication companies—conflict grew at the ITU. Core capitalist powers, led by the United States, began to consider alternatives. These first included political bodies like Intelsat, a global communication satellite organization whose rules permitted Western control, and, more recently, private corporations such as ICANN (Internet Corporation for Assigned Names and Numbers), which essentially establishes standards for the Web. The goal of these organizations has been to set standards to advance the interests of business and to do so without sacrificing global credibility. But it is more and more difficult to accomplish this.

Digitization is increasingly global, and the competition to dominate markets for the short term, by controlling one phase of a rapidly changing technical system, or for the long term, by setting a critical standard (such as for a computer operating system), is intensifying. Furthermore, the diversity of global interests is expanding so that even something as seemingly innocuous as setting a national suffix for a Web address becomes a political question (one particularly contentious case is the petitioning of Palestinians for the suffix ".pa"). Moreover, should the common ".com" suffix expand to include ".union"—as one public interest group proposed? Private businesses hoping to depoliticize these issues by setting up Western-controlled private or quasi-public standards organizations are actually only displacing tensions and contradictions. As a result, seemingly technical questions are caught up in political economic maelstroms that, at the very least, slow the process of global technological development. But the alternative, setting up genuinely public national or international regulatory authorities, a central feature in the expansion of communication during Fordism, invites turning this arena, widely recognized as critical to capitalist expansion, into a highly contested terrain (Lessig 1999).

This problem is evident not only in the struggle over standards; it has also marked debates about how to expand access to technology in order to build markets and about how to ensure some measure of privacy to create consumer confidence in the technology. In the early days of radio, business felt it did not need the state to regulate frequencies. The result was chaos, as broadcasters poached each other's frequencies and the air was filled with worthless static. Business brought the state in to regulate the mess, and it succeeded. But in doing so, it opened this private arena to the wider public, which used the opportunity to fight for public broadcasting and the regulation of private station content. The technology has indeed changed, but the underlying political and economic dynamic has not. Thus, the same tensions and contradictions mark the process of digitization. Consider the recent collapse of the telecommunications bubble, where one-time industry giants like Nortel, Cisco, and Lucent have seen their market values drop by close to 90 percent in one year, with Nortel declaring the largest quarterly loss in the history of business and the once proud Lucent, heir to the legendary Bell

Labs, seeing its shares reduced to junk bond status. Their decline, the overall crisis in the dotcom and telecommunications industries, and, most important, the yawning chasm between the massive glut of high-speed, long-haul information lines and the shortage of high-speed, local access connections needed to gain access to the Web can be directly traced to the almost religiously driven neoliberal strategy that the market would do a better job of regulation than traditional forms of state intervention. With no political or social policy check on investment decisions, a situation cemented into law in various forms, including the U.S. Telecommunications Act of 1996, companies went on a long-haul building binge. Much of this was done by small companies holding few assets, but with Wall Street flush with "new economy fever" (after all, this was the end of history), capital was remarkably easy to raise. One company, Global Crossing, founded in 1997 (led by a protégé of junk bond felon Michael Milken), managed to raise $750 million almost overnight, went public, reached a value of $30 billion, built a transatlantic fiber-optic network valued at much less, and with a glut in capacity (95 percent of fiber-optic network capacity goes unused) dropped to 10 percent of its peak value. In 2002, Global Crossing, like many of its competitors, filed for bankruptcy. (A newly constituted Global Crossing is expected to emerge from bankruptcy in early 2003.) In one year, June 2000 to June 2001, more than 100,000 jobs disappeared from the U.S. communications industry. And the promise of universal access to broadband communication remains just that (Romero 2001). Meanwhile, in another demonstration that the "new economy" is not all that new, a Canadian federal government task force, most of whose members come from the telecommunications and computer industries, recommended in June that the government spend $2.5 to $4 billion to expand broadband access in Canada, presumably by spending the money to bail out the companies that would build broadband networks.

A similar conundrum shapes the issue of privacy. The drive to use communication, particularly the new media of cyberspace, to expand the commodification process inevitably leads to the commodification of personal identity. The production and distribution of information about consumers and workers takes on a value related to, but distinct from, the value of their purchases and their labor. The threat to privacy is not just an offshoot of technology or a correctable oversight, but is rather intrinsic to the commodification process. Consequently, the fight for personal privacy is part of a wider struggle against the expanding commodity form. Among the many examples of the link between commodification and the struggle over privacy, consider the January 2001 Nortel Networks announcement of a new line of "personal content" network software, which the company will sell to Internet service providers in order to package online services to suit individual preferences. The software tracks every choice a user makes on the Internet and configures the network to deliver efficiently the kinds of material a user typically selects. In essence, Nortel is adding to the value of the Internet by making it more responsive to customer profiles. But in doing so, the company makes it possible to gather, package, and share information on customer choices, thereby posing a privacy threat. The response of one privacy activist focuses on the company's responsibility, charging that it is "unacceptable" to enable Internet service providers to watch where their customers are going. But Nortel's behavior is less a matter of corporate irresponsibility and more the response of a company that needs to expand the commodification of its major resource, the Internet. But even more than this, Nortel's product reflects a fundamental contradiction besetting the business of cyberspace: the conflict between the need to build consumer confidence in order to turn the Internet into a universal marketing tool and the need to commodify without government intervention whatever moves over the Internet, including personal identity.

If we step back from this analysis and recall Roland Barthes's description of myth as depoliticized speech, we might conclude that he did not get it entirely right. For this discussion, which began with the myths of globalization and cyberspace, was able to peel back the glossy cover of these phenomena and move from there to the politics of globalization and cyberspace. Yes, these myths demonstrate Barthes's claim that they are depoliticized speech, because myths purify social relations by eliminating the tensions and conflicts that animate the political life of a community. But if myths evacuate politics, then the critique of mythology restores and regenerates it. In this regard, I would agree with Doniger (1998), who concludes that we need to replace Barthes's vision of myth as *apolitical*—in essence, what is left after the politics is eliminated—with the view of myth as *prepolitical,* as an early step in a process that, when examined with a critical eye, can restore with every critical retelling the political grounding that myths leave out. In essence, myths can foreclose politics, can serve to depoliticize speech. But they can also open the door to a restoration of politics, to a deepening of political understanding.

Peeling away the myths of cyberspace reveals the messy, buggy politics of digitization, commodification, concentration, and contradiction. Let's conclude by saying something about the politics of convergence. I won't repeat the familiar and practically banal arguments about technological and institutional convergence, arguments that have been repeated so often that they are approaching the status of mantras. Rather, I want to consider convergence of a different sort, the kind that leads one to wonder about the potential for a new cultural politics, if not a new internationalism. The recent demonstrations in Seattle, Prague, Quebec, and Genoa, as well as the global movements organized around culture jamming, are grounded in a powerful and unprecedented broad-based understanding of the convergence of labor and consumption in the world today. Participants in these demonstrations and movements understand the links between Nike ads and sweatshops making running shoes, between slave labor and familiar brands like Wal-Mart, Esprit, K-Mart, and J.C. Penney. This happens, in part, because participants extend the analysis that Marx began in Volume 1 of *Capital,* where he described the commodity as a fetish (one might substitute the word *brand* or *myth*) that, when its glossy skin was peeled back, revealed an exploitative labor process. Today's global social movements are based on a similar ability to strip the gloss from a brand to reveal not only the exploitation of labor, but also the commercialization of life worldwide and the destruction of the earth's environment.

Convergence does not just mean plugging a cable modem into a PC; it also means the global convergence of labor and consumption practices that, in a multimediated world, drive home for the many what only a few understood over a century ago. Today, commodity production brings knowledge workers together and makes transparent the divide between them and the unskilled. It also brings consumers together and makes transparent the divide between them and those who have little. In essence, it makes it possible to unite the politics of labor, which, as Michael Denning reminds us, energized social movements of the first half of the twentieth century (Denning 1996), and the politics of consumption, which drove much resistance in the second half, to create a politics of citizenship that transcends both labor and consumption with the active construction of a democratic world order. The convergence of labor and consumption and the politics of citizenship, which seem to mark so much of what simplemindedly gets called the antiglobalization movement, may be the most significant form of convergence to understand today. Perhaps it is laying the groundwork for a new internationalism.

References

Barthes, R. 1972. *Mythologies.* Trans. A. Lavers. New York: Noonday Press.
Cairncross, F. 1997. *The Death of Distance.* Boston: Harvard Business School Press.
Carey, J.W. 1992. *Communication as Culture: Essays on Media and Society.* New York: Routledge.
Crozier, M., S.P. Huntington, and J. Watanuki. 1975. *The Crisis of Democracy.* New York: New York University Press.
Denning, M. 1996. *The Cultural Front.* London: Verso.
Doniger, W. 1998. *The Implied Spider: Politics and Theology in Myth.* New York: Columbia University Press.
Douglas, S. 1987. *Inventing American Broadcasting 1899–1922.* Baltimore: Johns Hopkins University Press.
Fisher, D.E., and M.J. Fisher. 1996. *Tube: The Invention of Television.* New York: Harcourt Brace.

Friedman, T. 1999. *The Lexus and the Olive Tree: Understanding Globalization.* New York: Farrar, Strauss, Giroux.

Fukuyama, F. 1992. *The End of History and the Last Man.* New York: Avon Books.

Gates, B., with C. Hemingway. 1999. *Business @ the Speed of Thought: Using a Digital Nervous System.* New York: Warner Books.

Gates, B., and N. Myhrvold. 1996. *The Road Ahead.* New York: Penguin USA.

Gilder, G. 2000. *Telecosm: How Infinite Bandwidth Will Revolutionize Our World.* New York: Free Press.

Hardt, H., and B. Brennen, eds. 1995. *Newsworkers: Toward a History of the Rank and File.* Minneapolis: University of Minnesota Press.

Klein, N. 2000. *No Logo.* Toronto: Knopf Canada.

Kurzweil, R. 1999. *The Age of Spiritual Machines.* New York: Viking.

Lessig, L. 1999. *Code and Other Laws of Cyberspace.* New York: Basic Books.

Longstaff, P.F. 2000. *Convergence and Divergence in Communication Regulation.* Cambridge, MA: Harvard University Program on Information Resources Policy.

MacIntyre, A. 1970. *Sociological Theory and Philosophical Analysis.* New York: Macmillan.

Martin, M. 1991. *"Hello, Central": Gender, Technology, and Culture in the Formation of Telephone Systems.* Montreal: McGill-Queen's University Press.

Marx, K. 1973. *Grundrisse.* Trans. M. Nicolaus. New York: Random House.

Marx, L. 1964. *The Machine in the Garden: Technology and the Pastoral Ideal in America.* New York: Oxford University Press.

McChesney, R. 1999. *Rich Media, Poor Democracy.* Urbana: University of Illinois Press.

McKercher, C. 2000. "From Newspaper Guild to Multimedia Union: A Study in Labour Convergence." Ph.D. diss., Concordia University, Montreal.

Miege, B. 1989. *The Capitalization of Cultural Production.* New York: International General.

Mitchell, W.J. 1989. *City of Bits.* Cambridge, MA: MIT Press.

———. 1999. *E-topia.* Cambridge, MA: MIT Press.

Mosco, V. 1996. *The Political Economy of Communication.* London: Sage.

Mosco, V., and D. Foster. 2001. "Cyberspace and the End of Politics." *Journal of Communication Inquiry* 25: 218–236.

Mosco, V., and D. Schiller, eds. 2001. *Continental Order? Integrating North America for Cybercapitalism.* New York: Rowman and Littlefield.

Mouffe, C. 2000. *The Democratic Paradox.* London: Verso.

Negroponte, N. 1995. *Being Digital.* New York: Knopf.

Ohmae, K. 1990. *The Borderless World.* New York: HarperCollins.

———. 1995. *The End of the Nation State.* New York: Free Press.

Romero, S. 2001. "Shining Future of Fiber Optics Loses Its Glimmer." *New York Times,* June 18, A1, A17.

Schiller, D. 1999. *Digital Capitalism.* Cambridge, MA: MIT Press.

Standage, T. 1998. *The Victorian Internet.* New York: Walker.

Sunstein, C. 2001. *Republic.com.* Princeton, NJ: Princeton University Press.

Sussman, G., and J. Lent, eds. 1998. *Global Productions.* London: Sage.

Teilhard de Chardin. 1959. *The Phenomenon of Man.* New York: Harper.

Toffler, A., and H. Toffler. 1995. *Creating a New Civilization: The Politics of the Third Wave.* Atlanta: Turner Publishing.

Wertheim, M. 1999. *The Pearly Gates of Cyberspace.* New York: Norton.

4

The PBS Brand and the Merchandising of Public Service

William Hoynes

In the early twenty-first century, public television in the United States is in the midst of a dramatic transformation. This is the result, in part, of the continuing changes in the structure of the broadcast industry and of the development of new digital media technologies. At the same time, the changes in public television are shaped by a broader ideological environment that celebrates the free market and produces a concomitant suspicion of the public sector. In this climate, thirty-five years after the initial Public Broadcasting Act, public television is, once again, in search of a mission. And rather than turning to the tradition of public service broadcasting, public broadcasters are looking to the world of advertising and marketing as they define their new vision of public television.

This chapter explores the evolving strategy within public television aimed at competing in the new media landscape. As public television makes an effort to become more market-oriented and commercially savvy, it is instructive to examine these developing strategies, for they tell us how far we have come from previous conceptions of public service broadcasting. Indeed, a quick glance through the original Carnegie Commission (1967) report, *Public Television: A Program for Action,* highlights the ways that the discourse surrounding public television has changed over the past three decades (Blakely 1971; Macy 1974).

While the founding documents of public television centered on democratic values—including a vision that the enterprise would "be a forum for debate and controversy," provide a voice "for groups in the community that may otherwise be unheard," and "help us see America whole, in all its diversity" (Carnegie 1967)—the current discourse around public television often lacks a core sense of the urgency with which this noncommercial broadcasting system can contribute to a democratic public sphere. In fact, the utopian impulse that helped create public broadcasting, the belief that a healthy democracy requires a genuinely public media system, now centers almost exclusively on the Internet. In much the same way that public television was in the 1960s, new digital media are now heralded as potential sites for enhancing our communication environment by providing opportunities for citizens to participate in public life.

What we need, in this time of rapid change, is to revisit the very reasons for the existence of *public* or *noncommercial* broadcasting in the first place. This will help us—scholars, critics, public broadcasters, and citizens alike— to think more clearly about the future of public broadcasting in this era of multimedia conglomerates. Indeed, if public television is to survive as a genuinely public institution, one that is structurally and substantively different from the commercial media, a clear articulation of its fundamental mission is long overdue.

In *Public Television for Sale* (1994), I argued that the most significant threat to our public television system was not the influence of the federal government, despite recent high-profile efforts by conservatives in Congress to reassert control over public broadcasting (Hoynes 1994). Instead, I made the case that the real challenge for public television was the continuing intrusion of market values within public broadcasting. By the early 1990s, with some forms of commercialization increasingly taken for granted, it was clear that we were headed toward a more thoroughly market-oriented public television system. However, in 1994, I could not have imagined how fast this commercialization was going to move forward. Since 1995, public television's shift toward the market has accelerated at a remarkably rapid rate.

The Weak Link: Funding for Public TV

Since its inception, U.S. public broadcasting has been plagued by a weak funding structure. Ever since the Public Broadcasting Act's passage in 1967, supporters of public broadcasting have sought, unsuccessfully, a federal commitment to long-term, stable funding. Instead of this kind of stable public funding, public broadcasters rely upon various revenue sources, each of which brings its own pressures and incentives.

There are two fundamental weaknesses to the funding structure of public broadcasting. One is the politicization of federal funding for the industry. Approximately 12 percent of the system's revenues come from the federal treasury, through annual congressional appropriations. At several points over the past thirty years—most notably in 1972, when President Nixon vetoed a bill authorizing funds for public broadcasting (Stone 1985), and in 1994, when House Speaker Newt Gingrich announced his intention to "zero out" public broadcasting—the White House and members of Congress have used the appropriations process as an opportunity to threaten cutbacks or total elimination of federal funds in response to supposedly "biased" programming (Witherspoon, Kovitz, Avery, and Stavitsky 2000). As a result, public broadcasters face a standing implicit threat from their federal patrons. While this implied threat does not dictate programming decisions in any direct way, political pressure has been frequent enough that the threat lingers around the edges, engendering an atmosphere of timidity. The potential for government intervention nurtures persistent concern, leading public broadcasters to routinely keep in mind the consequences of their programming choices.

Just as important as the political pressure surrounding federal funding is the fact that the annual congressional appropriation still accounts for only a small fraction of total public broadcasting funding. With the federal government providing $250 million in fiscal year 1999—albeit an important $250 million that helped to generate other revenue—for a public broadcasting system with total 1999 revenue of $2.1 billion, public broadcasters, quite simply, can neither worry too much about the federal government nor neglect other potential revenue sources. As Table 4.1 shows, federal funding through the Corporation for Public Broadcasting has been shrinking as a percentage of total public broadcasting revenue for the past two decades. Most of the nonfederal revenue for public broadcasting comes from state and local governments (many of which operate stations), foundations, corporations, and "subscribers." In fact, the largest single chunk of public television revenue comes from these subscribers, "viewers like you" who contribute to their local stations in pledge drives each year.

The increasing significance of viewers as donors provides incentive for PBS stations to broadcast upscale programming that will attract high-income viewers and motivate them to "join" or contribute. The focus on viewers as direct contributors encourages PBS and its member stations to develop programs aimed at potential *donors* instead of a *public* that is more broadly conceived. While total subscriber contributions have grown significantly over the past two decades, the number of individual contributors to public television stations has actually declined. As Table 4.2 indicates, the key change is the average size of individual contributions to public television stations, which

Table 4.1

Public Broadcasting System Revenues, 1982–1999
(as a percentage of total system revenue)

	1982	1990	1999
Corporation for Public Broadcasting	20.3	14.5	11.6
Other federal funds	3	2.4	2.4
Local governments	5	3.8	2.7
State governments	19.7	16.6	13.9
Public colleges and universities	10.9	9.6	8.8
Private colleges and universities	1.5	2	1.5
Foundations	2.6	4.5	5.7
Business	11.9	16.6	14.7
Subscribers	16.8	21.6	25.6
Auctions	2.4	1.4	0.8
Other private sources	5.8	7.1	12.3

Sources: Corporation for Public Broadcasting; Public Broadcasting Policy Base.

increased by 45 percent between 1989 and 1999. (Public radio stations have experienced a similar increase in the average contribution, but this has been accompanied by a substantial growth in the number of contributors as well.) From a purely revenue-generating perspective, viewers with high levels of disposable income are more valuable to PBS stations than those who lack the resources to contribute regularly. While PBS undoubtedly views its viewers as more than a simple source of revenue, public broadcasters have responded to their uncertain financial picture by emphasizing, both in the program development process and in the discursive construction of the public, the ways that viewers are, indeed, a valuable audience.

Public broadcasters also depend upon corporate sponsorship, or "underwriting," as a key source of revenue for program production. In 1999, corporate support for public broadcasting constituted 14.7 percent of total revenue, accounting for a larger piece of the funding pie than the Corporation for Public Broadcasting. In the increasingly cluttered media marketplace, there is a growing sense within public television that in order to attract sponsorship dollars, PBS stations need to provide corporate sponsors with more than simply a positive image in exchange for program funding. With a PBS viewership that is known to be highly educated and economically well-off, the attention of a small, but highly desirable audience segment has become one of PBS's most valuable assets. As a result, efforts to attract corporate underwriters provide another incentive for PBS to develop programs that will deliver an upscale audience.

Table 4.2

Member Contributions to Public Television Stations, 1989–1999

Year	Number of contributors (in thousands)	Average contribution (in current dollars)
1989	4,927	53.16
1991	4,904	58.29
1993	5,033	59.08
1995	4,938	63.15
1997	4,659	71.07
1999	4,657	77.05

Source: Corporation for Public Broadcasting.

The "New PBS"

Public television survived the high-profile assault from conservative critics, which was front-page news in the early 1990s. Organized efforts to eliminate or privatize public broadcasting in 1992 and 1994 were ultimately unsuccessful. However, the campaign against public television, waged to a large degree on the floor of the U.S. Congress and in the national media, did have lasting consequences. Public broadcasting did receive federal funding after the acrimonious debates in 1992 and 1994, emerging with renewed political support from both Democrats and Republicans. But the industry's leaders relearned a lesson that their predecessors had grasped from the 1972 Nixon veto: without an independent funding structure, federal funding would always be precarious, shifting in response to the changing political terrain.

As a result, public television executives began to build a "new PBS" in the mid-1990s, redirecting the public television system to be more market-savvy, more focused on revenue-generating possibilities, and more entrepreneurial. In the wake of the campaign that almost destroyed public television, PBS developed a plan to remake itself into what the 1998 PBS Annual Report called a "modern media enterprise" (Public Broadcasting Service 1998). The effort to restructure public television represented both the implementation of a strategy to insulate PBS from political pressure and a vision for the future of public broadcasting. The key to both this evolving strategy and to this vision of the future is the PBS *brand*.

The new PBS is, by its own definition, more commercially oriented than ever before. The PBS brand is the key to the growth of this multimedia enterprise, a sign that public television has adopted the newest language and strategy of the advertising industry. Indeed, managing and monetizing the PBS brand is more than just a means to generate revenue that is independent of government. A careful look at how PBS is trying to leverage its brand suggests that PBS is not just using the language of the advertising industry, but also adopting the same business practices as the commercial media and developing a series of strategic alliances with the major media conglomerates. At the new PBS, the brand becomes the primary asset of the system, marking the shift to a conceptual framework that renders public service a kind of value-generating activity and makes the idea of noncommercial broadcasting increasingly anachronistic.

This branding strategy at PBS has helped to transform the very idea of what's public about public broadcasting. This new focus on the value of the PBS brand is particularly significant because it represents a commodification of public service within public broadcasting. In essence, the notion of public service itself is increasingly being packaged and sold to consumers who are brand-loyal to PBS.

Extending the PBS Brand

As PBS develops a strategy for leveraging its brand, the organization's leaders have worked to extend the brand beyond television and to cash in on consumer loyalty to PBS. This is part of a broader strategy to create new revenue streams by licensing the PBS logo on a wide range of merchandise, selling new forms of advertising, and developing several PBS brand-name product lines. By 2001, PBS was engaged in an elaborate branding effort, with new products in various media aimed at key market segments.

One of the signature elements of the PBS branding effort is the growing PBS Online series of Web sites. PBS quickly adopted an active online presence, building www.pbs.org into a multilayered site with several online "neighborhoods" and Web pages for most of its programs. The various PBS online pages are clearly commercial ventures. While PBS continues to use the terms "underwriting" and "sponsorship," it is clear that advertising space is for sale on PBS Online. In its own promotional material, PBS woos potential sponsors with references to the high quality of its online content, noting that pbs.org has won several prestigious "Webby" awards. PBS promotional literature also tells sponsors about tens of thousands of pages of content, millions of visitors, an online audience that has "dream demographics," and an audience that is extraordinarily loyal to the PBS brand (Public Broadcasting Service 2001).

Sponsors of PBS Online can buy space for prominent display of their corporate logos on a pbs.org page of their choice; these logos are hyperlinked to the sponsor's corporate Web site. For example, the Web page for the science program *Nova* contains logo-links to Sprint and Northwestern Mutual Life Insurance. In addition, PBS touts the power of its brand as a means of enhancing the corporate image of sponsors, noting that PBS brand trust and loyalty will be transferred to these companies. PBS also promotes the popularity of its PBS Kids Web site, the most popular PBS brand site, as a selling point for potential sponsors. Although PBS continues to identify its children's programming as noncommercial, many of the PBS Kids Web sites include full-color corporate logos that link to the sponsor's Web site. The Web page for the popular children's program *Arthur*, for example, has prominent logo-links to Juicy Juice, Alphabits, and Lego. The *Barney* page has links to Chuck E Cheese's and Kellogg's cereal, and the PBS Kids Web page for *Between the Lions* has a logo-link to Cheerios (links from PBS Kids Web pages go through a "bridge page" that alerts users that they are leaving the PBS Kids Web site). While the viewer is online at one of the pbs.org sites, PBS merchandise is only a click away at Shop PBS (www.shoppbs.org), which provides an online store for purchasing PBS-related products.

PBS has also extended its brand into the sky. In the late 1990s, PBS worked out separate agreements, under the name PBS Aloft, to provide brand-name programming for in-flight viewing on the domestic and international flights of US Air and United Airlines. Since PBS is well known for its regular business news programs, the high volume of business travelers makes PBS Aloft a product that can reach business people in new settings.

PBS maintains a brand-name record label, PBS Records, a joint venture with Warner Bros. Records (a division of AOL Time Warner). The new record label releases music from PBS performance programs and soundtracks from other PBS programs.

In addition, PBS created a brand-name video and DVD line, PBS Home Video, a joint venture with Warner Home Video, to distribute programming to consumers for in-home use. This home video line, and the distribution that Warner Home Video can provide, will help to make PBS brand programs, especially those aimed at children, a much more significant player in the growing home video market. (This venture is separate from PBS Video, which licenses PBS programming for educational use.)

In 2000, PBS entered a strategic alliance with AOL (now AOL Time Warner) to become a "content partner." Under the terms of this alliance, PBS will provide content for various AOL services, and PBS and AOL will establish a series of online links between the two companies' various Web pages. In this alliance, the two companies established a cobranding partnership: AOL will promote the PBS brand online and AOL will receive on-air branding on popular PBS programs.

As a means of increasing the visibility of the brand, PBS licenses the use of its logo, copyrights, and program characters for a wide range of products. Children's products that build upon parental and child trust in the PBS brand—

from books, games, and toys to toothbrushes, cups, and clothing—have been a particularly attractive source of revenue. Retail stores such as Learningsmith and Store of Knowledge sell PBS brand products and, more generally, help to circulate the PBS brand. And PBS maintains a strategic relationship with Microsoft to manufacture and distribute "Actimates"—character toys from popular PBS programs that interact with both the television programs and the program Web sites.

Perhaps the most elaborate component of the PBS branding effort is the growing series of PBS Kids products. PBS is extending its brand, leveraging its reputation as a longtime producer of noncommercial children's programming, by developing a comprehensive PBS Kids *franchise*. This PBS Kids franchise is a genuinely multimedia effort. It features a distinct PBS Kids logo that gets widespread promotion on the lineup of PBS Kids television programs. One of the core components is the new PBS Kids digital television channel, available on the DirecTV satellite service—a sign of PBS's preparation to benefit from the emerging digital television era. PBS Kids features a separate online presence, pbskids.org, which is promoted heavily on PBS Kids television programs. The franchise includes PBS Kids Home Video, which distributes PBS children's programming for in-home use. In addition, the new PBS Kids Books, a joint venture with Simon and Schuster (owned by Viacom), will develop a line of books based upon popular PBS Kids television programs (much like Simon and Schuster does for its Viacom sibling company, and PBS competitor, Nickelodeon).

As they develop forward-looking plans to extend and leverage their brand, PBS executives are employing the same strategies, and making use of the same brand management consultants, that the major corporate media use. Indeed, it is increasingly difficult to discern the difference between public broadcasting executives and their counterparts in commercial broadcasting, with whom they share training and terminology, and follow the same underlying strategies to succeed in the marketplace. In this context, public service often becomes little more than a slogan used to justify federal funds and stimulate viewer contributions.

Merchandising Public Service

As PBS moves toward this more full-fledged market model, its branding strategy involves more than simply extending the brand to new products and making it more visible in a variety of arenas. PBS has adopted several other key components of the commercial media approach. As we have seen, PBS is developing joint ventures and strategic alliances with the major media conglomerates to develop and distribute new PBS brand products, including various television coproduction agreements with major commercial media. Upon announcing the appointment of a new vice president in charge of strategic partnerships in 2001, PBS executive vice president Judy Harris noted that "strategic partnerships are the key to success in today's competitive environment" (PBS News 2001). Indeed, PBS increasingly views commercial television networks as friendly competitors for market share, rather than as representatives of a model of broadcasting for which PBS provides an alternative.

As PBS further embraces the market model, public television has become a program service that targets specific market segments. Following the lead of successful cable channels that have built programming for a narrow demographic, PBS has moved even further away from a broad public orientation, focusing its general approach to "upscale" viewers by targeting two specific audience segments: businesspeople and children. PBS has long been a supplier of innovative children's programming; indeed, parents and young children are among its most loyal viewers. But as the market for children's media has exploded in recent years, PBS has been in a position to cash in on this loyal audience and PBS's reputation for quality educational programming. The growth of the PBS Kids franchise—and the interest among major national advertisers in sponsoring various PBS Kids ventures—testify to the increasing focus at PBS on children as potentially valuable consumers. The regular menu of business programs on PBS stations is another avenue through which public television directs its programming and sponsorship activities toward a highly desirable demographic.

As PBS builds its brand across multiple media platforms, the corporate temptation to take advantage of synergies through cross-promotion and cross-media sponsorship is increasingly evident. PBS, working with its counterparts in public radio and an online marketing firm, now offers sponsors the opportunity to develop integrated advertising campaigns utilizing public television, public radio, and PBS Online. Such cross-media revenue-generating strategies, bringing together the sales possibilities of these three media, are one of the driving forces behind the continuing consolidation of the global media industry.

In this age of media conglomerates, the new PBS is pursuing a strategy that may lead to short-term financial success. Efforts to monetize brand loyalty and a new entrepreneurial spirit within public broadcasting are bringing in new revenue streams and positioning public television to compete in the rapidly evolving media marketplace. However, these strategies are producing a PBS that is losing its distinctive public service identity, as it becomes just another brand competing for attention and consumer dollars in an increasingly cluttered commercial marketplace. The principal discursive framework within PBS now revolves around a definition of the media world as an intensely competitive marketplace. In this climate, competition for audiences, demographics, advertising revenue, and "talent" become the currency, while concerns about how best to serve the multifaceted public become increasingly marginal.

What we are witnessing is a new stage in the commercialization of public television in the United States. And, in tandem with recent threats from conservatives in the U.S. Congress to privatize public broadcasting, public television executives—looking for ways to ensure the survival of the public television system—are leading the way toward a new, market-oriented version of public television. The advent of the digital era promises a wide range of new commercial ventures for public television. In 2001, the Federal Communications Commission (FCC), in response to a petition from the Association of America's Public Television Stations and PBS, announced that it will permit noncommercial, educational license holders (public television stations) to carry advertising on their ancillary or supplementary digital services. These services include subscription video, interactive material, data transmissions, and future services other than free, broadcast video (Federal Communications Commission 2001). The FCC's decision opens the way for a new source of revenue for PBS stations and provides renewed incentives for PBS to develop commercialized segments among the evolving digital extensions of public television.

As PBS becomes more integrated into the commercial media system and develops a business model that sees public television as an increasingly commercial enterprise, the foundations of the public service model are deteriorating. Indeed, the branding strategy is an attempt to turn the cultural value of the old PBS into financial value for the new PBS. This exchange is a means of transforming public service, and the trust that accompanies such public service, into a marketable commodity. In the midst of this transformation, PBS runs the very real risk that its aggressive branding strategy will undermine the trust and loyalty that make its brand so valuable.

The commercial strategy is now so well developed at PBS that it is becoming harder to detect the public service model of broadcasting at work. Indeed, the rise of the new PBS raises important questions about the meaning of such concepts as "public service" and the "public interest." As public broadcasters continue to refine their commercial activities, building their brands and selling their audiences, they will inevitably face questions about how and why they serve the public in any distinctive manner. This new generation of market-savvy public broadcasters is likely to meet renewed challenges to the legitimacy of its claim on public funding. An entrepreneurial PBS—with multiple revenue-generating, brand-name product lines, an increasingly commercial presence in the digital media landscape, and an upscale audience whose attention is exchanged for sponsorship dollars—will become increasingly difficult to define as a public institution to either a skeptical Congress or a public that is barraged with so many niche-oriented media services.

PBS's branding strategy, much like public television itself, is rife with contradictions. The brand identity that PBS is trying to leverage is built on a noncommercial foundation. Indeed, the very core of trust in the PBS brand, which makes the extension of the brand such a valuable revenue-generating strategy, lies in public television's roots as an institution that is identified more as a public service than a corporate brand. PBS's multimedia branding effort—spanning the range of media platforms including television, the Internet, home videos, music, and books—is now fully developed. In this context, we need to begin to make sense of the meaning of public service broadcasting in a context where public service becomes a form of merchandise. This branding strategy may be the result of public television's longtime funding uncertainty. Nevertheless, it shows with great clarity that public television is in the business of catering to audiences and advertisers more than serving citizens.

References

Blakely, R.J. 1971. *The People's Instrument: A Philosophy of Programming for Public Television.* Washington, DC: Public Affairs Press.

Carnegie Commission on Educational Television. 1967. *Public Television: A Program for Action.* New York: Bantam.

Federal Communications Commission. 2001. Report and order, "Ancillary or Supplementary Use of Digital Television by Noncommercial Licensees." FCC 01–306. October 11.

Hoynes, W. 1994. *Public Television for Sale: Media, the Market, and the Public Sphere.* Boulder, CO: Westview Press.

Macy, J.W., Jr. 1974. *To Irrigate a Wasteland.* Berkeley: University of California Press.

PBS News. 2001. "PBS Names Marketing Executive Adrienne Cleere Vice President, Strategic Partnerships." Alexandria, VA: Public Broadcasting Service, May 21.

Public Broadcasting Service. 1998. *Doing Good While Doing Well: The PBS 1998 Annual Report.* Alexandria, VA: Public Broadcasting Service.

———. 2001. "Stand Out Online." sponsorship.pbs.org/online_only_ benefits.htm (April 19).

Stone, D.M. 1985. *Nixon and the Politics of Public Television.* New York: Garland.

Witherspoon, J., and R. Kovitz, with an update by R. Avery and A. Stavitsky. 2000. *A History of Public Broadcasting.* Washington, DC: Current.

5

The FCC and the Public Interest

A Selective Critique of U.S. Telecommunications Policy-Making

Robert K. Avery and Alan G. Stavitsky

This chapter serves as a brief snapshot of a work in progress. Our purpose is to examine selected primary documents from the public broadcasting community and the Federal Communications Commission (FCC) in various policy matters, in order to determine the underlying values that drive the arguments advanced and the decisions set forth. Our approach can be described as a critical close reading of these documents, as a means to determine the extent to which the actual language used is consistent with the existing broader critique of public broadcasting's continued disenfranchisement. We situate our analysis within contemporary critical writings that afford a basis for interpretation. Our objective is to offer a context for this study, to provide some examples of the kinds of documents under review, to suggest some preliminary findings, and then to relate them to larger discussions about contemporary public broadcasting.

Public Interest in Communications Policy

Wick Rowland (1986) provides a devastating critique of the way noncommercial educational broadcasting has been systematically disenfranchised by communication policy-makers in the United States. Departing from the neutralist historiography of the U.S. broadcasting research tradition, Rowland offers a historical account that significantly reinterprets events and actions, that places new emphasis on themes and nuances that, up until then, were typically glossed over or ignored in the literature of American broadcasting history. Working closely within the popular critical and cultural perspectives

of the time, he demonstrates the relevance of questions about public authority, corporate, political and economic interests, the mythologies of democratic culture, pluralism, and broadly conceived public service ideals. Rowland
(1986, 1993b) argues that this revisionist view of broadcast history reveals a
long-standing minimalist orientation toward public radio and television, one
that demonstrates a callous disregard for developing policies to safeguard
and nurture an alternative broadcasting service.

The fundamental themes contained in Rowland's essay are expanded and
recontextualized by Robert McChesney (1993) in *Telecommunications, Mass
Media, and Democracy,* and by Thomas Streeter's (1996) communication
policy critique, *Selling the Air.* Both authors provide penetrating analyses
and convincing explications of how corporate liberal ideology pervades the
entire policy establishment, which routinely privileges private interests at
the expense of the public interest. In other works, McChesney (1997) and
Herman and McChesney (1997) further develop the themes of capitalism,
media concentration, and threats to democracy.

Our own interpretive framework draws heavily from these and other authors who argue that the shared value system of corporate liberalism can be
found in the decisions and practices of our policy-makers. This study, then,
attempts to contribute to a growing body of literature that advances the proposition that while capitalist philosophy is central to the workings of government, there should be a reasonable balance between two fundamental
perspectives of what constitutes the "public interest" in America. These two
perspectives have been described as the "instrumental view" and the "program service view."

According to Rowland (1993a), the "instrumental view" equates the interest of the public with that of the industry being regulated. The theory here
is that the public cannot be served unless the broadcast service provider is
economically healthy. If the company prospers financially, it will be able to
offer quality products that render the greatest good to the public. This perspective suggests that the public is represented, at least indirectly, in the regulatory process, with fiscal soundness and profitability being a general marker
of public approval. The competing view of the public interest, and the one
we in the academy most frequently associate with broadcasting, is wedded
to the nature of the program services provided. Here the public's well-being
is seen through the "diversity of programming, the range of social, cultural
and political interests served, educational and informational richness, and
overall quality" (Rowland 1993a, 2). While regulatory language has always
drawn from both perspectives, the actual practices of the Federal Radio Commission (FRC), and later the FCC, demonstrate a definite preference for the
instrumental view (Stavitsky 1994).

The regulatory charade of license renewals and periodic public hearings served to mask the underlying values of corporate liberalism until FCC Chairman Mark Fowler and his legal associate David Brenner decided to go public with their policy bias in 1982. Against the deregulatory backdrop of the Reagan administration, Fowler and Brenner (1982) unleashed language that brought advocates of the public service ideal to their knees. These authors argued that the public trustee model of broadcast regulation was in reality a sham and that its continued use could not be justified in an era of channel abundance. For them, the use of the "public interest, convenience, or necessity" standard served merely to encourage broadcasters to promote the public interest myth, thus misleading Americans about the real role and function of broadcasting in this country—to make money. Making clear their position that broadcasting was first and foremost a business, the authors went on to explain how continued adherence to the trusteeship model would only perpetuate the regulatory shortcomings that have undermined open competition. In their words, "Our thesis is that broadcasters as community trustees should be replaced by a view of broadcasters as marketplace participants. Communications policy should be directed toward maximizing the services the public desires. . . . The public's interest, then, defines the public interest . . . . The first step in a marketplace approach to broadcast regulation, then, is to focus on broadcasters not as fiduciaries of the public . . . but as marketplace competitors" (Fowler and Brenner 1982, 3–4). Later in their essay, Fowler and Brenner write at some length about the potential virtues of a noncommercial public broadcasting service that might take on the responsibility of providing programming that has absolutely no commercial viability, and they concede that such programming might be of value to those segments of society that obviously would be excluded from consideration under the market forces model. But ultimately, they wash their hands of any obligation to public broadcasters, stating that the well-being of an alternative system of noncommercial broadcasting is the responsibility of Congress and not the FCC.

A Template for Critical Analysis

The marketplace language of unbridled competition first introduced by Fowler and Brenner provides us, then, with the first portion of the template used to examine the exchange of documents between public broadcasting and the FCC. A second segment of the template is that of the trusteeship model itself, emanating largely from the early writings (e.g., Reith 1942 and Briggs 1961) on British and other Western European models of public service broadcasting. This traditional noncommercial view of the public interest standard was based on an overarching ideal of the cultural and intellectual enlightenment of society. The fundamental principles that served as the hallmark of this philosophy are universality of service, diversity of programming, provision for minorities and the disadvantaged, the sustaining of an informed electorate, and cultural and educational enrichment (Avery 1993). Authors of the early and mid-1900s borrowed heavily from these writings, as did Dallas Smythe and Charles Siepmann when drafting the FCC's famous "Blue Book" (Federal Communications Commission 1946) about the public service responsibilities of broadcasters. One month after this report was published, Siepmann (1946) released *Radio's Second Chance*, a volume that, like the Blue Book, criticized the American broadcasting industry.

The third and final part of our template is the language contained in Subpart D, Section 396 of the Communications Act itself, introduced by the Public Broadcasting Act of 1967. Given that the Federal Communications Commission is mandated to uphold this law, several statements are of particular interest:

(1) it is in the public interest to encourage the growth and development of public radio and television broadcasting, including the use of such media for instruction, educational, and cultural purposes;

(5) it furthers the general welfare to encourage public telecommunications services that will be responsive to the interests of the people both in particular localities and throughout the United States, which will constitute an expression of diversity and excellence, and which will constitute a source of alternative telecommunications services for all the citizens of the Nation;

(6) it is in the public interest to encourage the development of programming that involves creative risks and that addresses the needs of unserved and underserved audiences, particularly children and minorities; [and finally]

(7) it is necessary and appropriate for the Federal Government to complement, assist, and support a national policy that will most effectively make public telecommunications services available to the citizens of the United States. (Communications Act, Sec. 396, p. 115)

In summary, then, we are guided in our analysis by the actual language contained in (1) the overarching principles of public service broadcasting that represent a trusteeship orientation to the public interest standard, (2) the language of the Communications Act, (3) and the initial philosophical statement that articulated the FCC's commitment to deregulation of the broadcasting industry, along with its policy shift to a market forces orientation.

Our actual methodology might best be described as a form of discourse analysis wherein we seek to determine the values embedded in the discourse that underlies the arguments and beliefs of the rhetor. Unlike formal content analysis, which conforms to quantitative measures articulated at the outset of the study, our analysis takes the form of a critical close reading, with decisions made about the overall relevance of documents as the reading progresses. We draw our methodological approach from the work of Sillars, Ganer, Sandeen, and Armstrong (Sillars 1991; Sillars and Ganer 1982; Ganer 1988; Sandeen 1997; Armstrong 2002), who argue that while texts may contain any number of values or beliefs, only those germane to the investigation need be noted. We also recognize that the researcher must be aware of the presence of "subtexts" that are not immediately apparent in the discourse, and that ultimately the purpose of the analysis is to explicate the values that enable the researcher to answer the question, "So what?"

The documents selected for this study were drawn from the legal files of America's Public Television Stations (APTS). According to APTS records, the legal counsel's office participated on behalf of the public broadcasting community in a total of thirty-nine separate FCC rule-making proceedings between January 1, 1990, and July 1, 1999—the period selected for analysis. Within these rule-making proceedings, a total of 159 filings were made on behalf of public television and public radio interests. In selecting our sample of documents, we were guided by the desire to examine those documents that (1) might best afford APTS and the FCC the chance to set forth statements that contained public interest positions and interpretations, (2) afforded a range of regulatory contexts and issues, and (3) provided enough opportunity for the development of the respective arguments advanced. Using these criteria, we selected nine rule-making proceedings that represent 105 separate filings, or about two-thirds of the filings during the period of study.

The nine rule-making proceedings under examination are as follows: Advanced Television Systems and Their Impact upon Existing Television Service (29 filings); Direct Broadcast Satellite Services (23); The Reexamination of Existing Policies on Comparative Broadcast Hearings (20); Local Multipoint Distribution Service (12); The Telephone Company—Cable Cross Ownership Rules (a.k.a. Video Dialtone) (9); The Cable "Must Carry" Rules (8); Inquiry into the Use and Management of the Radio Spectrum (2); and the Proposed Rulemaking Related to the Public Telecommunications Facilities Program (2). These documents, along with the FCC's corresponding requests for comments, notices of proposed rule-makings, memoranda of opinion and reconsideration, and rule-making notices, constitute the data for this study.

Discussion of Results

While our analysis remains a work-in-progress, we can offer some preliminary findings. In broad-brush strokes, we can state with confidence that the values underlying the respective discourses of the FCC and the public broadcasting community are distinctly different. The FCC's statements reveal values that are overwhelmingly tied to such market-oriented concepts as maximizing competition, enhancing market power, promoting investment incentives, insuring competitive rate structures, removing barriers to entry, and encouraging new service providers. Although the FCC frequently makes reference to the "public interest," it is almost without exception within a market-related context. Such phrases as "the Commission's policy in this matter is to further the public interest goals of increased competition, improved infrastructure, and greater diversity in service providers" are exceedingly commonplace. Indeed, the 1982 Fowler and Brenner essay can be seen as a blueprint for the values that pervade the entire range of FCC documents examined to date. Despite the language of Section 396 of the Communications Act—which gives emphasis to the importance of an informed citizenry, the needs of minorities and other underserved audiences, the general welfare of all citizens, and the assurance of access to instructional, educational, and cultural services—the FCC consistently privileges the concept of "consumer" rather than the concept of "citizen." In fact, one could easily conclude that the core values that provide the foundation for the creation of an alternative public broadcasting system in the United States are totally absent from the majority of the documents reviewed.

In contrast, the public broadcasting filings cling repeatedly to the well-rehearsed language of the public trusteeship model. Throughout the collection of documents generated on behalf of public broadcasting interests, the values of universal service, an informed citizenry, diversity of programming for minority audiences, and cultural and educational enlightenment are invoked repeatedly in a wide variety of contexts and applications. While the FCC apparently avoids the language used in the Communications Act, APTS employs it directly in a majority of its filings. But beyond the routine invoking of language drawn directly from the act and previous rulings, such as the 1952 Sixth Report and Order, the public broadcasting documents create a positive value that repeatedly enhances the strength of the arguments advanced. Despite the widely held position in the public broadcasting community that there is growing disregard—if not outright hostility—toward public broadcasting within the agencies of the federal government, those drafting the public broadcasting statements never provide any suggestion that anything other than unanimous and totally uniform endorsement and support of noncommercial educational broadcasting might exist. In addition, the careful juxtaposition of recognizing and underscoring government involvement in the protection and safeguarding of an alternative noncommercial educational system—with skillfully crafted language that embodies concepts of "citizenship" and the "welfare of people"—suggests an imagined partnership between public broadcasting and the federal government in promoting the principles of American democracy.

While the public broadcasting documents reveal an intentional avoidance of the term "consumer," several filings employ marketplace values to support the positions advanced. For example, while making statements to remind the commission of the "unique" and "nonmarket" character of public broadcasting itself, the educational offerings of public broadcasting are depicted as providing U.S. citizens with valuable information that will enable them to be "competitive in the global marketplace."

Other evidence of public broadcasters' attempts to co-opt the marketplace value orientation of the commission is apparent in the projected self-image of public broadcasters as "broadcast industry leaders," "innovators," and "risk takers." And when arguing against diversity of ownership as a criterion for awarding new noncommercial educational licenses, APTS states: "Diverse ownership will facilitate a diversity of voices only if the market will support the separate stations . . . As the history of public broadcasting has shown, the marketplace will not support public broadcasting operations or the programming it offers [sic] . . . given the economic imperatives of [noncommercial educational] broadcasting, the Commission cannot rely on diversity of ownership as a means to promote diversity of viewpoints for noncommercial applicants."

Conclusion

On the basis of our preliminary findings, we feel comfortable in reporting that two fundamental interpretations of the "public interest" are clearly revealed in the documents selected for this study. As expected, values reflecting the instrumental view are embedded in the FCC's statements, and the values of the trustee model pervade the set of public broadcasting filings. While these results in and of themselves are hardly surprising, they take on additional meaning when seen within the context of a growing rigidity and apparent lack of interest on the part of FCC decision-makers and of a Congress that continues to back away from providing the long-term, insulated funding that was a central component of the Carnegie proposal on which the Public Broadcasting Act of 1967 was based.

Given this climate of continued disenfranchisement, the public broadcasting establishment is systematically painting itself into a box. There is a growing public outcry about the ever increasing commercialization of public broadcasting in America. Virtually every segment of public discourse now contains critical commentary about the blurring of program services between commercial and public broadcasters. Faced with the economic realities of generating more and more funding through enhanced corporate underwriting, the collection of unique, noncommercial, educational, alternative broadcast programming that projects the values of the public service model is quickly eroding before our eyes. With the adoption of the PBS/Station Equity Model in 1996, the public television system formally embraced the instrumental view of the public interest—a commitment that is demonstrated most vividly in the programming and station underwriting practices that have dramatically moved away from the ideals of public service broadcasting. National Public Radio's opposition to low-power FM radio is, in part, a recognition that public broadcasting does not adequately represent or serve the general public, and that even 100-watt stations would "compete" with NPR for listeners (Stavitsky, Avery, and Vanhala 2001). While the products of the nation's public broadcasting stations become increasingly indistinguishable from commercial broadcasting fare, the FCC and congressional filings submitted on behalf of the public broadcasting community continue to advance protectionist arguments based on public interest values that are no longer well supported by the services rendered. This, in our minds, is a trajectory of self-destruction.

If public broadcasting is to survive in this country, it must have the freedom to abandon the competitive strategies that have been imposed by the values of the commercial marketplace. Only then can the system regain the integrity and respect that a genuine noncommercial educational program service deserves. To do this will require the creation of a long-awaited trust fund that will free public broadcasting to pursue its original public service mission.

Numerous scholars, including Aufderheide (1991, 1999), Balas (1999), Engelman (1996), Hoynes (1994), McChesney (1999), Starr (2000), and Streeter (1996), have called for the kind of serious reform that would enable public broadcasting in the United States to finally achieve its potential as a genuine public interest media service. Yet, until now, those calls have gone unheeded. What is needed above all is a citizens' movement that can reenergize the role of the public in public broadcasting. If the conference that inspired this book is to be remembered for its impact on the future of public service broadcasting in America, it will be due to the fact that the people who took part helped empower such a movement with the knowledge and leadership they are fully capable of providing.

References

Armstrong, J. 2002. "Localism, Community and Commercial Television, 1948–1960: A Value Analysis." Ph.D. diss., University of Utah.

Aufderheide, P. 1991. "Public Television and the Public Sphere." *Critical Studies in Mass Communication* 8: 168–183.

———. 1999. *Communications Policy and the Public Interest: The Telecommunications Act of 1996.* New York: Guilford Press.

Avery, R., ed. 1993. *Public Service Broadcasting in a Multichannel Environment: The History and Survival of an Ideal.* White Plains, NY: Longman.

Balas, G. 1999. "The Recovery of Institutional Vision for U.S. Public Media: Three Moments of Purpose and Failed Resolve." Ph.D. diss., University of Iowa.

Briggs, A. 1961. *The History of Broadcasting in the United Kingdom.* London: Oxford University Press.

Engelman, R. 1996. *Public Radio and Television in America: A Political History.* Thousand Oaks, CA: Sage

Federal Communications Commission. 1946. *Public Service Responsibility of Broadcast Licensees.* Washington, DC: Government Printing Office.

Fowler, M., and D. Brenner. 1982. "A Marketplace Approach to Broadcast Regulation." *Texas Law Review* 60, no. 2: 207–257.

Ganer, P. 1988. "An Analysis of the Role of Values in the Argumentation of the 1980 Presidential Campaign." Ph.D. diss., University of Utah.

Herman, E., and R. McChesney. 1997. *The Global Media: The New Missionaries of Global Capitalism.* London: Cassell.

Hoynes, W. 1994. *Public Television for Sale: Media, the Market, and the Public Sphere.* Boulder, CO: Westview Press.

McChesney, R. 1993. *Telecommunications, Mass Media, and Democracy: The Battle for Control of U.S. Broadcasting, 1928–1935.* New York: Oxford University Press.

———. 1997. *Corporate Media and the Threat to Democracy.* New York: Seven Stories Press.

———. 1999. *Rich Media, Poor Democracy: Communication Politics in Dubious Times.* Urbana: University of Illinois Press.

Reith, J. 1942. *Broadcast Over Britain.* London: Hodder and Stoughton.

Rowland, W. 1986. "Continuing Crisis in Public Television: A History of Disenfranchisement." *Journal of Broadcasting and Electronic Media* 30: 251–274.

———. 1993a. "The Meaning of 'The Public Interest' in Communication Policy—Part II: Its Implementation in Early Broadcast Law and Regulation." Paper presented at the International Communication Association conference, Washington, DC.

———. 1993b. "Public Service Broadcasting in the United States: Its Mandate, Institutions, and Conflicts." In *Public Service Broadcasting in a Multichannel Environment*, ed. R. Avery. White Plains, NY: Longman, 157–194.

Sandeen, C. 1997. "Success Defined by Television: The Value System Promoted by PM Magazine." *Critical Studies in Mass Communication* 14: 77–105.

Siepmann, C. 1946. *Radio's Second Chance.* Boston: Little, Brown.

Sillars, M. 1991. *Messages, Meanings and Culture: Approaches to Communication Criticism.* New York: Harper and Row.

Sillars, M., and P. Ganer. 1982. "Values and Beliefs: A Systematic Basis for Argumentation." In *Advances in Argumentation Theory and Research*, ed. R. Cox and C.A. Willard. Carbondale: Southern Illinois University Press, 184–201.

Starr, J. 2000. *Air Wars: The Fight to Reclaim Public Broadcasting.* New York: Beacon Press.

Stavitsky, A. 1994. "The Changing Conception of Localism in U.S. Public Radio." *Journal of Broadcasting and Electronic Media* 38: 19–33.

Stavitsky, A., R. Avery, and H. Vanhala. 2001. "From Class d to lpfm: The High-powered Politics of Low-power Radio." *Journalism and Mass Communication Quarterly* 78: 340–354.

Streeter, T. 1996. *Selling the Air: A Critique of the Policy of Commercial Broadcasting in the United States.* Chicago: University of Chicago Press.

6

Pacifica Radio's Crisis of Containment

Matthew Lasar

On the evening of July 13, 1999, I stood at the corner of University Avenue and Martin Luther King Jr. Way in Berkeley, California, and became, for all practical purposes, two people. My first persona was a participant, a long-time volunteer for listener-supported KPFA-FM, one of five stations in the Pacifica Radio network, watching the most bizarre, horrific scene I had ever witnessed in all my years of work with countercultural institutions. The frequency's regular broadcast had been terminated by its administrators for reasons I still do not understand. Squadrons of police ran in military formation toward the station while hundreds of KPFA supporters pressed against hastily erected barricades (see Lasar 2000).

I ran toward the building. From my vantage point I could see station staff and armed guards stumbling about inside; the staff, waiting to be arrested, tossed various items out of windows to friends while the guards prepared to close the building down. Longtime KPFA classical music programmer Mary Berg walked to a ground floor door and grimly passed me her handbag and a sack full of books. She asked me to hold them until later.

I wandered about this chaotic scene in a state of shock that gradually evolved into a mood of deep disappointment. I had hoped, with the collapse of the Soviet Union in 1991, that we on the left had learned a fundamental lesson: you cannot bludgeon good people into progress. Whatever it is you say you want to accomplish—diversity, greater relevance, bigger audiences—if you pursue this goal via secrecy, fiat, bureaucratic tricks, then purges, censorship, and ultimately a police raid, in the end your actions bury your stated intentions. Your meanness, rather than your medium, becomes your message.

But while my first persona remained a partisan in this conflict, my second identity witnessed this awful event as an observer, an institutional historian struggling to understand the present, to construct a teleology that would adequately explain why experienced, intelligent people made the series of decisions leading to this crisis: from the idiotic dismissal of KPFA general manager Nicole Sawaya two weeks before KPFA's fiftieth anniversary to a shutdown that provoked the biggest demonstration in Berkeley since the Vietnam War era. Searching for models that would facilitate an understanding of the Pacifica National Office and Board of Governors, I thought of scholars who analyzed the decision-making process that led to the disastrous Bay of Pigs invasion in 1961. What were the broader historical factors that made those at the helm of Pacifica see what they were doing as something that made sense?

What follows here is a narrative in service of that question.

Over any discussion of Pacifica's revered founder Lewis Hill hovers the question of whether we have veered from Pacifica's original intentions and goals. The answer is that of course we have, and if we had not, the organization would not have lasted five years. It has always been adaptability, not rigid adherence to stated plans, that has saved Pacifica. No one demonstrated a greater genius for institutional veering than Hill himself. Lewis Hill's original mission for the Pacifica Foundation came out of his accurate perception that 1930s-era pacifism had failed to convince people of the futility of war. During World War II, Hill and other conscientious objectors (COs), stuck in remote concentration camps administered by Quakers under government jurisdiction, argued over the extent to which they should cooperate with their captors, staging walkouts and strikes over the four years of the war.

Hill wanted to build postwar pacifist institutions that would transcend this marginality, that would, through public dialogue, demonstrate as well as advocate the possibility of what he called a "pacific world in our time." His early fund-raising literature warned against "ivory towerism" and the kind of isolated, newsletter pacifism he regarded as ineffective (Hill 1946). Early on, KPFA, which would ultimately become the founding station in the five-station Pacifica Radio network, struggled to produce town hall-style discussions that would represent what Hill called "the wholeness of the political problem," the full range of perspectives from left to right, always centered around pacifist questions (personal letter to Henry R. Finch, February 18, 1951, 2).

But in practice KPFA, and subsequently WBAI in New York and KPFK in Los Angeles, functioned in the 1950s and early 1960s as cultures of refuge, serving alienated, hypereducated audiences a mix of classical and folk music, radio drama, and erudite commentary that I call "hybrid highbrow" (Lasar 1998, 46). And as McCarthyism intensified, as the government systematically retaliated against Pacifica's broadcasting of voices of the left, the organization devoted less time to left/right dialogue and, by necessity, more resources to publicly defending its right to air the voices marginalized by the Cold War. Dialogue radio became "free speech, First Amendment radio," the voice of the dissenter, remembered and understood as such up to the present ("Pacifica Says Goodbye" 1996).

By the mid-1960s, this remarkable evolution had drawn to it a new generation of student activists whose formative experiences had taken place during their struggles with universities in the Cold War era, largely over the Vietnam War and campus free speech issues. They differed from Lewis Hill in that, inspired by the civil rights movement, they spoke in the language of democracy and populism. They personally identified, as well as sympathized, with the socially dispossessed. "We have been too academic in the past," declared KPFA's news director in 1975, "and now it is time to go to the people and get their feelings" (Snitow 1984).

"The people"—African-Americans, Latinos, gays, lesbians, and others—replied that they could express their feelings quite well without the assistance of professional mediators. The protracted conflicts that WBAI experienced in the late 1970s as a result of this demographic shift are well narrated in Jeff Land's *Active Radio: Pacifica's Brash Experiment* (1999). They also took place to varying degrees at Pacifica's other older stations and the new ones: KPFT in Texas and WPFW in our nation's capital. To borrow a phrase from another historical period, in the 1970s "the world rushed in" to the Pacifica network (Holliday 1981). KPFA was now governed by a program council whose meetings attracted as many as eighty people. When the dialectical smoke cleared, Pacifica had moved into its third phase: "community radio"—the voice of diverse cultural constituencies.

But at the same time that a new generation of women and people of color made their presence known, the government began containing the amount of available space for community radio, or what I call local access broadcasting.

The walls began rising with the Federal Communications Commission's (FCC) banning of low-power FM in 1978, followed by the gradual relaxing of public service requirements for commercial stations. Next came the abandonment of the FCC's Fairness Doctrine in 1987, along with public broadcasting's increasing preference for satellite-fed programs over local fare. In the 1990s we saw the Corporation for Public Broadcasting's gradual ratcheting up of audience-level requirements for grantee stations and the disastrous Telecommunications Act of 1996, with its radical relaxation of antitrust protections. All of these policies encouraged radio stations—

public, community, and commercial—to curtail local broadcasting and to opt for more profitable, but less community-oriented fare (Douglas 1999; Engelman 1996).

This containment left community radio in general, and Pacifica in particular, with the impossible task of managing institutions besieged by suitors of every cultural and political variety, all excluded from most other broadcasting venues. In the 1980s, I saw the best community radio minds of my generation—general managers, department heads, program directors, advisory board chairs, national board members—become weary under these circumstances, increasingly inclined to see their constituents, with whom they struggled every day, as the enemy; less inclined to sense the corporate state, which in fact was gradually strangling Pacifica, as the true source of the problem.

By the early 1990s, the Pacifica Foundation had, in a way, come to resemble the network of CO camps in which Lewis Hill and his comrades had languished in the 1940s: small concentrated spaces in which residents fought with each other over resources and over the extent to which they should cooperate with their jailers. Desperate to escape its fate as an exercise in cultural power sharing, Pacifica faced two possibilities. It could act like a movement organization and put its resources in service of a renewed struggle against this containment of the airwaves. Or Pacifica could accept the containment, take advantage of its possession of scarce frequencies, and centralize the network, purging itself of rough edges in the process.

The organization chose the latter road. "The expansion of media trusts simultaneously illuminates the distinctiveness of Pacifica's programming and mission," read a sidebar quote from the organization's 1997 *Strategic Plan.* "By diminishing the supply of informational programming—Pacifica's and public radio's stock-in-trade—the commercial trusts have paradoxically increased audience demand for Pacifica and other public radio services" (Bunce 1997, 12). In fairness, this enlightened opportunism produced some good results: most notably the network-wide inauguration of the news and public affairs program *Democracy Now!* and the construction of new headquarters for two of the foundation's stations. But the Pacifica network is too steeped in the rhetoric of democracy and free speech to sustain a governance system that would make the Vatican blush and a management style that would make a commissar grin. It just doesn't seem to be working, unless you regard as signs of institutional success lawsuits, arrests, stringer strikes, mass demonstrations, and the worst national press clips short of Bill Clinton's.

The fruits of this unwise policy speak for themselves. In November of last year, Pacifica wreaked havoc at its New York station, WBAI, by dismissing its general manager against the wishes of key staff (Sadasivam

2001). Then it appointed a new manager, who, as at KPFA in 1999, installed guards, fired programmers who protested the change, and sparked a listener boycott of the station. Several months ago, WBAI's Amy Goodman, host of the network's highly successful program *Democracy Now!*, declared the station unsafe for herself and her staff after an altercation with the station's new general manager (Hinckley 2001). Goodman moved the program to studios outside WBAI's headquarters, while Pacifica management convinced four of the five network-owned stations to remove the program from their schedules—a ban that lasted for almost six months (*Democracy Now!* 2002). One result: Pacifica Network News lost at least fifteen of its affiliate subscribers. These community radio stations had already protested the termination of PNN's executive director in November 1999, shortly after he allowed the airing of a brief report admitting to dissatisfaction with the news service among some affiliates. The exile of *Democracy Now!* proved the last straw, provoking the affiliates to abandon the network completely. In addition to all this, the Pacifica Foundation faced three lawsuits challenging the legality of its board structure (Behrens 2000).

A growing national mass movement for a democratic Pacifica spread. A national boycott of listeners and donors was launched and by the spring of 2001, picketing outside each station became commonplace (Gonzalez 2002). Pacifica's "mainstreaming" board members, having spent a fortune on lawyers, public relations firms, and guards to defend their attempt to dilute Pacifica's radical politics and community programming, could not withstand the national protest. In December 2001, Pacifica was saved. The entire board resigned, replaced by an interim body consisting of five dissidents, five representatives of the old majority, and five elected from the station's local advisory boards. The new Pacifica board reinstated many employees who had been fired to their previous positions and replaced those who had been involved in the dismissals and censorship. The board also began work on a new set of by-laws that will permit local boards to appoint members to the national governing board and to hold the first-ever listener elections of local advisory boards at all stations (Thompson 2002, 14). Pacifica's acting executive director claims the network hovered on the brink of financial collapse in early 2002, but cost-cutting measures and record pledge drives have now made the financial picture more stable (Pacificia Radio Acting Executive Director Report 2002; Record 2002). I feel good about the future of Pacifica Radio for the first time in a long while.

Undoubtedly, the larger conditions that created this crisis still prevail. The systematic assault on public and locally accessible noncommercial media in the United States has left Pacifica isolated. The network shoulders the burden of being too many things to too many people, within the context of too little space. This condition threatens to demoralize future generations of Pacifica station managers and governors, as it has in the recent past. But there is renewed hope. Pacifica's affiliate stations are coming back into the fold because of positive changes in management and the return of *Democracy Now!* ("Pacifica Radio Acting Executive Director Report" 2002). The remarkable grassroots energy directed toward restoring the country's only independent noncommercial radio network can now be put to work democratizing the larger public media sphere. It seems only appropriate that a renewed Pacifica once again claim its role as a leader in the struggle for a broad, democratic, noncommercial domain.

References

Behrens, S. 2000. "Three Suits Deny Legitimacy of Pacifica's National Board." *Current.* www.current.org/radio/radio020pac2.html (October 30).

Bunce, D. 1997. "The Crisis of Democratic Communications." In *A Vision for Pacifica Radio: Creating a Network for the 21st Century,* (n.p.). Berkeley, CA: Pacifica Foundation.

Democracy Now! 2002. *WBAI—e-News.* www.wbai.org/parts/news5.htm (March 21).

Douglas, S. 1999. *Listening In: Radio and the American Imagination.* New York: Times Books.

Engelman, R. 1996. *Public Radio and Television in America: A Political History.* Thousand Oaks, CA: Sage.

Gonzalez, J. 2002. "Back on the Air at Pacifica." *In These Times,* February 18, 11.

Hill, L. 1946. *Pacifica Foundation Radio Prospectus.* San Francisco: Pacifica Foundation.

———. 1951. February 18 letter to Henry R. Finch Jr., 2. Pacifica National Office Papers, Box 11, Folder 2.

Hinckley, D. 2001. "BAI Dissident Hides Out." *New York Daily News Online.* www.nydailynews.com/2001–08–15/New_York_Now/Television/a-121838.asp (August 15).

Holliday, J.S. 1981. *The World Rushed In: The California Gold Rush Experience.* New York: Simon and Schuster.

Hopkins, V., ed. 1984. *The Pacifica Radio Sampler.* Los Angeles: Pacifica Foundation.

Land, J. 1999. *Active Radio: Pacifica's Brash Experiment.* Minneapolis: University of Minnesota Press.

Lasar, M. 1998. "Hybrid Highbrow: KPFA's Reconstruction of Elite Culture." *Journal of Radio Studies* 5: 46–67.

———. 2000. *Pacifica Radio: The Rise of an Alternative Network.* Philadelphia: Temple University Press.

"Pacifica Radio Acting Executive Director Report to the Interim Pacifica National Board." 2002. Pacifica Radio Web site, March 8. www.pacifica.org/info/releases/iEDreport030802.html (March 21).

"Pacifica Says Goodbye to First Amendment Radio." 1996. Leaflet distributed by Take Back KPFA, Berkeley, CA, February 23.

"Record Fund Drives Continue at Pacifica Radio." 2002. Pacifica Radio Web site, June 12. www.pacifica.org/info/releases/020612_recordfunddrive.html (August 12).

Sadasivam, B. 2001. "Morning Sedition: WBAI Fights Management's Move to Turn the Station into NPR Lite." *Village Voice.* www.villagevoice.com/issues/0103/sadasivam.php (January 23).

Snitow, A. 1984. "Pacifica Radio: Purpose and Goals, 1946–September 1947." In *The Pacifica Radio Sampler,* ed. Vera Hopkins (n.p.). Los Angeles: Pacifica Foundation, 1984.

Thompson, C. 2002. "War and Peace." *The East Bay Express,* January 9–15, 14.

Part II

Critical Dimensions

7

Introduction

Eric E. Peterson

From its varied beginnings, public broadcasting has been shaped by a utopian impulse. Practitioners and academics, advocates and critics, politicians and policy analysts from across the political spectrum share in this utopian impulse when they imagine a future in which what we think of as "broadcasting" in general would be improved through the growth and development of "public broadcasting" in particular. Part of the impulse to imagine a better future for public broadcasting in the United States comes from a political tradition concerned with how a democracy organizes communication systems. The emphasis on "free speech" and a "free press" illustrates this traditional concern. Tradition holds that social groups and individuals will gain opportunities for expression and self-representation, for debating the common good, and for realizing collective goals if they have unfettered access to diverse information in a "marketplace of ideas." However, the development of communication systems in the United States did not result in a democratic or open marketplace of ideas; instead, the marketplace came to dominate the ideas. In this context, the turn to public broadcasting was one way to counter the domination of commercial interests in broadcasting. The move to establish noncommercial radio and television was seen as a way to restore the democratic potential of broadcasting to serve the interests of the public.

Before turning to the ways in which this utopian impulse to serve the interests of the public shapes the essays in this section, let us briefly consider (1) what is meant by the idea of *the public* that broadcasting should serve, (2) how *broadcasting* is conceptualized as a system of communication, and (3) the importance of a critical understanding of *public broadcasting* for democracy.

The use of the term "the public" contains several ambiguities. It can be used to refer both to people, as in "the voting public," and to a situation or context, as "I am going out in public." And even as a reference to people, "public" is ambiguous; it can mean a particular group of people that share common interests, as in "a reading public," and it can mean the people as a whole. This ambiguity becomes troublesome when it is used to hide the ideological slippage in which one particular public is taken for a universal or The Public. An obvious and often cited example of this ideological slippage can be seen in the writing of the U.S. Constitution, where one particular group of people—white, European, heterosexual, male landowners—see themselves as universal, as constituting "we, the people."

The ambiguous use of language here to construct The People or The Public obscures the reality of competing interests and peoples within which any one group of people or public can be located. Taking one group as universal collapses this context of diversity into an opposition between one group or public and other possible groups or publics. Members of one public are thus positioned as normal and neutral, while members of other possible publics within the context of competing interests are positioned as "other" and biased. Under these circumstances, anyone who is not part of the supposedly universal group faces an uphill struggle when trying to enter the marketplace of ideas. From the beginning, such others are suspect because they are, by definition, not part of what is considered neutral or normal. They are outside the status quo; they are unreasonable and irrational. Furthermore, there is an economy to discourse that hides privilege in addition to the well-recognized privilege that comes from access to economic resources. That is, it is easier to speak within the status quo and to maintain existing interests than it is to challenge what is considered normal, neutral, and of The People. If I speak outside the status quo, then I run the risk of being seen as impolite, unreasonable, and irrational.

The placement of other publics as outside the status quo links the ambiguity of a public as The Public with the ambiguity of "public" as referring to both a people and a situation. The use of "public" to refer to a situation or context is perhaps most easily seen in the common opposition of public and private. The public interest, from a situationally based formulation of the public, lies outside the home and other sites of self-interest. Of course, this easy opposition is belied by situations that are neither public nor private. For example, shopping in a suburban mall takes place in a commercial space that is regulated in ways that public streets in a downtown shopping area are not. Broadcasting is not public in that it is dominated by a small number of corporations organized around advertising and commercial interests. Furthermore, the high cost of capitalization and industry regulation severely restrict any public that desires entry into broadcasting. And, perhaps more significantly for this discussion, this opposition also breaks down when we consider situations that are both public and private, such as our mundane experience of radio and television. Public broadcasting, ironically enough, takes place not in public but in homes.

The ambiguous meanings of the word "public" as a situation or context suggest our second concern: that is, how broadcasting is conceptualized as a system of communication. Listening to the radio or watching television in my home is not the same thing as listening to a public speech down at the town hall, nor is it the same as engaging in a conversation at a local coffee shop. Broadcasting, as the name suggests, is a communication system in which material is "cast broadly" to dispersed audiences. It is unlike a public communication situation in that, as an audience member, I cannot turn to another community member in the audience to ask a question or discuss what the speaker is saying. Nor can I, as I would in a face-to-face situation, engage the speaker in a conversation in order to clarify my understanding or to persuade the speaker to a different understanding. Yet the idealization of both public communication and face-to-face communication haunts our understanding of broadcasting.

Let me illustrate how the ideal communication situation haunts our understanding of broadcasting. Maine Public Radio describes itself as "The Station You Listen To!" This formulaic use of "you" is quite common across all types of broadcasting: "your television news station," "music you want to hear," "your source for local news," and so on. As in the ambiguous use of "public," the use of "you" positions listeners in at least two ways: it suggests a collective "you" of an audience (as in public communication) and it suggests a specific "you" or person (as in face-to-face communication). Thus, broadcasting constructs its audiences—it addresses you—by conflating the collective "you" with the specific "you." Broadcasting speaks *to* me by speaking *for* me and for what I can do. "The Station You Listen To!" and the programs "you" hear on Maine Public Radio are designed for a particular someone who can be anyone happening to listen. Broadcasting constructs its audience by addressing a group of people (the public communication ideal) as if they were a particular person (the face-to-face ideal). Conceptualized in this manner, broadcasting reduces the variability of the group to a singular person and it abstracts from individual interaction the interests of the group.

But, of course, broadcasting is not truly broad; it is not equally interested in everyone, in all those who happen to listen. As we discover in the marketing plans of commercial broadcasters and, increasingly, during public broadcasting fund-raisers, some audiences are more important than others. The conjunction of "public" and "broadcasting" makes the selectivity of broadcasting a central concern: what publics can be audiences? what publics can fund and produce? what publics are the focus of coverage? whose interests are served? Furthermore, the situational meaning of the word "public" suggests additional questions: where is this public situated? what economic and historical conditions constrain who participates? to what extent is the context of diverse publics addressed in broadcasting content?

As important as these questions are, they do not go far enough in untangling the challenge that public broadcasting faces. As phrased, these questions tend to assume the constitution of public and of broadcasting as given. They do not ask how the ways we talk about and conceptualize public broadcasting constrain possibilities for change. The turn to a critical perspective on public broadcasting requires that we examine the discursive conventions of broadcasting and the idealization of communication systems embedded in them. The challenge here is to conceptualize the conjunction of *public* and *broadcasting* in ways that do not dissolve or ignore the importance of diverse publics in society and the importance of multiple affiliations by members of those publics. The face-to-face communication ideal tends to ignore multiple publics either by treating audience members as individuals apart from social affiliations or by reducing such affiliations to characteristics of the individual. The public communication ideal tends to ignore how audiences are dispersed by reducing the public to a spatially defined community or by collapsing divergent interests into a representative speaker or program. These idealizations can be productive, however, if we make them explicit and use them to combine the opportunities for mutual self-definition and expression that emerge in face-to-face communication with the collective debate and determination of common goals that emerge in group communication.

The point of a critical perspective on public broadcasting, then, is not to moralize or condemn from some transcendent or universal standpoint. Rather, as the following chapters illustrate, a critical perspective participates in the utopian impulse to imagine a better future for public broadcasting. This effort to imagine a better future is not fanciful speculation or mordant cynicism, but rather the engaged work of interpretive explication—a way of making sense of a troubling situation. To elucidate this better future, a critical perspective may examine what public broadcasting *claims* to do in light of what it *does* or what it *could* do. Or a critical perspective may vary elements of public broadcasting to determine their significance and efficacy; for example, it may compare the U.S. version to other national versions of public broadcasting, or it may compare one historical or economic context with another. Yes, this work is critical in the sense that it does not accept that public broadcasting has to be the way it currently is, but it is also critical if we hope to transform how public broadcasting serves the interests of diverse publics in a democracy.

In "The Public and Its Problems," B. Lee Artz takes up the question of diverse publics that constitute the public body. He challenges the way public broadcasting in the United States hides race, class, gender, and youth. He argues that while the public is *subject to* public broadcasting, it is not the *subject of* such broadcasts. As presently constituted, the public can be the site but not the author, the body but not the mind of public broadcasting. Artz contrasts his experience at a U.S. public broadcasting station with his experience at Community Radio Nicaragua in order to highlight alternate ways to open up access and participation that would engage all of the "body" of the public. Judi Puritz Cook also questions the definition of public when she asks, given the current state of commercialization and "enhanced underwriting," whether the audience of public broadcasting is better described as a market than as a public. The evidence she presents in "Advertising on Public Television" is highly persuasive. Her study of WGBH-2 (PBS Boston) suggests that public television is interested in children, but not as potential citizens nor as a public to be served. In an effort to find funds for programming, public television targets children as consumers—an audience to be served up to advertisers rather than a public to be served.

Mary E. Hurley's study of a public radio affiliate in California provides a radio counterpart to Cook's television-based study. Hurley carefully details the changing mission at KUOP-FM by contrasting pre- and post-1998 programming and audiences. KUOP significantly reduced local programming in favor of network programming, and both the diversity and amount of music in favor of more news and information programming. These changes reflect how the concern for funding resulted in a shift from a local or spatially defined community to a lifestyle market—the professional-managerial class, a "virtual" community that is seen as most likely to patronize underwriters.

The final two chapters address the impact of new technologies on the democratization of public broadcasting. Steve Pierce explores the opportunity that satellite television systems, such as Dish Network, offer for expanding available content and reaching geographically isolated audiences not served through broadcast reception or cable. Pierce suggests that this technology can be utilized by activists to network and share alternative content and voices ignored by mainstream media. Free Speech TV and Deep Dish TV are two examples of this possibility for creating a dispersed public oriented around common goals. Gary P. Poon argues that pragmatic concerns for funding need not conflict with the effort to reach a diverse audience. He cites the changing demographic and population projections for the United States, which suggest that public broadcasting must address these new audiences or risk losing an increasingly important public. Poon also finds an opportunity to increase diversity in the enlarged programming stream made possible by the transition to digital transmission. These changes also present opportunities to increase access to diverse publics through interactive formats similar to those on the Internet.

These chapters, taken together with the others in this volume, begin to mark out the contributions and importance of a critical perspective on public broadcasting. The critical perspective they demarcate is one based in engagement, participation, and the constitution of a diverse public. Nearly all of the writers come from backgrounds in broadcasting; they share in a utopian impulse to imagine a future that better serves the public. The critical analysis of public broadcasting is thus tempered by a shared interest. The understanding that critical analysis generates is vital if public broadcasting is to move toward realizing its democratic potential.

8

The Public and Its Problems

Race, Class, and Media Access

B. Lee Artz

It has been at least ten years since I worked in industry, but I still understand the world as a machinist, a labor unionist. I make sense of the world from the perspective of the working class. My understanding of economics, politics, news, entertainment, and advertising is informed by fifteen years of working in production alongside black workers, Mexican-American workers, and women workers—and by our collective recognition that our lives and concerns never played on the silver screen or appeared on the little blue screen in our living rooms. I laugh when I see the McDonald's commercial showing young, energetic, smiling McDonald's employees identified as "future stock broker" and "future scientist." I particularly like the realistic part where a child is identified as a "future McDonald's employee"—flipping burgers as the ultimate safety net for the United States. Unemployed stockbrokers, scientists, machinists, or even college professors always have McDonald's to fall back on! More importantly, although we may not be future McDonald's employees individually, as part of the American public we are already being McDonaldized (Ritzer 2000). Work and play, private and public life, are increasingly rationalized for market efficiency and institutional control. The conference upon which this book is based is a tacit recognition of the McDonaldization, the privatization, of public communication.

Indeed, the public has a communication problem because of privatization. I am not speaking here of the amorphous public referenced on network television, nor I am talking about the public constituted by Public Broadcasting System (PBS) funding appeals. No, I am speaking of the *real* public in its ethnically diverse working-class majority. That public has a serious problem: we have no media.

To talk about the future of public media, we need to begin by realizing that we have no public media, no public broadcasting. Perhaps I feel this way because of my fifteen years as a steelworker, but I do not believe that public broadcasting as currently practiced has much connection with the public as it currently exists. The public in today's public broadcasting appears as an adjective, a simulated site where a particular kind of broadcasting takes place. Public certainly does not refer to the subject, to those doing the broadcasting, nor even to the audience they seek. Broadcasting *to* the public? Only if you mean the donors. In no way can it mean broadcasting *by* the public.

So what is the public? President Clinton had a public mandate, right? Eleven percent of all registered voters voted for President Clinton. President Bush has a public mandate? A few years ago there was a poll that asked, "If you had the ability and the resources, would you leave the United States?" Twelve percent replied, "Yes." More people would leave this country than voted for Clinton or Bush! What kind of public mandate is that? Twelve percent say, "Get me outta' here!"

You know the figures: Five percent of the world's population lives in the United States; 25 percent of the world's prison population lives here. One percent of the U.S. population owns 20 percent of the wealth; 20 percent have about 1 percent of the wealth. In the next few years, some states will have people of color as majorities. Already most big cities are majority non-white with an average age in the twenties. So I ask you to think about the demographics of today's diverse public. . . . Now think about what parts of that public have access to broadcasting, either commercial or public. You see the problem? The majority of the public has no media.

The American public is working-class. I did a recent study on the character of the information society in Chicago. I found that more than 30 percent of the residents of Chicago and surrounding Cook County are directly involved in industrial manufacturing. About an equal number are involved in servicing some industrial manufacturer—transportation, distribution, retailing, and the like. Sure, there are fewer workers in the United States than elsewhere because technology allows us to be more productive, more skilled, more socially powerful. That means we produce more goods and services with fewer hours of labor. (Of course, CEOs and their university economists want to keep that detail bracketed from discussions about democracy.) At any rate, the vast majority of Americans still work for a living, for a wage.

The American public includes black, Puerto Rican, Mexican-American, and Asian-American—all exceedingly young—working people. When we consider the public body we have to consider all of its parts. We cannot talk about a body and lop off its left arm, cut off a toe. Of course, some would like the public to have no tongue, to be silent, and let the relatively small percentage of Americans who vote in presidential elections speak for all. Or, if we do speak, it should be in monosyllables about inconsequential topics, as in the Budweiser commercial where working guys sit around asking "Wha's up?" and answering, "True, true." Or in the Acura ad, aimed at a more up-scale public that is also expected to be quiet. There is no talking; you just see a sleek car winding up the Maine coast with the tag line: "Do nothing." We get a vision of a well-tended woman lying on a bed and a handsome fellow looking at the ocean. Buy an Acura—then you too can "do nothing—sooner!" This is network casting for the public.

Unfortunately, the public is largely silent and unheard. It is comprised of all those people who do not appear on PBS's *News Hour*, who will not be on Brokaw, who will not be guests of Jay Leno. Public discourse on "E!" or cable, anyone? The public preferred by the networks, including PBS, is a mass of spectators. Their public is spectating, watching, buying, and self-indulgent—and doing nothing (except shopping) sooner. Spectatorship and consumerism are destroying the public as a body politic.

What we are witnessing, and all too frequently participating in, is a relent-less cultural construction of a citizenry reduced to a consuming public, a passive, watching public. The outcome could mean the destruction of a po-litical, decision-making, socially active public capable of doing something about its conditions of life.

We see the consequences of this at WLUW-FM at Loyola University in Chicago—and I'm sure other college stations have had similar experiences. Station personnel and supporters fought a battle with the administration over the purpose and character of the radio station. We said, "Let us get away from the twenty-four-hour dance music, let us have community radio, let us get students to do broadcasting of consequence, let us invite people from the community in to do broadcasts for their neighbors." Well, we won and we did it. We set up a Lakeshore Community Media Project and estab-lished the framework for community radio, but nobody really knew what to do with it once we had it. Yes, we have had successes: we broadcast Pacifica's *Democracy Now!,* we have student programming, an Ethiopian show, a Ko-rean show, a Haitian show, a Puerto Rican show, and more—but there is a disconnect. It is not the orchestrated disconnection at National Public Ra-dio, but it is similar: Where is the public? Where is the community? Ethio-pian, yes, the show host is Ethiopian; but it is not an Ethiopian community show. He speaks the language, he plays the music, but there is no public participation in setting the format or carrying it out. We struggle with that. Here, we have the resources, the format, but we do not yet have public communication in terms of production. Why? Largely because the public has learned to be passive through years of training in school and in front of the TV. First-year students come in expecting to be a top-40 DJ, or Howard Stern, or have their own show. They do not immediately see this as an opportunity to work with or for the public. Public service broadcasting must be learned, experienced.

Public broadcasting needs a politically conscious public such as the one that grew out of the revolution in Nicaragua from 1979 to 1986 (Artz 1994). The twenty-three stations of CORADEP (Community Radio Network) arose in the course of campaigns for democracy by farmworkers, students, urban workers, and professionals. CORADEP radio stations were part of a revolution. They featured "community correspondents" just learning to read and write, writing their own stories, relying on their own community sources, speaking out as partisans of independence and equality. Of course, this situation is not the same as the one at WLUW or other stations throughout most of the United States today. Public campaigns for an improved quality of life are diffuse and disjointed for the time being. The point here is that *real* public broadcasting as a means of communicating the concerns and experiences of the working majority in the United States is virtually nonexistent. There is no public broadcasting in the sense of a public constituted by blacks, workers, females, and young people who broadcast to a larger audience with similar social backgrounds. Public broadcasting does not exist in the United States.

In fact, if advertisers have their way, democracy will be privatized along with public broadcasting and the public. Democracy appears mostly as a code word for consumer choice. Coke or Pepsi? Bud? True, true. Unless you are limiting choice to consumer products, including the entertainment formats of radio and television, there is no democratic, institutional decision-making in the United States today. To be heard and counted, working people must rely on organized mass movements and create their own independent media—excluding broadcasting that is legally monopolized by a handful of media entities (Herman and McChesney 1997). There are few government institutions (none at the national level) that permit debate, discussion, and democratic decision-making. There is little public space left that has not been filled with advertising—the highways in Maine a notable exception. Where is the soapbox for the public speaker? You cannot put a soapbox at the mall. That is private property. In Chicago, if you are a young person, you cannot be with a group of more than three persons or you are considered to be engaged in a criminal gang activity. Where is public space? Anything more than a dyadic conversation and you are carrying out a crime? There is no public space there. Unless you are on the short list for approved guests, you might get thirty seconds on some *vox populi* talk show before the host cuts you off. Otherwise, broadcasting is strictly off-limits to real public discourse.

I do not want to pick on National Public Radio (NPR). I listen to it. I like Terry Gross, Michael Feldman, Garrison Keillor, the *Car Talk* guys, and the rest. I love the avuncular tenor voices on the newscasts, one minute caring and the next amused, the next minute concerned. I appreciate NPR. It does in-depth pieces more than any other service on the radio dial (with the exception of community radio, KPFA, and some others). That is a positive read. But another, more balanced read is that NPR still offers standard mainstream fare that marginalizes the working class. Reports on life outside the beltway are invariably touching, hopeful, and oh, so telling about the tragic life of the masses, as the white urbane uncle clicks his tongue, saying, "Isn't that sad, isn't that bad, isn't that just too bad." Maybe I am wrong, but I challenge you to make a list. Make a list of the black, Asian-American, female, young, working-class voices that are hosts or guests on NPR.

Of course, some representation of the public interest occasionally appears on some of the better NPR shows. WBEZ in Chicago has *Chicago Matters,* an annual public information series, which focuses on some of the changes wrought by gentrification, immigration, and globalization (although *Chicago Matters* does not refer to it in those terms). Recently the program did a story on how the Buck Town neighborhood is improving. What was one of the best indicators? Starbucks. Starbucks opened shop in Buck Town. Such improvements will help rid Buck Town of gangs and crime. Another WBEZ show called *848* aired the same day with a wonderful piece on the architecture of Chicago's South Side auto row in the 1950s. In the course of the commentary, the host and the guest agreed that the community went downhill when people moved to the suburbs. Think carefully for a minute. The people moved . . . . Which people? Thousands of people stayed in Chicago's South Side— unless blacks and Mexican-Americans are not people. The people moved out! The community declined! It was not intentional . . . the host and guest didn't reflect on this, but they gave absolutely no context for changes other than the fact that white people left. What about the closing of U.S. Steel's South Works, the rail mergers and closings, the refinery shutdowns, and other socially and culturally disruptive corporate decisions? A real public radio station would feature a *public* discussion about the *public* consequences of corporate decisions. As it is, the "public" audience of WBEZ or any other NPR station just does not seem to include most of the public living in its broadcast radius. Few hosts live in the black, brown, working-class neighborhoods of Chicago. There is no interest at all in talking with Chicago's young people, who are notorious for not contributing during pledge week. Who questions NPR's fabrication of public interest? Certainly not the actual Chicago public, which finds little connection with WBEZ. Of course, according to WBEZ donor lists, the listening audience does drink at

Starbucks, did move to the suburbs (or now lives in gentrified townhouses and condos), and gives money over the Internet to shows like *848*. And that audience segment does not experience or recognize the conditions of Chicago's working-class life. So NPR further disconnects public interest and public service by broadcasting to its donor base. This is not politically intentional, although it has certain cultural tendencies, that are further verified by the half dozen lawsuits against NPR by black and female employees over bias in hiring, promotions, and pay. It seems public broadcasting is run like commercial radio with cronyism, favoritism, discrimination, and all. NPR correspondent Nina Totenberg says, "Well, yeah, NPR is an equal opportunity abuser, but it is still a better place to work than network radio"— all things considered!

Given the economies of scale, public television is even further from the public. Take any PBS evening schedule: opera, bugs, volcanoes, *Nova,* and *The American Experience.* Occasionally you might find *I'll Make Me a World* or some other social history, but even in those cases (with the exception of Bill Moyers), most of them are depoliticized greetings. Above all, there is little connection to the diverse public as an audience, a political entity, and none as a potential news source or programming producer.

I suggest that even while we battle for funding for public radio and public television—which remains a problem, as Hoynes (1994) clearly demonstrates—the larger battle is to change who runs the major networks. NPR sounds like National Professionals Radio and PBS looks like a Patrician Broadcasting System; neither provides media access to the American public in all of its ethnic and class diversity. I refer you to repeated studies by Fairness and Accuracy in the Media in their publication, *Extra!,* if you have any doubts about this claim. Control over production and broadcasting is also an issue at some community radio stations, as Pacifica's crisis clearly demonstrates.

Our experience at Loyola was different. The battle was won when we moved away from a discussion about Arbitron ratings, job placements, and corporate sponsors. The battle was won when we stopped arguing with the administration and took the case to the students and the faculty—when we took it to the public. The Pope and the Jesuits at Loyola believe "blessed are the poor," so we said it was better if the poor were organized than blessed, right? We won when we presented the call for democratic communication to audiences of students and ethnic communities around Loyola.

My argument is basically that public broadcasting today dismisses the character of the public. Race, class, and youth affect the conditions, experiences, identities, concerns, and solutions of the public in its entirety. Public broadcasting today hides the public from the view of its audience. With the absence of the actual public from broadcasting, so-called public broadcasting denies that a public actually exists.

What would real public broadcasting look like? One model might be CORADEP in Nicaragua. You could look at the examples of some community radio stations. Public broadcasting must be representative, participatory. In the United States, public broadcasting must mean solidarity. It means going beyond that 11 percent solution. It means broadcasting for the majority, the other 80 percent of the population. You have 10 percent Republicans, 10 percent Democrats, and they have access to all of the corporate media in the country. That leaves 80 percent of the population that is not in the conversation. As public media advocates, as scholars and researchers, as media workers, we should not be in that conversation either. We should be talking to the 80 percent, to the working people of the United States that currently have no media access. What does that mean? It means building a community of the nonelite, a community that includes everyone except the corporate class exclusionists, a community with a public, decision-making democracy based on participation and equal access—a community of public solidarity and public struggle. Such a public broadcasting network would regularly report on wages, education, healthcare, the environment, and other quality-of-life issues—and just as importantly, it would necessarily help organize public action to address public issues. How will it happen? If public broadcasting advocates raise their polemic against the market system in different terms, advocating institutional media independence based on a different class, we can shift the focus of the debate about public broadcasting. We should talk with Congress or the FCC only as a means of talking with the public, to encourage public knowledge of the divisions of race, class, and youth in America. Realistically speaking, we should do nothing for the marketers—and we should do it sooner. What is the public and what is its problem? It is that the voices of the public are silenced, muted at best. The public is not just a group of individual consumers. The public cannot be represented by celebrities, nor by the VIPs and newsmakers certified by broadcasting networks, whether NBC and ABC, or NPR and PBS. The public is black, it is brown, it is female, it is young, and above all, it is working-class. The problem with the public is that we have not recognized our own social position and our own power. The public needs leadership to organize this conversation for and by the public.

Wha's up? The public and its problems need to be addressed by a politically organized public power, a power that comes from mobilizing in solidarity with the needs of the majority in all of its diversity of race, class, gender, and youth. And we should say to that public, "True, true."

References

Artz, L. 1994. "Communication and Power: Popular Radio in Nicaragua." *Journal of Radio Studies* 2: 205–228.

Herman, E., and R. McChesney. 1997. *The Global Media: The New Missionaries of Corporate Capitalism.* New York: Cassell.

Hoynes, W. 1994. *Public Television for Sale: Media, the Market, and the Public Sphere.* Boulder, CO: Westview Press.

Ritzer, G. 2000. *The McDonaldization of Society: An Investigation into the Changing Character of Social Life.* 3d ed. Thousand Oaks, CA: Sage.

9

Advertising on Public Television

A Look at PBS

Judi Puritz Cook

Underwriting. Enhanced underwriting. Sponsorship. Whatever name Public Broadcasting System (PBS) stations choose for the fifteen-second spots airing on public television, the reality is that public broadcasting on PBS looks more like commercial television than ever before. As PBS stations feel pressure to compete with an abundance of new commercial stations and face a decrease in federal funding, many air soft-sell "commercials" for companies like Ace Hardware, Healthtex, Juicy Juice, and Kellogg's. Through content analysis of WGBH-2 (PBS Boston), this chapter examines the reality of commercial influences on PBS. Results of the content analysis are used to illustrate the extent to which corporate sponsorship has made a presence on PBS. The chapter concludes with a discussion of the ramifications of the commercialization of public television on American culture.

The History of Public Television Underwriting

As commercial television established itself in the 1950s and 1960s, it became clear that advertisers influenced the range and quality of programs offered to viewers. Several authors, most notably Hoynes (1994, 1999), McChesney (1997, 1999), and Ledbetter (1998) provide insight into the history behind public television and the Carnegie Commission (1967), which was established to address this issue.

Certainly, the Carnegie Commission envisioned that public television would provide an alternative to commercial television. Its 1967 report specifically identified public television as programming "of human interest and importance which is not at the moment appropriate or available for support by advertising, and which is not arranged for formal instruction" (Carnegie Commission 1967, 1).

The commission described a public television system committed to promoting diversity and cultural enrichment. It clearly positioned public television as a noncommercial alternative to the market-driven content of commercial television. And yet, as Ledbetter (1998) argues, the public broadcasting system was never fully equipped to operate without the help of corporate sponsorship. McChesney (1999) draws a similar conclusion, arguing that public broadcasting in America was "handicapped" when plans for funding the Corporation for Public Broadcasting with a tax on television receivers were abandoned. The original recommendation in the Carnegie report called for a manufacturer's excise tax on television sets that would start at 2 percent and rise to 5 percent. However, this plan was not followed through when the Corporation for Public Broadcasting was established.

From the beginning, then, public broadcasting was reliant on contributions from corporate sponsors in order to fill the funding gaps. Early underwriting guidelines were strict with regard to the types of sponsors suitable for particular programs. PBS underwriting rules through the late 1970s prohibited corporations with a direct interest in the program's content to serve as sponsors. Such restrictions helped to ensure that programming decisions were not being influenced by underwriters. Yet over the years, PBS relaxed the rules in order to bring in heavy-hitting underwriters like the computer company Unisys, which in 1992 sponsored the broadcast of *The Machine That Changed the World,* a history of the computer, for $1.9 million (Ledbetter 1998).

If the rules have changed, so too has the look of the underwriting. Prior to 1984, PBS limited the promotion of underwriters to "dull, tombstone-like on-screen promotions" (Ledbetter 1998). In the 1980s PBS allowed underwriters to add their logos, store locations, and even descriptions of their products. Today, corporations produce full-motion video productions for their PBS underwriting spots. For example, a spot for the antibiotic Zithromax (a product of Pfizer Pharmaceuticals) features children in front of a chalkboard learning the "ABC's of antibiotics."

Corporations now consider the public television audience to be a market segment worthy of reaching through advertising. In other words, underwriters no longer support public television for charitable reasons (Everhart Bedford 1997). Perhaps this is because PBS serves as a viable option for creating brand identity and awareness. This connection is not lost on PBS, either. The *1999–2000 PBS Sponsorship Guide* highlights underwriter Libby's Juicy Juice in a section on "results." The authors write, "What better way, then, for Juicy Juice to reach millions of parents and children and reinforce the brand's quality than to sponsor PBS's most popular children's program, *Arthur?*" (Everhart Bedford 1997, 32).

Audience As Market vs. Audience As Public

In *Desperately Seeking the Audience*, Ien Ang (1991) offers a detailed examination of the commercial television industry's relationship with audiences. She presents two ways of viewing the audience: audience-as-market and audience-as-public. On commercial television, one can expect that the audience will be commodified and viewed as merely a means to a profit. On public television, however, there is an assumption that the audience-as-public model will prevail. Or will it?

One does not need to look far for proof that PBS audiences have been turned into a commodity for sale to corporate America. The *1999–2000 PBS Sponsorship Guide* states that "PBS sponsors are remembered long after the screen goes dark. And that recognition means that our viewing audience of nearly 100 million people every week can consider your PBS sponsorship in making their buying decisions" (*1999–2000 PBS Sponsorship Guide*, 1). A later section titled "Expand Your Reach" continues to feature the audience as commodity: "PBS delivers highly educated and highly influential audience. Our diverse programming attracts viewers who are equally diverse— including mothers watching their children, business decision makers, and minorities" (*1999–2000 PBS Sponsorship Guide*, 2). The *1999–2000 PBS Sponsorship Guide* provides tables and charts profiling the PBS audience in comparison to other channels' audiences. It carves up the PBS audience by age, income, occupation, and education.

This document best demonstrates how public television has shifted from being content-driven to being audience-driven. As is the case in commercial television, audience members have been reduced to a viewing public. Moreover, audience members are viewed not as citizens, but as consumers. This leads to a conflict of interest, if the goal of public television is to serve the public (not *serve up* the public).

The purpose of this chapter is to quantify the advertising that takes place on one PBS station, WGBH-2 Boston. Through quantification, we can shed light on how commercialized public television has become. In analyzing the underwriting spots themselves, we can show similarities between underwriting spots and the "commercials" on commercial television. In analyzing the placement of the underwriting spots, we can understand which PBS market segments are being targeted by which companies. While one station may not be representative of the entire population of local PBS stations, it certainly opens the door for further analysis.

Method

A sample of content from WGBH-2 was drawn from February 12–26, 2000.[1] A rotated schedule was employed, in which two-hour time blocks were randomly selected each day until a twenty-four-hour composite day was achieved. Such a schedule was chosen in order to guarantee that the sample included the same variety of programs offered on any given day.

All content was timed and recorded as either an underwriting spot, programming, or station promotion. Underwriting spots were coded along several dimensions. First, each spot was associated with a genre of programming in order to determine which genres received the most underwriting. Next, underwriting spots were categorized as either static images of company logos or full-motion videos. The full-motion videos mirror the commercials aired on commercial television most closely, while one might associate the static version with underwriting spots of a previous era.

Each underwriting spot was also coded by product category. The product categories offered in the *1999–2000 PBS Sponsorship Guide* were employed for this study, including Aerospace, Agricultural, Apparel and Jewelry, Automobiles, Automotive, Education, Entertainment, Financial and Insurance, Food and Beverage, Healthcare and Pharmaceuticals, Homebuilding and Hardware, Home Furnishings, Industrial and Manufacturing, Legal and Professional Services, Office Systems, Photography, Shipping and Transportation, Technology, and Telecommunications. The coding instrument recorded whether or not product features were mentioned in the spot, if the product itself appeared in the spot, and if there were any calls to action. Additionally, the appearance of Web addresses, 800 numbers, corporate logos, and statements in support of PBS, or of learning, were coded.

Results and Discussion

Segment Types and Times

As mentioned earlier, all segments in the twenty-four-hour sample were coded as either an underwriting spot, a PBS promotional spot, or a program. Because the majority of underwriting spots were only fifteen seconds long, the total amount of time attributed to underwriting appears small at 2 percent (t = 22.8 minutes). However, when one considers the frequency with which these spots are run, the appearance of these advertisements becomes more suspect.

Underwriting spots accounted for 47.8 percent (n = 97) of the sample. PBS promotional spots accounted for 32.5 percent (n = 66). The sample contained 19.7 percent (n = 40) programming. This ratio of almost 2:1 of

Figure 9.1   **Frequency of Underwriting Spots at Different Times of the Day**

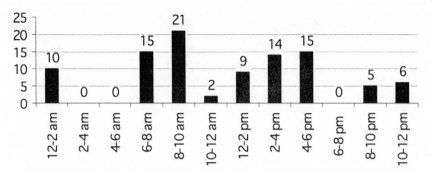

underwriting spots to programming (in terms of simple frequency) suggests that almost every show is flanked by underwriting spots. In actuality, however, the data suggest a different kind of relationship: of all the two-hour time segments recorded, the largest amount of the underwriting appeared in the 8:00–10:00 A.M. slot (21.6 percent, n = 21; see Figure 9.1). One of the two next largest slots for underwriting spots was the 6:00–8:00 A.M. slot (15.5 percent, n = 15). Given the fact that children's programming appears during these segments, it would appear that children are being targeted the most as consumers. In further support of this claim, several segments (6:00–8:00 P.M., 2:00–4:00 A.M., and 4:00–6:00 A.M.) contained no underwriting spots at all.

Genre

Interestingly, underwriting spots appeared to be associated with only three genres: arts and culture, children, and history. This may be due to the small sample size. Table 9.1 presents the frequencies for each genre. Other programming genres in the sample that appeared without the support of underwriting included drama, exploration, public affairs, science and nature, and comedy. The finding that 82.5 percent (n = 80) of the underwriting spots appeared during children's programming again suggests that children are the targeted consumers of PBS underwriting. However, one must also consider that children's programming makes up much of what is on PBS anyway.

Slightly more than half (56.7 percent, n = 55) of the spots appeared prior to the airing of a program. The remaining 43.4 percent (n = 42) of the spots ran after the programs they were associated with. All underwriting spots were associated with a particular program by way of an introduction such as, "*Barney and Friends* was made possible by. . . ." Such an association assists in targeting the particular audience being sought.

Table 9.1

Underwriting and Genre

Genre	Frequency	Percent of sample
Children's programming	80	82.5
Arts and culture	15	15.5
History	2	2.1
Totals	97	100.0

Visual

As mentioned in the literature review, early underwriting spots appeared "tombstone-like" (Ledbetter 1998). In comparison, more modern underwriting spots incorporate full-motion video, music, actors, graphics, and so on to convey their message. The departure from the older, more static underwriting spots of the past suggests that today's underwriting spots resemble "commercials"—so much so that they could perhaps be aired on commercial television stations without anyone noticing the difference. Underwriters are hiring agencies to produce these spots in the same manner that they would for commercial television. This is not simply a function of changes in technology that make it easier to prepare full-motion video ads; these ads require a budget for production. Underwriters are willing to invest in the production of these spots because they view sponsorship as a legitimate way to reach audiences.

In effect, public television has become just another option for advertisers in the commercialized media matrix. And, while these spots strongly resemble commercials in terms of production, they often are also "linked" to the underwriters' true commercial nature through the appearance of Web addresses. Deployed in this manner, the Web addresses serve as an extension of the ad.

The Web Address: An Extension of the Ad

All underwriting spots were examined for any types of call to action or extensions of the ad, including visiting a Web page or calling an 800 number. Only 8.2 percent (n = 3) of the ads featured an 800 number, but 33 percent (n = 32) included a Web address. Despite the rules and regulations underwriters follow for producing their spots on public television, the Web address allows them to promote themselves in any manner they see fit on their web sites, often providing a seamless link back to the PBS site as well. Of course, viewers must access a computer and intentionally visit the address appearing on the screen.

Table 9.2

Underwriting and Business Category

Category	Frequency	Percent of sample
Food and beverage	34	35.1
Toys	12	12.4
Technology	11	11.3
Telecommunications	8	8.2
Healthcare and pharmaceuticals	8	8.2
Retail-General	8	8.2
Financial and insurance	7	7.2
Entertainment	3	3.1
Apparel and jewelry	2	2.1
Automobiles	2	2.1
Education	2	2.1
Total	97	100.0

In terms of PBS and the Web in general, McChesney (1999) argues that public television stations have made their Web sites "the most commercialized aspects of their operations" (254). He explains that many PBS Web sites, including the CTW Web site that makes *Sesame Street* characters available for children, are commercially supported.

Business Category

A significant number (35.1 percent, n = 34; see Table 9.2) of products advertised could be classified as "food and beverage." The second largest product category represented in the sample was toys at 12.4 percent (n = 12). Technology products came in third at 11.3 percent (n = 11). These results support the idea that children are being targeted as consumers on public television. Companies like Juicy Juice, Kellogg's, Chuck E. Cheese, and KB toys are using public television to tap their best target audience: kids. While children may not possess the financial means to purchase products directly, they can be very influential with mom and dad at the grocery or toy store.

Of all the underwriting spots, all but two were repeated at some point in the sample. The average number of times a spot appeared was 3.2. The most often repeated spot was for DirecTV, making eight appearances in our sample. Since DirecTV is a satellite television system that could very well add to PBS's problems, the fact that DirecTV ads appear on PBS was initially surprising. Satellites deliver more channels, and more channels equal more competition. On the other hand, PBS can also increase its offerings over direct broadcast systems. In fact, some additions available on DIRECTV include the PBS Kids channel and the PBS You channel. PBS Kids runs only children's programming; PBS You offers telecourses on a variety of subjects, along with personal enrichment programs.

The toy company KB Kids appeared seven times in the sample of underwriting spots. Two spots ran six times each: one for Kellogg's Frosted Flakes and the other for Chuck E. Cheese restaurants. Such repetition helps to ensure that the messages in the underwriting spots are ingrained in the minds of viewers. Given that this sample recorded only twenty-four hours of PBS, one can only imagine how often a frequent viewer is exposed to the same message over time. While messages may be just fifteen seconds long, the practice of repeating them several times a day imbues them with all the power of a longer spot.

Corporate Symbols, Product Depictions, and Benefits

Corporate symbols and logos were present in 93.8 percent of the spots (n = 91). However, only 34 percent (n = 33) of the spots mentioned specific product benefits. In addition, the actual products were present in only 24.7 percent (n = 24) of the spots.

The presence of corporate symbols is significant for a variety of reasons. Since the target audience appears to be children, many of whom may not even be able to read, the symbols serve as something they can understand. Additionally, the symbols aid in memory retention and message identification. One does not have to invest much in the way of concentration to interpret an Ace Hardware logo. Finally, the corporate symbols provide a visual bridge to other marketing efforts of the companies using underwriting spots. When viewers see the logo on PBS, on commercial television, in print advertising, and in other venues, it becomes an important part of a company's wider marketing effort.

The fact that only a third of the spots mentioned product benefits, and only a quarter of them featured the actual products advertised, is not surprising. The rules for underwriting restrict product comparisons, and statements of benefit and product depiction may seem too close to the line. Many advertisers still put up the front that they are being "charitable" by sponsoring PBS, and roughly half (47.4 percent, n = 46) of the underwriting spots included statements in support of PBS or learning in general.

Conclusion

The findings presented in the previous section suggest that advertising is alive and well on public television. It is hard to imagine that the business of accepting underwriters does not influence the content of public television in some way, perhaps indirectly censoring the content of PBS programming. Like commercial television, which avoids controversial topics in an effort to please advertisers, PBS may find itself catering to underwriters instead of audiences.

Perhaps the most disturbing result is the targeting of children as consumers, suggested by the timing of the spots, the types of products advertised, and the program genres aired at the times in which the spots run. Reducing children to commodities and serving them up to underwriters is not exactly something one normally associates with public television. And yet, this appears to be the way of the future. In October 2001, the Federal Communications Commission approved a plan to allow public television stations to run commercials on some of the new channels they will obtain after converting to digital transmission. What may be at stake is PBS's future as a nonprofit organization. McChesney argues that, "as the commercial logic expands from within, it almost certainly means that what they broadcast will increasingly be indistinguishable from what is being broadcast by the commercial media giants" (1999, 255). If public television continues to employ the logic of commercial television, it will surely be unable to justify itself as a nonprofit organization worthy of federal subsidy.

What is at stake, then, is the very existence of public broadcasting as it was conceived by the Carnegie Commission. Ironically, public television became more commercialized in an effort to compete with the expanding commercial television market.

The issues raised in this chapter are not meant to be interpreted as an attack on any PBS station. We cannot blame PBS for doing its best to survive. With dwindling federal support and the increase in commercial competition, PBS stations may feel they have no choice but to turn to underwriters. The commercial model does provide the money necessary to fund programming. It is, however, a deal with the devil. We may not realize the cultural ramifications of commercializing public television until it is too late.

Additionally, we must consider that the content analyzed in this study came from many different sources; some of the programming was local, while other shows were national. Underwriting spots often come packaged with the shows themselves, especially if the sponsorship was arranged by a particular show's producers (e.g., Exxon Mobil's sponsorship of *Masterpiece Theater*). Therefore, we must view the problem of increased commercialization at PBS as multidimensional, with issues to be considered at the local, national, and production levels.

Since the future of television promises more channels and therefore more competition, it would be a shame to see public television serving the needs of the market over the needs of the public. As Hoynes (1999) concludes, increasing the number of television channels does not necessarily increase the diversity of offerings. We could improve the future of television with a host of public broadcast offerings, but as long as the market is the driving force of the future, this will not happen. Perhaps now, more than ever, public television needs to revisit its past and renew its commitment to serving the public interest. As this chapter has shown, PBS has drifted off course.

Note

1. A taping error occurred on February 19. To replace that time block, another segment was taped on February 26.

References

Ang, I. 1991. *Desperately Seeking the Audience.* New York: Routledge.
Beyond TV. 2000. *Sponsorship Guide 1999–2000.* Alexandria, VA: PBS.
Carnegie Commission on Educational Television. 1967. *Public Television: A Program for Action: The Report and Recommendations of the Carnegie Commission on Educational Television.* New York: Harper and Row.
Everhart Bedford, K. 1997. "'The Question of Length Is Really Settled': It's True That 30–Second Spots Abound on Some Local Stations, But They Divide the Public TV System." http://www.current.org/mo/mo703s.html.
Hoynes, W. 1994. *Public Television for Sale: Media, the Market, and the Public Sphere.* Boulder, CO: Westview Press.
———. 1999. "Democracy, Privatization, and Public Television." *Peace Review* 11: 33–39.
Ledbetter, J. 1998. *Made Possible By . . . The Death of Public Broadcasting in the United States.* New York: Verso.
McChesney, R.W. 1997. *Corporate Media and the Threat to Democracy.* New York: Seven Stories Press.
———. 1999. *Rich Media, Poor Democracy: Communication Politics in Dubious Times.* Chicago: University of Illinois Press.
Streeter, T. 1996. *Selling the Air: A Critique of the Policy of Commercial Broadcasting in the United States.* Chicago: University of Chicago Press.

10

Should One Size Fit All Audiences?

A Study of KUOP

Mary E. Hurley

The University of the Pacific (UOP) in Stockton, California, had a tradition of innovative radio broadcasting since the 1920s; it offered the first radio production major in the West and held the first Federal Communications Commission-licensed FM station in California's San Joaquin Valley. For many years KUOP's unique programming held multiple appeals for specific local communities. But on August 17, 1998, KUOP embraced a mission of audience and revenue development by narrowing its programming, ignoring its spatial community, and seeking an audience comprised entirely of members of the professional-managerial class.[1]

This is a study of KUOP-FM, Stockton-Modesto, a station that was, until June 1, 2000, an independent affiliate of National Public Radio (NPR) and Public Radio International. Since that date, KUOP has been operated by Capital Public Radio (CPR), a broadcast service of California State University, Sacramento. But, in truth, the old KUOP had long ceased to exist. This study examines shifting conceptions of public radio's mission, community, and audience, and the resulting changes in its programming, by contrasting the findings of public radio audience research with a 1997 survey of KUOP members. The discussion is informed by experience gained as a part-time worker at the station from 1996 to 1998.[2]

(Re)Defining the Mission of Public Radio

Public radio costs money and someone has to pay the bill. From its inception, the Corporation for Public Broadcasting (CPB) has had difficulties with funding and political interference. In recent years, public radio stations have also come under increasing financial stress.[3] In 1988, public radio's mission was to "provide meaningful services to significant numbers of listeners efficiently and effectively" (Giovannoni, Liebold, Thomas, and Clifford 1988, 3). By 1998, its mission was articulated as "significant programming for significant audiences" (Giovannoni 1997). This rhetorical refinement implies that mere numbers of listeners are not a significant measure of a station's success. The repeated message of *Audience 98*, a major research project in the public radio industry, is that public radio listeners are most likely to be highly educated, self-actualized professionals with healthy incomes who consider public radio to be personally valuable and are willing to support it.[4] A mission of audience and revenue development privileges this class, electing to serve it over those listeners less likely to pay for the programming.

Funding is also a prime variable in organizational structure at on-campus radio stations. Recognizing the development potential in the fast-growing Modesto market, KUOP-FM moved its transmitter to Mt. Oso, southwest of Stockton, in the early 1980s. In late 1996, when KUOP was removed from the Communication Department—a division of UOP's School of Liberal Arts and Sciences—to the Office for Institutional Advancement, the station underwent an unexpected change from an educational mission to one of institutional development, a move that was motivated by the university's concerns about financial resources. After a lengthy search, a former manager of radio projects and programming for CPB was hired as general manager (GM) of KUOP in October 1997.[5] The new GM soon articulated a significant shift in direction, suggesting to staff that a change in mission was appropriate for KUOP and stating that service to a community that "shared meaning" was its new mission. In order to serve the preferred community, undisclosed major programming changes would be coming to KUOP.[6]

Community

In 1988, public radio users were highly concentrated in the suburbs. Wealthy or artsy urban and "new melting pot" neighborhoods were locations of heavy public radio use, as well (Giovannoni, Liebold, Thomas, and Clifford 1988; Liebold 1988). Although in 1990, "the composition of the population and the availability of other stations" (Giovannoni 1990, 6) were considered to be essential in the definition of a station's community of service, *Audience 98* ignores these factors, asserting that "geographic localism is a more compelling concept among many public broadcasters than it is among most listeners" (Giovannoni, Youngclaus, and Peters 1998a; also Youngclaus, Peters and Giovannoni 1998c). Network public radio programming creates a virtual sense of community. A resource- and research-driven mission has transformed the public radio community into a social space for the reification of a particular worldview (Stavitsky 1994).

KUOP reaches a spatial community that is more ethnically diverse and more rural than the suburban and urban enclaves described in national audience research. Hispanics constitute 25 percent of the population in the listening area. Five percent of Stockton's citizens are African-American and 21 percent are of Asian-Pacific descent. Stockton is a "second city" that lies at the edge of the larger Sacramento, Silicon Valley, and San Francisco Bay areas. It is home to upscale white-collar workers, affluent retirees, and mid-income and working-class families of all ethnic backgrounds. Modesto is a suburban mix of white- and blue-collar families and the upwardly mobile people who are among public radio's frequent users. The entire listening area encompasses more farm and ranch towns than the national norm.[7] Although Modesto's affluent suburbanites are closer to the typical public radio user, Stockton's populations of landed gentry, second city elites, gray power retirees, new immigrant families, and college town singles present a significant audience for public radio.

And the Survey Says . . .

In April 1997, I conducted a survey of the members of KUOP at the request of Program Director Dennis Easter, who gave me complete access to the station's audience research data. Approximately 3,300 questionnaires were sent to members in the April 1997 edition of *The Voice*, KUOP's monthly program guide. A total of 528 surveys were completed and returned for a 16 percent response rate. The Statistical Package for Social Sciences, SPSS, was used to perform all statistical operations for the survey, and Cramer's V, a chi square-based measure of association, was used to illustrate the strength of the relationships between variables. Although it is impossible to generalize the results of this member survey to all listeners, it is useful to compare KUOP's particular audience with the typical public radio audience described in audience research funded by the CPB.

Respondents were asked to indicate their age, gender, and zip code (see Table 10.1). Zips were then coded to indicate eight general areas of residence.[8] KUOP members were asked to indicate their level of education and their family income for 1996 (see Tables 10.3 and 10.4 for categories). Respondents were asked to indicate their ethnic or racial heritage based on six categories, but because the frequencies of individual ethnic categories were slight, responses were recoded as Nonwhite and White.[9] Members indicated their frequency of listening to each show on KUOP's schedule[10] and their preferences concerning news over music, and network over local programs.[11]

Table 10.1

Sample Statistics

	Mean	Standard deviation	N
Gender	1.51	0.50	513
Age	55.80	16.45	506
Ethnicity	0.97	0.18	500
Education	3.13	0.88	515
Income	4.22	1.72	478
Zip code	*95350		515
News vs. music	2.11	0.74	501
Network vs. local	2.15	0.90	504

*Mode

Audience

The average public radio listener is a male with an annual household income of $67,000. Sixty-two percent of listeners have graduated from college or hold advanced degrees. Baby boomers in their forties comprise the largest listening cohort, but nearly 50 percent of public radio's audience was born before 1945. By 1998, 3 million nonwhite listeners tuned to public radio each week; this figure has doubled since 1988. Still, only one in seven public radio listeners is a person of color.[12]

Lifestyle and values research identified the two types of listeners, Actualizers and Fulfilleds, who do 72 percent of all listening and provide more than 80 percent of public radio's membership support. The ideal public radio listeners, Actualizer-Fulfilleds, are a combination of these two types; on average, fifty years old with an annual household income of more than $100,000. Seventy percent held advanced degrees, 50 percent were current public radio contributors, and two-thirds of these gave at least $50 per year.[13]

KUOP members who responded to the survey were most likely to be fifty-six-year-old, white, female college graduates who earned between $45,000 and $59,000 per year and lived in Modesto; they were older, less affluent, and less educated than the typical listener described by CPB-funded audience research. KUOP members were also more likely to be female. Ninety-seven percent of the responding KUOP members were white, compared to a national estimate of 86 percent (Tavares and Giovannoni 1998). In a region that has substantial Hispanic, Asian-Pacific, and African-American populations, younger people, as well as these large communities of color, were not significantly represented in KUOP's membership survey. Long before the format switch, the station seemed to have consciously targeted the white,

Table 10.2

LEWF and Program Streamlining at KUOP from 1996 to August 17, 1998
(in percent)

		LEWF	1996–97	1997–98	8-17-98
Source of total	Local	—	48	44	23
programming	Network	—	52	56	77
Source of "prime time"	Local	75	42	42	—
	Network	25	57	57	100
Format of total	News/Info	27	35	35	72
programming	Music	74	60	60	23
	Entertainment	—	5	5	5
Music formats	Americana	—	—	—	23
	Folk	13	6	10	—
	Classical	13	20	18	—
	Jazz	10	13	5	—
	Rock	18			
	Other*	20	21	28	—

Note: Other* includes Latino, reggae, world, blues, and New Age.

middle- and upper-class audience members that most resemble the typical listener identified by research.

Programming

The use of research as a predictive tool has led public radio to adopt the practice of narrowcasting, "the 'superserving' of particular audience segments to the exclusion of many others" (McCauley 1997, 8; also see Current Publishing Committee 1997). In 1992, 570 public stations participated in a study that revealed nine distinct programming cohorts in public radio. KUOP was located in the category "Local Eclectic with Folk," or LEWF, a "Mixed Format." There were seventy stations within the LEWF program cohort, comprising 12 percent of total stations, 10 percent of total listeners, and a low figure of 9 percent of nonfederal funding sources. Music was heard 74 percent of the time on LEWF stations, and local programs outstripped network programs three to one in 1992. It was predicted that formats would become streamlined and that LEWF would focus and expand its news, information, and classical music programming (Giovannoni, Thomas, and Clifford 1992, 12).

KUOP streamlined its dayparts to include only network news and locally programmed classical music in 1996, confirming the predictions of format focusing (Giovannoni, Thomas, and Clifford 1992, 28–29, 41). Table 10.2

compares the streamlining of program content at KUOP from 1996 to 1998 with the features of the LEWF program cohort as described in 1992. Format genres and musical formats are presented as a percentage of total programming.

"Programming economics," a research concept that conflates financial support with quality and value to the listening public, justifies the ascendance of network programming over local fare. *Audience 98* reported that two of five listeners preferred network programming, which, in turn, grossed nearly twice the listener-sensitive return (in funds from listener pledges and underwriting contracts) per hour of locally produced programming. This difference, however, was not due as much to a lack of listener financial support as it was to weaker underwriting support for locally produced programming. Two in five listeners acknowledged no preference between local and network programming, and members contributed one-half cent less, on average, for local programming than for network programming (Giovannoni, Youngclaus, and Peters 1998a; Giovannoni 1997). Upon examination, "listener-sensitive return" becomes a skillful rhetorical spin on "underwriter-sensitive return."

Of five programming appeal cohorts identified in the 1992 study, KUOP was determined to be a Multiple appeal station. Multiple appeal stations were predicted to target more whites with advanced degrees, and fewer young and poorly educated listeners. Public radio broadcasters cannot afford to waste resources targeting audiences whose financial support is less reliable. *Audience 98* warned programmers against potential damage to the target audience if public stations adopted a different "sound" in order to attract these less demographically desirable listeners.[14]

The locally produced programming that often constitutes a station's Multiple appeal has been the subject of criticism because wild shifts in audience appeal from program to program lead to "tune-out." Discernible seams between otherwise appealing programs are seen as counterproductive when research measures privilege audience size and "time spent listening." Public stations that depend on listener support need to maximize listening and minimize tune-out. Thus, research has rendered local block programming an endangered species. Indeed, all local public radio production declined 10 percent between 1986 and 1996.[15]

Table 10.3 presents the KUOP member survey findings on the relationship between the independent variables of gender, age, ethnicity, education, income, and zip code and the dependent variables of network or local programming. Relationships with age and education were determined to be statistically significant. The statistical mean of 2.15 suggests that the average respondent enjoyed both network and local programming. While those KUOP members who expressed a preference enjoyed network programs over local by a two to one margin, nearly half of the respondents expressed no particular preference.

Table 10.3

Audience Characteristics by Network or Local Program Preference
(in percent)

	Network	Local	No preference	Total	N	V
Gender						
Male	32	22	46	100	242	.11
Female	35	14	52	101	249	
Age						
18 to 30	28	17	56	101	18	.18**
31 to 40	59	7	35	101	58	
41 to 50	35	19	47	100	153	
51 to 60	34	12	55	101	95	
61 to 70	29	23	48	100	90	
71 and older	17	26	57	100	69	
Ethnicity						
White	35	17	49	101	467	.06
Nonwhite	21	29	50	100	14	
Education						
High school	27	27	47	101	15	.13*
Some college	25	23	53	101	114	
College grad	28	16	56	100	150	
Advanced degree	42	16	42	100	213	
Income						
Under $15,000	21	0	79	100	19	.13
$15,000–29,999	27	0	53	100	55	
$30,000–44,999	36	18	47	101	114	
$45,000–59,999	36	17	47	100	81	
$60,000–74,999	24	14	62	100	66	
$75,000–99,000	34	19	47	100	62	
$100,000+	43	18	39	100	61	
Zip code						
Bay area	13	50	38	101	8	.10
Butte	0	0	100	100	1	
Mother Lode	31	18	51	100	71	
Sacramento	33	22	44	99	18	
San Joaquin	33	19	47	99	156	
Stanislaus	36	15	50	101	210	
Yosemite area	31	10	59	100	29	

Note: $*p < .05$, $**p < .001$.

The relationship between network or local program preference and age was statistically significant ($p < .001$). The thirty-one to forty-year-old cohort expressed a strong preference for network programming over local. This cohort also preferred news to music, and since KUOP's only local news elements were weather and traffic reports inserted into breaks in NPR network news programs, members who preferred news programming necessarily preferred network programming. Other age groups expressed no preference.

The relationship between education and program preference was statistically significant as well ($p < .05$). Preference for network programming seemed to rise with education. KUOP members with advanced degrees strongly preferred network to local programming—by a margin of 42 percent to 16 percent. However, an equal number of highly educated members (42 percent) expressed no preference.

Local musical programs appealed to more diverse audience members than the type of survey respondent most likely to prefer specific network programs —a white, middle-class, fifty-something Modesto resident with an advanced degree. Two of the programs with the greatest appeal to members were produced locally and were the only programs in the KUOP Top Ten that attracted different audiences than the norm.[16] Daytime classical music attracted sixty-one- to seventy-year-old members. Male respondents enjoyed Americana music.

Within a year after the survey, KUOP had eliminated locally produced jazz, Latino, opera, New Age, and "pops" programs, along with network-based children's, folk, New Age, and early music programs. By early 1998, all promotional announcements for locally produced programs had been removed from the classical music programs that aired Monday through Friday. Local promos still ran at night and on the weekends, when the station's "typical" listeners were less likely to be tuned in. Further, most local evening programs were not "pitched" during KUOP's membership drives.

Audience 98 reported superior financial returns for network news, information, and entertainment programs. Local news and call-in shows were also well supported. News and information programs deliver desirable audience members, including a growing population of Generation X listeners. Public radio stations have abandoned musical dayparts for news and information formats.[17]

Table 10.4 presents the survey's findings on KUOP member preferences for news or music programming, cross-tabulated by gender, age, ethnicity, education, income, and zip code. Of these variables, gender, age, and education proved to be statistically significant.

Males responding to the survey preferred music to news by more than two to one ($p < .01$). Cross-tabulations to the independent variable of age were extremely significant statistically ($p < .001$). Only one age cohort, KUOP members aged thirty-one to forty, expressed a strong preference for news programming. Eighteen- to thirty-year-olds were evenly split between news, music, and no preference; forty-one- to sixty-year-olds had no preference. Nearly 70 percent of the oldest respondents, aged sixty-one and above, were music lovers. Equally significant were the findings regarding the indepen-

Table 10.4

Audience Characteristics by News or Musical Program Preference
(in percent)

	News	Music	No preference	Total	N	V
Gender						
Male	23	50	27	100	243	.15*
Female	23	37	40	100	246	
Age						
18 to 30	33	33	33	100	18	.28**
31 to 40	47	16	37	100	57	
41 to 50	27	33	40	100	154	
51 to 60	23	37	41	101	93	
61 to 70	10	69	21	100	89	
71 and older	9	68	23	100	69	
Ethnicity						
White	23	43	34	100	467	.01
Nonwhite	20	47	33	100	14	
Education						
High school	13	73	13	99	15	.16**
Some college	11	57	32	100	111	
College grad	21	41	38	100	152	
Advanced degree	31	36	33	100	210	
Income						
Under $15,000	11	37	53	101	19	.14
$15,000–29,999	19	50	32	101	54	
$30,000–44,999	26	44	30	100	113	
$45,000–59,999	28	46	26	100	80	
$60,000–74,999	11	42	48	101	65	
$75,000–99,000	26	37	37	100	62	
$100,000+	31	39	31	101	62	
Zip code						
Bay area	25	75	0	100	8	.14
Butte	0	0	100	100	1	
Mother Lode	14	51	34	99	70	
Sacramento	21	42	37	100	19	
San Joaquin	29	42	29	100	158	
Stanislaus	20	44	36	100	206	
Yosemite area	24	24	52	100	29	

*Note: *p < .01, **p < .001*

dent variable education ($p < .001$). Consistent with audience research findings, those with higher levels of education expressed a greater preference for news programming.[18] More than twice the number of members with a high school education (73 percent) preferred music than did members with advanced degrees (36 percent). However, even those KUOP members who had advanced degrees preferred listening to music.

During 1998, news and network programming came to dominate KUOP's positioning and promotional statements. Listeners were invited to "stay tuned" to NPR news during commuting hours. The frequent forward promotion of network news and information programming became a noticeable feature of the classical music program. A short pledge campaign held in the spring of 1998 totally eliminated funding messages for the station's music programming.

The Day the Music Died

KUOP launched its new mission on August 14, 1998, when, without notice to volunteers, part-time staff, or listeners, management announced that it would switch to a news and information format on August 17. This announcement, delivered in a letter to the KUOP membership, was front-page news for Stockton's *The Record* and prompted protest from longtime listeners. Management justified the sudden format change by citing increasing competition from the Capital Public Radio classical station, KXPR, and falling ratings during the two most recent Arbitron measurement periods. However, KXPR had planned to improve its transmission into KUOP's market for at least two years, and KUOP's weekly audience had increased by more than 3,000 listeners between 1997 and 1998. The issue was not the number of classical listeners, but rather their advanced age and lower economic status.[19] Within a year of the change, KUOP lost substantial listener support and eventually leased its transmitter to its competitor, Capital Public Radio.[20]

KUOP's switch to a network news and information format eliminated service to demographically unattractive listeners so the station could focus on those listeners that conformed to the *Audience 98* ideal. Until August 17, 1998, KUOP served both music-loving seniors and network news-loving thirty-one- to forty-year-old listeners with the programming they preferred. Since then, KUOP's entire midday schedule has been switched from local classical music to network news and information. Network programs filled 77 percent of KUOP's weekly broadcast schedule, and only 23 percent of KUOP's airtime was occupied by locally produced Americana music. Since its takeover by Capital Public Radio, KUOP devotes about 33 percent of its weekly schedule to music.[21]

Conclusion

Public radio's new mission is less concerned with quality of service and quantity of listeners, and more concerned with the quality of those listeners whom it serves in quantity. Community has been redefined as a social space, "shared meaning" among members of demographic clusters most likely to pay for the service or to patronize those most likely to underwrite it. The current emphasis on audience research limits the notion of "the public" that might be reached by public radio programs, along with the program formats by which this public may be addressed.

Is it ethical, or practical, for a public radio station to ignore large populations of less statistically valorized listeners in order to chase those who may not live within its market in significant numbers? Public radio, in theory and in practice, must accept that there are differences among audiences—both the diversity within a single audience group and the diverse number of potential audience groups. For example, it is foolish to think that the audience for public radio in Atlanta derives from only one class or cultural group, or that it shares every demographic, ethnic, and cultural feature with the audience for public radio in San Francisco. It is just as wrong to assume that rural and small-town audiences share every feature with those in great urban centers. This study of KUOP suggests that one size does *not* fit all. As Gilbert Seldes claimed: "A medium of entertainment that can serve everybody and chooses to serve primarily 'the civilized minority' is contradicting its own nature" (Seldes 1951, 232). Public radio is, indeed, contradicting its own nature when it uses audience research to construct a pattern that tailors its garments to the civilized minority.

Notes

1. Brewer (1977); Kita (1998); "Back in Time: 1951" (1997); Beymer (1997/1998); see Ohmann (1996).

2. From July 27, 1996, through August 17, 1998, I served KUOP as a program host, programmer, and engineer on a volunteer and part-time basis: mainstream and traditional jazz programs; network news and entertainment programs; reggae, world, blues, classical, and Americana music; production and operations tasks; music library.

3. McCauley (1997, Chapter 3); McChesney (1995); Conciatore (1997, 9); Ledbetter (1997); Russell (2001); Twentieth Century Fund Task Force on Public Broadcasting (1993).

4. Arnold (1998); Giovannoni (1987, 1998a); Giovannoni, Liebold, Thomas, and Clifford (1988); Peters, Youngclaus, and Giovannoni (1998); Robinson (1996); Smith (1998).

5. Dennison (1992, 15, 59); Dennis Easter, KUOP program director, personal communication with author, November 1996; DeRosa (1996, 1997/1998); Spence (1997, 1998); Wills (1997/1998).

6. Dennis Kita made these statements during a meeting for KUOP staff on April 16, 1998.

7. Audience research conducted for KUOP, Stockton, CA, 1997; Sue Kelly, *Claritas Corporation*; Giovannoni, Liebold, Thomas, and Clifford (1998, 10); Liebold (1988, 9); Stockton Chamber of Commerce, telephone interview with author, June 11, 1997.

8. The Bay Area comprises members from Alameda, Contra Costa, Marin, San Francisco, and Solano counties. The Mother Lode represents Amador, Calaveras, El

Dorado, Nevada, Placer, and Tuolumne counties. The Yosemite Area includes Madera, Mariposa, and Merced counties. All other counties are listed individually.

9. The original six categories were Hispanic/Latino, African-American, Asian/ Pacific Islander, White/Caucasian, Native American, and Other.

10. Categories included Often, Sometimes, Rarely, Never. The categories Often and Sometimes were recoded as Most Listening; Rarely and Never were recoded as Least Listening. The favorite programs of KUOP members were those with the highest frequencies in the category Most Listening.

11. Each of these dependent variables—"news or music" and "network or local"— was cross-tabulated with the demographic independent variables.

12. Current Publishing Committee (1997); Giovannoni (1998b); Giovannoni, Youngclaus, and Peters (1998b): Peters, Youngclaus, and Giovannoni (1998); see Lakey and Youngclaus (1998); Tavares and Giovannoni (1998).

13. Peters (1998b); Audience Research Analysis (1998); Youngclaus (1998).

14. Giovannoni, Thomas, and Clifford (1992, 39–42, 58, 97); Giovannoni (1998a); Giovannoni, Peters, and Youngclaus (1998); Hansen and Burch (1998); Peters (1998a); Peters, Youngclaus, and Giovannoni (1998); Youngclaus, Peters, and Giovannoni (1998c, 1998d).

15. Giovannoni (1993); Hein (1998); Giovannoni, Thomas, and Clifford (1992, 39–42); McCauley (1997, 8); Stavitsky (1994, 25); Youngclaus, Peters, and Giovannoni (1998c); Current Publishing Committee (2001).

16. The two programs were *Morning/Afternoon Classics* and *Prairie Fires and Paper Moons*. The rest of the Top Ten were *All Things Considered, Morning Edition, Prairie Home Companion, Weekend Edition, Fresh Air, Car Talk, Thistle and Shamrock, Schickele Mix*.

17. Giovannoni (1997); Youngclaus, Peters, and Giovannoni (1998a); Conciatore (1997, 10); *KXJZ Format Change* (2001).

18. Giovannoni (1997); Giovannoni, Peters, and Youngclaus (1998); Peters (1998a); Youngclaus, Peters, and Giovannoni (1998a, 1998b).

19. Dennis Kita, letter to the members of KUOP, August 14, 1998; Spence (1998); Fitzgerald (1998); Flint (1998); "Letters to the Editor" (1998); "KUOP Turns Off Loyal Listeners" (1998); McCoy (1998); "The Mission of Public Radio" (1998); KXTV—ABC-TV (1998); "On August 17" (1998); Bring Back the Music (2000); Dennis Easter, KUOP Program Director, personal communication with author, November 1996; Dennis Kita, personal communication with author, April 16, 1998; "Topline Release" (1998, 1999); Audience research conducted for KUOP, 1996–1997.

20. Louie (2000); Carlson (2000); Ferraro (2000).

21. Dennis Kita, letter to the members of KUOP, August 14, 1998; Spence (1998, A8); "Capital Public Radio to Change Programming" (2001); *KUOP Program Schedule* (2001).

References

Arnold, M. 1998. "Listening More or Less." *Audience 98: Report 4*, February 2. www.aranet.com.

Audience Research Analysis. 1998. "VALS2: An Abbreviated Guide." *Audience 98: Sidebar*, September 7. www.aranet.com.

"Back in Time: 1951." 1997. *Pacific Review* 85, no. 1: 32.

Beymer, L.J. 1997/1998. "Intangible Art: 'One-of-a-Kind' Program Pushes the Broadcast Envelope by Spotlighting Experimental Formats." *Pacific Review* 85, no. 2: 12–15.

Brewer, K.P. 1977. *Pioneer or Perish*. Fresno, CA: Pioneer Publishing.

Bring Back the Music. 2000. *KUOP Protest Page* (last updated January 7). protest@mindsync.com.

"Capital Public Radio to Change Programming." 2001. *Sacramento Business Journal*, August 28. sacramento.bcentral.com/sacramento/stories/2001/08/27/daily14.html.

Carlson, K. 2000. "Deal Puts KUOP in Capital Group." *Modesto Bee Online*, May 31. www.modbee.com/metro/story.

Conciatore, J. 1997. "Radio Sharpens Formats to Keep CPB Grants." *Current*, March 17, 9–10.

Current Publishing Committee. 1997. "Looking Back at the Audiences of Public Broadcasting." *Current Online*, April 5. www.current.org.

———. 2001. "Producers Defy the Trend Against Local Shows." *Current Online: Briefing*, August 14. www.current.org/local/index.html.

Dennison, C.F. 1992. "Administrative Patterns of On-Campus Radio Stations and the Leadership Behaviors of the Managers." Ph.D. diss., West Virginia University. *Dissertation Abstracts International*, 54–11A, 3940.

DeRosa, D. 1996. "President's Perspective." *Pacific Review* 84, no. 2: 2.

———. 1997/1998. "President's Perspective." *Pacific Review* 84, no. 3: 2.

Ferraro, C. 2000. "Capital Public Radio to Operate Stockton's KUOP." *Sacramento Bee Inside Business* (May 31). www.sacbee.com/ib/news

Fitzgerald, M. 1998. "The Day the Music Died on KUOP." *The (Stockton, CA) Record*, August 16, B1.

Flint, J.M. 1998. "We're Losing a Radio Legend." *Modesto Bee*, August 21. protest@mindsync.com.

Giovannoni, D. 1987. "What Makes Public Radio Personally Important?" *Current*, February 10, 5.

———. 1990. "A Tale of 3 Cities: And 1 Radio Station." *Current*, October 22, 6.

———. 1993. "Appeal and Affinity." www.aranet.com.

———. 1997. "The Value of Programming." *Audience 98: Report One*, September 11. www.aranet.com.

———. 1998a. "Basic Principles." *Audience 98: Adagio*, August 10. www.aranet.com.

———. 1998b. "Wait 'til You're Old Enough." *Audience 98: Sidebar*, August 10. www.aranet.com.

Giovannoni, D., L. Peters, and J. Youngclaus. 1998. "Yield Not to Temptation." *Audience 98: Report Ten*, July 8. www.aranet.com.

Giovannoni, D., T.J. Thomas, and T.R. Clifford. 1992. *Public Radio Programming Strategies: A Report on the Programming Stations Broadcast and the People They Seek to Serve*. Washington, DC: Corporation for Public Broadcasting. www.aranet.com.

Giovannoni, D., J. Youngclaus, and L. Peters. 1998a. "A Question of Place." *Audience 98: Sidebar*, June 22. www.aranet.com.

———. 1998b. "Public Radio's Older Audience." *Audience 98: Report Thirteen*, August 31. www.aranet.com.

Giovannoni, D., L.K. Liebold, T.J. Thomas, and T.R. Clifford. 1988. "Terms and Concepts." *Audience 88: A Comprehensive Analysis of Public Radio Listeners*. Washington, DC: Corporation for Public Broadcasting.

Hansen, J., and E. Burch. 1998. "Reality Check." *Audience 98: Sidebar*, July 8. www.aranet.com.

Hein, D. 1998. "A Place in Question." *Audience 98: Sidebar*, June 22. www.aranet.com.

Kita, D. 1998. "What's in a Name?" *The Voice* 14: 3.

KUOP Program Schedule. 2001. October 14. www.csus.edu/npr/grid5.html.

"KUOP Turns Off Loyal Listeners." 1998. *The (Stockton, CA) Record*, September 8, A4.

KXJZ Format Change Frequently Asked Questions. 2001. September 29. www.csus.edu/npr/kxjzfaq.html.

KXTV—ABC-TV. 1998. *Eleven O'clock News*, September 25. Sacramento, CA: ABC-Capital Cities Corporation.

Lakey, I., and J. Youngclaus. 1998. "I Want My NPR." *Audience 98: Sidebar*, August 10. www.aranet.com.

Ledbetter, J. 1997. "As Long as Presidents Appoint Its Rulers, Public Broadcasting Will Remain a Hopeless Mess." *Salon*, November 7. www.salon.com/media/1997/11/10media.html.

"Letters to the Editor." 1998. *The (Stockton, CA) Record*, August 25, B4; September 8, A4; September 23, B4, B5.

Liebold, L.K. 1988. "Underwriting." *Audience 88: A Comprehensive Analysis of Public Radio Listeners*. Washington, DC: Corporation for Public Broadcasting.

Louie, E. 2000. "KUOP Deal Signals Move to All News." *The (Stockton, CA) Record*, May 31. www.recordnet.com/daily/news/articles.

McCauley, M. 1997. "From the Margins to the Mainstream: The History of National Public Radio." Ph.D. diss., University of Wisconsin, Madison. *Dissertation Abstracts International*, University Microfilms Number AAS-97–21881.

McChesney, R.W. 1995. "America, I Do Mind Dying." *Current Online*, August. www.current.org/why/why514m.html.

McCoy, B. 1998. "Looming Competition Killed KUOP's Classics." *The (Stockton, CA) Record*, August 28, G1.

"The Mission of Public Radio." 1998. *The (Stockton, CA) Record*, September 8, A4.

Ohmann, R. 1996. "Public Radio: A Cultural Medium for the Professional-Managerial Class." *Chronicle of Higher Education*, November 14, B10–B11.

"On August 17 the Soul of Public Radio in the Valley Was Torn Out!" 1998. Advertisement in *The (Stockton, CA) Record*, September 26, A6.

Peters, L. 1998a. "Cases from the X Files." *Audience 98: Sidebar*, August 10. www.aranet.com.

———. 1998b. "VALS Notes: Where Are the Soc-Cons?" *Audience 98: Sidebar*, September 7. www.aranet.com.

Peters, L., J. Youngclaus, and D. Giovannoni. 1998. "A Tale of Two Audiences." *Audience 98: Sidebar*, July 8. www.aranet.com.

Robinson, J.P. 1996. "Radio Songs." *American Demographics* 18 (September): 60–64.

Russell, J. 2001. "Who Are You Calling a Corporate Shill?" *Salon*, June 23. www.salon.com/tech/feature/2001/07/02/npr2/print.html.

Seldes, G. 1951. *The Great Audience*. New York: Viking Press.

Smith, I. 1998. "Getting to More with the Concept of Core." *Audience 98: Report 6*, March 9. www.aranet.com.

Spence, B.D. 1997. "UOP Proposes Eliminating 29 Majors: Students Protest Updated Hit List at Forum." *The (Stockton, CA) Record*, April 11, A1, A8.

————. 1998. "KUOP Changes Format: Public-Radio Station Turns Down Music for Talk, News." *The (Stockton, CA) Record*, August 15, A1, A8.

Stavitsky, A. 1994. "Changing Conception of Localism in U.S. Public Radio." *Journal of Broadcasting and Electronic Media* 38: 19–33.

Tavares, F., and D. Giovannoni. 1998. "Public Radio's Minority Audiences." *Audience 98*. www.aranet.com.

"Topline Release." 1998. *RRCOnline* (Spring). www.rrconline.org.

————. 1999. *RRCOnline* (Fall). www.rrconline.org.

Twentieth Century Fund Task Force on Public Broadcasting. 1993. "Summary of Recommendations, July 1993." *Public Broadcasting Policy Base*. www.current.org/pbpb/documents/tcf93.html. (October 20, 2001).

Wills, J. 1997/1998. "New Directions." *Pacific Review* 84, no. 3: 6.

Youngclaus, J. 1998. "Comparing VALS Types." *Audience 98: Sidebar*, September 7. www.aranet.com.

Youngclaus, J., Peters, L., and Giovannoni, D. 1998a. "Four Generations of Listening and Giving." *Audience 98: Sidebar*, August 31. www.aranet.com.

————. 1998b. "Public Radio's Generation X Audience." *Audience 98: Sidebar*, September 18. www.aranet.com.

————. 1998c. "What Do Listeners Think When They Think of 'Local' and 'National' Programming?" *Audience 98: Sidebar*, June 22. www.aranet.com.

————. 1998d. "Why Do Some Listeners Support Public TV But Not Public Radio?" *Audience 98: Sidebar*, July 8. www.aranet.com.

11

DBS and the Public Interest Opportunity in Satellite Television

Steve Pierce

In his 1961 statement on communication satellite policy, a few years after the first successful U.S. rocket launch, President John F. Kennedy announced that the primary guideline for his recommendations "was that public interest objectives be given the highest priority" (U.S. Senate 1973, 293). The tension between satellite technology's potential in this regard, and the reality of its implementation underlies my study.

Two features stand out in the contemporary global telecommunications landscape:

> Consolidation of ownership and control on an unprecedented scale, including the AOL Time Warner deal and other massive mergers.

> A small but vibrant community media movement, exemplified by independent media coverage of corporate globalization and the accompanying social protests.

These seemingly contradictory trends—corporate oligopoly and a promising public interest sector—characterize direct broadcast satellite (DBS) television as well. DBS television is best known as the consumer electronics phenomenon that brings hundreds of program choices into the home via a small dish antenna. Although commercialism now dominates the media industries, the development of DBS was an act of social construction by viewers themselves; quite literally, they built a new telecommunications system on a foundation of crude homemade receiving dishes. This development spotlights the potential of new telecommunications technologies for democracy, along with the social process through which public roles are defined.

The pioneering work of public access cable television advocates since the 1970s is largely responsible for carving out whatever electronic green space exists on DBS. These pioneers built a number of powerful media models that focus on people, not technology. To the extent that the many thousands of people working with community-based forms of radio, television, and computer networks are involved in designing new communications systems, and as long as their collective knowledge is applied to new technologies, the movement for media democracy will retain its vitality. But those who see new technologies as inherently liberating frequently overlook this human factor:

> Freedom and equality are frequently evoked in discussions of these emergent public media, as new technologies prompt a seemingly endless cycle of hope and disappointment over their ability to help citizens enhance communication, develop forms of community, and gain control over their lives. With each successive invention, from the printing press to the radio to the technologies of television, satellite and computer, every advance has generated fresh waves of speculation over new social potentials. Such is the myth of scientific progress ever advancing in human improvement. (Trend 1997, 105)

Building a vibrant public media sector in the face of rapid change necessitates recycling and extending existing models, even as the particular technologies around which they are wrapped are cast aside. As Bayles notes, "When citizens are mobilized, they will use whatever communications system is at hand. But by itself a new system is not likely to mobilize citizens" (in Melzer et al. 1999, 163). The largely unheralded pioneers of public interest communication have shown the way—the challenge is to build on the foundation they have created. In a culture obsessed with disposable commodities and constant change, this is not an easy task. If the key factor in building this vibrant public media sector is people, not technology, few in our wired world want to know about it.

Direct Broadcast Satellite Television

Media mogul Rupert Murdoch's hostile takeover of the Manchester United soccer team in 1998 signaled the arrival of DBS television as a major force in the global telecommunications industry. British football fans were outraged that their hometown team had become just another multinational corporate asset. But in the content-driven arena of electronic media, the purchase was a masterful strategic acquisition. Soccer is a worldwide obsession and Manchester United is its most popular franchise. Like the sex-and-violence-laden products that drive the global film industry, televised sports easily transcend language and other cultural barriers. By buying the team, Murdoch's pioneering DBS network secured a relatively inexpensive stream of programming with almost universal worldwide appeal. The acquisition was part of an effort that spanned more than a decade: five years earlier, when he spent half a billion dollars to take over the Star TV operation in Asia, the *New York Times* noted that "Mr. Murdoch has bought himself at least the potential of reaching two-thirds of the world's population" and that "as a result, he is now close to creating the first truly global television empire" (Shenon 1993).

DBS is a technology without borders. In the 1960s and 1970s, "free flow of information" was a political doctrine that sought to guarantee the unfettered passage of Western media products into developing countries—over local objections, if necessary. New technology rendered that debate moot:

> From a vantage point of 23,000 miles, many of the earth's major features are distinct, but its political boundaries are blurred. A modern communications satellite, hovering in synchronous orbit at that distance from the globe, sends a signal that can be received anywhere on the one-third of the earth's surface visible to it; it is no respecter of national, cultural, or linguistic barriers. (Pelton 1974, vi)

The application of DBS television to the commodification of culture on a global scale is particularly poignant, because the technology was commercialized in an early struggle between the cable industry and its viewers—at a time when advances in telecommunications promised much more than business as usual. DBS has traveled a fascinating path since the time, twenty-five years ago, when the grassroots movement that sustained it was accused of signal piracy. From the large home-brew wood and wire mesh backyard dishes of the late 1970s to today's inconspicuous mass-marketed antennas, home satellite television evolved into a billion-dollar consumer electronics market.

Along the way, possibilities for a unique public interest telecommunications infrastructure gave way to a delivery system essentially indistinguishable from cable television. This basic dilemma is as old as radio broadcasting and as up-to-the-minute as broadband computer networking, but the sheer complexity of satellite technology, coupled with its geopolitical reach, marks a watershed of sorts:

> Communication by satellite is one of the wonders of modern life. It is held to be, and is, a triumph of American technology. It is also held to be a triumph of American corporate capitalism, of American government, and of the working relationship between them. (Kinsley 1976, xi)

Figure 11.1   **Early Direct Broadcast Satellite Dish**

Source: John Wilson, W4UVV, Prince George, Virginia.

The first commercial satellite to accommodate television was deployed in 1962 through a working partnership between NASA and AT&T. It generated a groundswell of support for the Communications Satellite Act of 1962, leading to creation of the Communications Satellite Corporation (Comsat)—a private company charged with commercializing the new technology.

But if the underlying technology demonstrates a new level of cooperation between industry and the state, the evolution of satellite communication also shows that even large, affluent, educated, motivated, and well-organized groups of citizens have difficulty exerting influence on telecommunications system design. In the early 1970s, lobbying by public interest groups had little impact on the emerging communications satellite policy in the United States. One historian refers to the telecommunication industry's deliberate destruction of unwanted technological options as "corporate Luddism," noting that "the Comsat debate is remembered in Washington primarily because of the unsuccessful filibuster of a small band of liberals who believed that the then-unique organization created by the act permitted private companies such as AT&T and ITT to benefit from 'the biggest giveaway in the history of the United States'" (Kinsley 1976, 1). A more recent examination of direct broadcast satellite communication also supports the view that corporate self-interest drives technological decision-making: "The potential economic and cultural-power benefits of developing and implementing DBS technologies, although occasionally recognized, were more usually suppressed or diverted to protect these and other interests" (Comor 1998, 27).

The smorgasbord of commercial television programming available on satellite by the 1980s drove home viewers to build their own receive-only ground stations, creating the home satellite movement and paving the way for the DBS industry itself. The trade weekly *Broadcasting* hailed dish owners as "a public so committed to television but so impatient with its progress that it took things into its own hands." But in the same editorial these very people were excoriated as recipients "of perhaps the biggest electronic free lunch in history" ("Historic Moment" 1985). Rather than stimulating openness, active public participation in these technological developments had the opposite effect—it spurred more research on hardware and software controls designed to lock users into passive roles as consumers.

The deregulated telecommunications environment of the late 1980s, combined with the exceptionally high capital requirements of adapting DBS technology for a mass consumer market, resulted in an oligopolistic industry that was interested in programming only as a commodity form. With tens of millions of homes now equipped with DBS television receivers, the time for seriously considering the creative, noncommercial uses to which this technology could be put is long overdue.

Public Interest Uses of Satellite Television

A dramatic decrease in satellite "space/time" costs in the early 1980s (caused by a surplus of communications satellites in orbit)—coupled with the low cost and ubiquitous presence of receive dishes at schools, businesses, and cable systems—allowed media artists to begin experimenting with the technology. Like the telephone company, the satellite communications industry was organized as a "common carrier," meaning that anyone with the financial means could buy satellite time. At first, the uses were primarily one-time-only projects, typically "space bridges" between artists in widely separated countries. Linkups from coast to coast in the United States, between Eastern Europe and the West, and similar symbolic efforts were typical.

Then, in 1989, the solidarity group Nicaragua Network devised "Project Satellite." Grassroots political organizing against the Reagan administration's Central America policy was at an all-time high. Activists trying to respond to the administration's characterization of the Nicaraguan contras as "freedom fighters" were unable to get their message out, so, to bypass what they regarded as a corporate media blockade, they organized a live call-in show in Managua featuring Nicaraguan president Daniel Ortega. The show was televised in the United States using two satellite "hops," one above Latin America and another over North America. The goal was to allow American citizens to see and hear Ortega in a context unmediated by journalists and even, via long-distance telephone, to ask him questions. Through a vigorous campaign of community organizing, downlink sites were arranged throughout the United States. Local groups booked meeting rooms and rented portable satellite dishes and television screens. Some universities also sponsored the program, opening their facilities to the public. A few participants with home satellite dishes sponsored potlucks followed by the screening. Organizers thought the project was sufficiently successful to repeat it the following year, in cooperation with a group based in New York City called Deep Dish TV (Armstrong 1990).

Deep Dish TV's innovation was to connect public access cable television channels with DBS. Successful as they were, the early satellite projects were essentially variants of closed-circuit television. Anyone with a few hundred dollars could rent satellite time, but placement on cable television systems was practically impossible to arrange. Without cable distribution, only private dish owners could view programming distributed via satellite. Artists and organizers had formed the Deep Dish TV satellite network in 1986 to explore creative uses of new media technology. The network was established to create a national sense of community among activist television producers and public access cable stations.

One of the most impressive demonstrations of the potential uses for this kind of networked grassroots media infrastructure came in 1991 with the Gulf Crisis TV Project. Produced by Paper Tiger Television using tapes solicited through Deep Dish TV's social network, the Gulf Crisis TV Project was designed as an activist response to the uncritical U.S. media coverage of preparations for war in the Persian Gulf. The goals were to provide the critical analysis missing from mainstream media outlets and demonstrate the extent of nationwide opposition to war. The initial series of four half-hour television programs (six more were produced after the war began) was compiled from footage submitted by activists around the country. Using consumer camcorders as well as professional equipment from public access cable television and media arts centers, independent producers covered protest rallies and conducted interviews with war resisters in their hometowns. The footage was then shipped to New York for assembly into finished programs by the Gulf Crisis TV Project staff. Completed shows were then distributed by satellite to the hundreds of public access centers active in the Deep Dish TV network, and to home dish viewers nationwide.

The series was also offered via satellite as an independent feed to stations

Figure 11.2 **"The Deep Dish Process"**

Source: Deep Dish TV.

in the Public Broadcasting System. The project underscored the lack of local production infrastructure at the nation's "public" television stations—it offered virtually the only timely source of news and public affairs programming critical of the war. Even though fewer than a quarter of PBS stations aired the shows, it was enough exposure to unleash a tidal wave of supportive calls, for which Deep Dish TV's tiny staff was completely unprepared (Marcus et al. 1991). The project proved to be a watershed event in the history of community television: never before had so many activist productions been assembled on such short notice over such a wide area. Never before had the final product been edited so quickly and distributed so broadly; never before had public response been so widespread and favorable (Magnan 1992).

Following this success, Deep Dish TV extended its collaborations to include other community media organizations. Working with the Pacifica Radio network, it produced an interactive live telecast of *Slow Death in the Cities,* a panel discussion on the global environmental crisis at New York City's Borough of Manhattan Community College. A rented portable satellite uplink was connected to a mobile production van operated by volunteers and staff members from Staten Island Community Television. The two-hour program was transmitted simultaneously to several satellites, reaching noncommercial radio, cable access centers, home dish viewers, and PBS stations. For not much more than $5,000, a nationwide community radio and television network was assembled.

A few months later two New York City-based groups, The Kitchen and Visual Aids, created a live national television program in observance of World AIDS Day called *We Interrupt This Program: A Day Without Art.* Produced by volunteers in Manhattan, the program was supported by AIDS activist groups across the country. Downlink sites contributed live phone-ins to symbolize unity in the face of the epidemic. In some cities the program was sent out on cable; in others it was screened at universities and in other public spaces, while people in rural areas watched in groups at home, using their own satellite equipment.

These projects generated considerable excitement in the independent media community. The John D. and Catherine T. MacArthur Foundation went so far as to bring a group of activist television programmers to Chicago for a series of strategic planning sessions aimed at developing a full-time network. But the cost of establishing an ongoing independent satellite television channel, even if minimal by commercial standards, was seen as prohibitive. Instead, the Deep Dish TV network and other programmers continued with their strategy of offering limited series and specials. Widely screened independent television coverage of the December 1999 protests at the World Trade Organization (WTO) meetings in Seattle, and the April 2000 actions at the World Bank in Washington, D.C., showed existing models still had a great deal of potency. Yet without a regular stream of programming or spectacular special projects, the ad hoc network of cable access television stations and other outlets proved difficult to hold together.

By the late 1990s, the most consistent nationwide distribution of alternative television programming came from Free Speech TV. In spite of this organization's in-house expertise with a wide range of cutting-edge telecommunication technologies, Free Speech TV found the old standby of "bicy-cling" videotapes by mail from one station to another to be the most cost-effective means of regular distribution. The organization's founders had been exploring the margins of the telecommunications industry for more than a decade, looking for niches through which to distribute independent programming — particularly material supportive of progressive political causes. Free Speech TV was also one of the first access-oriented media outlets to begin the tran-sition to Internet-based distribution by offering streaming video on its Web site. That experience positioned the organization for a key role in the devel-opment of the online Independent Media Center movement that burst into view with Seattle's WTO protests. Free Speech TV is also a player in the new direct broadcast satellite television environment, having successfully lob-bied for one of the few channels reserved for public interest use.

In the decade following Deep Dish TV's first satellite-distributed televi-sion series for public access cable, DBS technology moved toward commer-cial viability. Improved scrambling technology made it possible to restrict satellite viewing to paying customers only, converting millions of "signal pirates" into subscribers. The familiar hulking backyard dishes gradually gave way to pizza-sized antennas, as digital compression and other technological improvements married many more channels to a more powerful satellite sig-nal. Following global trends, the DBS industry in the United States took a step toward monopoly status when DirecTV and its only competitor, Echostar (the parent company of Dish Network), signed a merger agreement in Octo-ber 2001—a deal that was later rejected by regulators. DBS providers are like a satellite and cable company rolled into one; with their emergence, independent producers cannot buy satellite time to reach home dish viewers. A new regulatory framework is now in place—no longer common carriers, these operators are instead subject to a public interest set-aside included in the congressional legislation that establishes spectrum for DBS use.

In late 1998, two years after commercial DBS television service was inau-gurated, the Federal Communications Commission (FCC) finally announced the public service standards mandated by Congress. These rules reserve 4 percent of the available channels for public interest use, but with enough ambiguity to arouse significant concerns (Aufderheide 2000). Foremost among them is the FCC's decision to allow a DBS operator to choose which services to offer under the new guidelines. The language on public interest obligations specifies that, as with cable access, operators are not allowed to exercise content control over the new channels, but critics of the policy's implementation argue that allowing them to choose the channels amounts to the same thing.

Another onerous aspect of the FCC rules is a provision allowing operators to charge noncommercial programmers 50 percent of the direct cost of providing the channel. The Dish Network charges public interest programmers more than $10,000 per channel per month, just for access to its system. Even at that, contracts are negotiated on a year-to-year basis, providing little security for large investments in operating expenses. As a result, most of the public interest DBS channels went to established televangelists with deep pockets and on-air fund-raising experience or to institutions like state universities, which are able to write off television programming expenses as a loss leader in service of their other interests.

With Free Speech TV's years of experience in programming a variety of distribution outlets, the public interest channel was a way to achieve a nationwide presence. In addition to reaching millions of homes directly, its DBS channel offers the potential for use as a real-time digital satellite network linking public access cable channels and other programming outlets that previously relied on unwieldy bicycled tapes. For around $200, individuals and organizations can purchase a digital satellite downlink capable of delivering programming live or automatically recording it for future use.

Though encouraging, even these new directions in DBS television leave much to be desired. The cost to an organization operating one of the public interest channels is exorbitant—more than $100,000 a year for distribution alone, with no clear way to recoup expenses. Add to this the costs of playback, personnel, and acquiring programming, and the challenge of running in the black seems even more daunting. Vying with hundreds of competitors for viewers, each channel must market itself aggressively and without the cross-promotional muscle of conglomerates like AOL Time Warner, which own popular cable services as well as print and other media.

More significantly, and despite the important content offered by Free Speech TV and other public interest programmers, these DBS channels are not structured for public use. Cable access allows any citizen or group to reach a television audience; nothing remotely similar exists on DBS. It is unclear how or if the viewing public can participate in choosing or producing DBS programming. After forty years of organizing, cable access advocates have successfully expanded the definition of media access to include not just channel time, but also training, equipment, and studio facilities. The DBS industry can now provide an outlet for independent projects, but does little to foster the creation of that work.

To the extent that perceived competition from DBS (and other new media technologies) provides justification for further deregulation of the cable industry, it is important from a public policy perspective not to lose the benefits of decades of media activism and organizing. "Level playing field" arguments can either raise the standard for public interest requirements or—

as is often the case, absent strong advocacy—trigger a race to the bottom. Public access cable organizations give local communities a focal point for education and outreach using television as a tool. New technologies should enhance the opportunities for democratic participation and dialogue at all levels of political discourse, rather than reduce communication to consumption and remand it to national programmers.

Potential DBS Models

A good start toward meaningful public access to direct broadcast satellite television would be to emulate the public, educational, and governmental access provisions that are already in place for local cable television. This might include:

1. Substantial (10 percent or more) set-asides of channel capacity for national noncommercial programming, whether video, audio, or data. Channels should be programmed by nonprofit public, educational, and governmental access entities with governance structures that guarantee open and accessible programming decisions. These access organizations should also be structurally insulated, as much as possible, from commercial and political pressure. The programmers of these noncommercial channels should have access to all the promotion and marketing technologies available to commercial channels (on-screen program guides, preview channels, bill inserts, telemarketing support, and so on).

2. Similar set-asides for local and regional noncommercial programming. Wherever DBS operators carry local commercial broadcast stations, they should be required to provide programming from the local cable-based public, educational, and governmental access organizations. After years of struggle, nonprofit, public interest advocates should benefit from advances in telecommunications technology; at the very least, they should not be pushed further into the margins.

3. Spectrum fees (10 percent or more of gross DBS revenues) allocated between national, regional, and local media access centers.

4. Media literacy education (on- and off-screen) to inform the viewing public about alternatives to commercial programming.

5. Outreach measures alerting subscribers to the availability of local program production training and distribution resources, for those inclined to create their own projects for local and national distribution.

6. Support for noncommercial community networks, both local and national, on DBS-delivered Internet services.

Establishing substantive media resources for individuals and groups of citizens depends on more than the regulation of any particular technology.

The inclusion of public, educational, and governmental access requirements in cable television legislation was an important first step decades ago, but it ultimately falls short of what is required to support a viable community media and technology infrastructure. The effort needs to be broad-based and sustained. The need for well-funded community-based media centers is now stronger than ever, since "public" broadcasting continues to drift further from its original mandate.

Public Broadcasting and DBS

The ascendance of new technologies is driving the electronic media environment through a transformation as radical as any since the dawn of broadcasting more than eighty years ago. Public broadcasting is struggling to integrate new media models, made possible by broadband Internet access and DBS technologies, into long-term strategic planning. Operating with bureaucratic systems and other infrastructure developed over the course of decades, present-day broadcasting networks present a powerful barrier to substantive change in the roles played by the electronic media in society. Professional broadcasters, commercial and noncommercial, often see new technologies and new applications of existing technologies as threats to be overcome, instead of opportunities for growth. Public television's alliance with commercial cable interests against backyard satellite dish owners in the late 1980s—and public radio's partnership with the National Association of Broadcasters to hobble the late 1990s microbroadcasting movement—bear witness to the extent to which technological inertia drives telecommunications policy.

In the staid world of the Corporation for Public Broadcasting and its client radio and television stations from coast to coast, public broadcasting exists primarily to fill gaps in the commercial media ecology. As niche services spring up to cover even the smallest demographic, the only remaining unserved audiences are those with no commercial appeal—groups as unattractive to public broadcasters as to their for-profit counterparts. By embracing, instead of questioning, the methods of the commercial sector, public broadcasting organizations at the national level have constructed a top-down network of repeater stations blanketing the country with a stream of programming that originates from their corporate headquarters. Whether in Los Angeles or New York City, Chicago or New Orleans, Laramie or Dubuque, public radio listeners and public television viewers hear and see essentially the same programming. This is precisely what direct broadcast satellite technology does, only more efficiently.

Public broadcasters now have a remarkable opportunity to reinvent themselves as *community* broadcasters, abandoning their bland programming in favor of a return to the mission they were created to serve. For, despite its many successes, public broadcasting has yet to fulfill its mandate. In a 1977 evaluation of modern public broadcasting's first decade, the second Carnegie Commission already found the industry "out of kilter and badly in need of repair," and suggested that

> the outcome of the institution of public broadcasting can best be understood as a social dividend of technology, a benefit fulfilling needs that cannot be met by commercial means. As television and radio are joined by a host of new technological advances, the need becomes even more urgent for a nonprofit institution that can assist the nation in reducing the lag between the introduction of new telecommunications devices and their widespread social benefit. (Carnegie Commission on the Future of Public Broadcasting 1979)

The new technological advances foreseen by the second Carnegie Commission a quarter century ago have arrived, now fully developed in their commercial forms. Preoccupied with self-preservation and internal conflict, existing public broadcasting institutions have failed to take the lead in defining the "widespread social benefit" of direct broadcast satellite television. With almost no resources, a contingent of grassroots producers and programmers has done so instead. Harnessing community radio, public access cable, DBS television, and streaming media on the Internet, an unprecedented coalition of media activists joined forces after September 11, 2001 to bring daily coverage of the global peace and justice movement to listeners and viewers around the world—this occurred under the banner of *Democracy Now!*'s "War and Peace Report." Public television could offer nothing like it.

Conclusion

In August 1998, media activists from around the world met in Italy and issued the Milan Declaration on Communication and Human Rights. Building on a section of the United Nations' Universal Declaration of Human Rights that calls for global "freedom of opinion and expression" as well as "the right to receive and impart information and ideas through the media regardless of frontiers," the Milan conference sought to establish the basis for a fundamental human right to communicate:

> This Right to Communicate is a universal human right which serves and underpins all other human rights and which must be preserved in the context of rapidly changing information and communication technologies. (Buckley 1998, 20–21)

As part of a dozen claims on behalf of noncommercial community-based media, the Milan declaration asserts that "all members of civil society should have just and equitable access to all communications media" and that "people must be seen as producers and contributors of information and not be defined solely as consumers."

The history of the media and democracy movement articulated here suggests that a two-pronged strategy is necessary to bring about the goals articulated at the Milan Conference:

- In the short term, existing technologies and forms of organization should be taken as givens; media activists should develop ways to work with and around them.
- In the long term, activists should organize to effect change via public policy and other means, as necessary.

The social movement that broke into public view during the December 1999 World Trade Organization summit in Seattle has a media auxiliary that epitomizes the short-term approach. Using life-size puppets and other forms of street theater, demonstrators attempt to manipulate mainstream press coverage of their civil disobedience actions. Having learned from experience that the substance of their political message cannot be communicated through sensationalism-oriented commercial media channels, activists have also created Independent Media Centers based on community media forms, in order to get out higher-quality information (even if to a smaller audience).

The organizers of the effort to redefine globalization in their own terms ("from the grassroots up") face daunting challenges to reach an audience, and they know it:

> "Six global corporations control all the media in this country," says Eric Galatas of Free Speech TV, who's been part of each media center so far. "We had a saying in Seattle: We were trying to break through the information blockade." (Carr 2000)

To address telecommunications reform in the long term, community media activists must engage directly with the political process on the level of public policy. The reserved, noncommercial portion of the FM radio dial; the public television system; the federal mandate for public, educational, and governmental access channels on cable systems; the public interest channel set-asides applied to direct satellite broadcasters; and, most recently, the establishment of a low-power FM radio service are all the result of tenacious organizing and lobbying.

The lack of enthusiasm with which community media are regarded in some quarters is understandable given the limited impact of some of these spectrum set-asides, particularly in contrast to the power of commercial media. Yet the doubters must come to appreciate the full scope of what has been accomplished against formidable odds. Otherwise, the decades of organizing embodied in successive waves of technology may be wasted. It is easy to dismiss public access cable television, for example, as an irrelevant media form because of the effort required to use it effectively and the attraction of the Internet's seemingly unlimited bandwidth. But lack of bandwidth is not the source of access problems confronting cabled communities—every municipality in the United States has a statutory right to demand channels for public use from cable providers, yet only one in five does. Whatever the form of a given technology, the underlying problems—powerful corporate interests, timid elected officials, political corruption, disinterested citizens, chronic funding shortages, lack of media education—will persist.

Historian David Noble (1983), writing about largely unsuccessful efforts in the 1970s to protect jobs in the face of industrial automation, argued that union leaders were dazzled by changing technology and made the critical strategic error of ignoring the familiar underlying social forces. Those who equate fundamental media reform with technological innovation face the same fate. A comparison of the pioneering half-inch reel-to-reel "guerilla video" coverage of the 1972 presidential conventions by Top Value Television with the hours of live programming distributed via satellite by the Independent Media Centers at the Republican and Democratic conventions in 2000 leaves no doubt that advances in technology have radically altered the playing field. Yet even the crisp, new, digital images at our disposal cannot mask the fact that the Portapack revolution heralded by TVTV and other early video enthusiasts has never fully materialized. Now, at a time when public access cable television has not yet achieved its promise, there are those ready to move on to the "next big thing" in communications technology.

The problem, as articulated by Andrew Feenberg, is the context in which technological development takes place: "I argue that the degradation of labor, education, and the environment is rooted not in technology per se but in the anti-democratic values that govern technological development" (1991, 3). Unfortunately, this view leads those who see democracy in media as a prerequisite for democratic renewal into a logical circle. To break out of this pattern, I offer the following criteria for communications system design as a starting point:

• A democratic steering process to guarantee open governance.
• Training to foster media production skills and critical thinking.

- Equipment and other support to facilitate the creation of programming.
- Distribution mechanisms to connect producers to consumers of information.
- Strategies to assure access to information while moderating overload.
- Funding to guarantee universal service.

The story of direct broadcast satellite television starts with spontaneous, uncoordinated moves by individual consumers to intercept transmissions intended for cable system operators. The rapid growth in the number of home satellite television viewers created a new medium, one with relatively autonomous and open characteristics, compared to what was then available on broadcast and cable television. Within a decade, this freewheeling and undercapitalized industry (epitomized by the rural phenomenon of mom-and-pop home satellite television stores) had become rationalized into just another part of the media landscape, a process completed with the emergence of DirecTV and Echostar's Dish Network. Satellite technology inherently promotes centralization, but there are strategies that can be adopted to take advantage of that tendency while minimizing adverse impacts. DBS has the potential to reinforce the worst aspects of the technology or to help transform it. It's our choice.

References

Armstrong, D. 1990. "Ortega to Go Live with Point of View." *San Francisco Examiner*, March 2, C8.

Aufderheide, P. 2000. *The Daily Planet: A Critic on the Capitalist Culture Beat.* Minneapolis: University of Minnesota Press.

Buckley, S. 1998. "From Managua to Milan: The Milan Declaration on Communication and Human Rights." *InteRadio* (December): 20–21.

Carnegie Commission on the Future of Public Broadcasting. 1979. *A Public Trust: The Report of the Carnegie Commission on the Future of Public Broadcasting.* New York: Bantam Books.

Carr, C. 2000. Get Me Download! Reporting the Real Philadelphia Story. *Village Voice Online*, July 12–18. www.villagevoice.com/issues/0031/carr.php (August 15, 2002).

Comor, E.A. 1998. *Communication, Commerce, and Power: The Political Economy of America and the Direct Broadcast Satellite, 1960–2000.* New York: St. Martin's Press.

Feenberg, A. 1991. *Critical Theory of Technology.* New York: Oxford University Press.

"Historic Moment." 1985. *Broadcasting*, December 9, 97.

Kinsley, M.E. 1976. *Outer Space and Inner Sanctums: Government, Business, and Satellite Communication.* New York: Wiley.

Magnan, N. 1992. "Alternative Television in America." *UNESCO Courier*, October 1992, 13.

Marcus, D. et al. 1991. *ROAR: The Paper Tiger Television Guide to Media Activism.* New York: Published by the Collective in association with Wexner Center.

Melzer, A.M. et al. 1999. *Democracy and the Arts.* Ithaca: Cornell University Press.

Noble, D. 1983. "Present Tense Technology." *Democracy: A Journal of Political Renewal and Radical Change* 3, no. 2, parts 1–3.

Pelton, J.N. 1974. *Global Communications Satellite Policy: INTELSAT, Politics, and Functionalism.* Mt. Airy, MD: Lomond Books.

Shenon, P. 1993. "Start TV Extends Murdoch's Reach." *New York Times,* August 24, D1.

Trend, D. 1997. *Cultural Democracy: Politics, Media, New Technology.* Albany: State University of New York Press.

U.S. Senate. 1973. President Kennedy's Statement on Communication Satellite Policy. Senate Report No. 1584, 87th Congress, 2d Session (pp. 25–27) July 24, 1961. In F. Kahn, ed., *Documents of American Broadcasting*, 3d ed. New York: Appleton-Century-Crofts, 293–295.

12

Making Money and Serving the Public Interest

Public Broadcasting Can and Should Do Both

Gary P. Poon

In October 2001, the Federal Communications Commission (FCC) issued a *Report and Order* clarifying the rules for the use of digital television (DTV) channel capacity by public television (PTV) stations (*Report and Order* 2001). While PTV stations are required to use their DTV channels for noncommercial educational programming, they may also use the excess channel capacity that all digital stations will have for moneymaking purposes. This chapter begins with a review of public broadcasting's original mission and then moves to an analysis of the FCC's *Report and Order*. Specifically, it contemplates whether a public television system that makes money through advertisements will necessarily "lose its soul." This issue will become more important (in years to come?) because of the diverse programming needs of a U.S. population that is undergoing rapid demographic change.

The Founders' Vision

> The utilization of a great technology for great purposes, the appeal to excellence in the service of diversity—these became the concepts that gave shape to the work of the Commission. In the deepest sense, these are the objectives of our recommendations. (Carnegie Commission 1967, 14)

A portion of this chapter originally appeared in *Current*. See Gary P. Poon, "Seize the Diversity Market—A Pragmatic View," *Current* (November 1, 1999).

During the mid- to late 1960s, members of the Carnegie Commission on Educational Television articulated a grand vision for noncommercial TV that was built upon the principles of diversity and multiculturalism. "America is geographically diverse, ethnically diverse, widely diverse in its interests," members observed. "American society has been proud to be open and pluralistic, repeatedly enriched by the tides of immigration and the flow of social thought. Our varying regions, our varying religious and national and racial groups, our varying needs and social and intellectual interests are the fabric of the American tradition" (Carnegie Commission 1967, 14).

Public television, members envisioned, should "help us see America whole, in all its diversity," should be "a mirror of the American style" and "should remind us of our heritage and enliven our traditions." Public television is a place "where people of the community express their hopes, their protests, their enthusiasms, and their will." It should provide "a voice for groups in the community that may otherwise be unheard." Its programs "should help us know what it is to be many in one, to have growing maturity in our sense of ourselves as a people." It should, in short, be the "clearest expression of American diversity, and of excellence within diversity" (Carnegie Commission 1967, 92, 93, 18).

Yet many of public television's critics—even some of its champions—claim that the industry has fallen far short of these ideals. While there may be some exceptions, public television programming, they say, tends to be dull, unimaginative, predictable, and safe. "The fear of alienating corporate underwriters, station subscribers and government officials reinforces . . . a 'logic of safety' and a culture of timidity inside public television," wrote one independent producer turned academician (Bullert 1997, 4). "Such timidity has not always been the norm," another observer added. "It is learned behavior, based on survival instincts" (Ledbetter 1997, 11).

While there may be some truth to these criticisms, it would be naive to expect public TV to ignore the now predictable threats to cut off its funding whenever a controversial or provocative program is aired. But if public broadcasting's self-censorship is a learned behavior, could it not also be unlearned?

The FCC's *Report and Order*

On October 17, 2001, the FCC clarified three areas that had been previously left unclear by its 1997 *Fifth Report and Order,* which had established the original rules for the transition to DTV. First, PTV stations must use their digital channels "primarily" for "nonprofit, noncommercial, educational broadcast services," but may use their excess channel capacity for remunerative purposes, such as subscription services. Second, PTV stations may not run commercial advertisements on their broadcast channels, but may do so in connection with their ancillary and supplementary channel capacity, such as fee-based subscription and data broadcasting services. Finally, like their commercial counterparts, PTV stations must pay a 5 percent fee on the gross revenues generated from their ancillary and supplementary services.

"Primarily" Nonprofit, Noncommercial, and Educational Services

Under Section 399B of the Communications Act of 1934, as amended, PTV stations have flexibility to generate funds for their operations by providing facilities and services in exchange for remuneration, so long as such uses do not interfere with the stations' provision of noncommercial, educational services. However, PTV stations cannot simply make their facilities "available to any person for the *broadcasting* of any advertisement."[1]

When rules for the transition to DTV were promulgated in 1997, the FCC allowed all broadcasters the flexibility to provide moneymaking services, including subscription television, provided that these services do not derogate free over-the-air programming. This left an ambiguity as to whether PTV stations could actually provide subscription services as part of their ancillary or supplementary DTV services, or whether they were restricted from doing so under the rules governing analog television.

After notice and comment, the FCC ruled that PTV stations must use their entire digital capacity *primarily* for nonprofit, noncommercial, educational broadcast services and that the excess capacity may be used for fee-based ancillary and supplementary services (*Report and Order* 2001, 4–9). However, the FCC specifically declined to define what "primarily" means, except to note that this concept *could* likely be operationalized and measured on a weekly basis. The commission believed this ruling would preserve the noncommercial, educational nature of PTV stations while giving them flexibility to make money with their excess digital capacity. The FCC declined to impose any further restrictions on the stations' ability to do so, but agreed to revisit the issue as part of its periodic reviews or on a case-by-case basis.

Advertising

The next question before the FCC was whether a public television station's excess channel capacity could be used for commercial advertisements. After reviewing the comments of various interested parties, the FCC concluded that the current ban on advertisements under Section 399B applies only to "broadcast" services provided by PTV stations, but does not apply to ancillary or supplementary services, such as subscription services or data transmission services (*Report and Order* 2001, 9–14). To be considered *broadcasting,* a service must be available indiscriminately to all members of the general public. Since fee-based subscription services, data transmission services, and other ancillary or supplementary services would not, by definition, be available to the general public, they do not meet the stated definition of broadcasting. Other services that could fall into this category include "computer software distribution, . . . teletext, interactive materials, aural messages, paging services, audio signals . . . and any other services that do not derogate DTV broadcast stations' obligations [to] transmit at least one over-the-air video broadcast signal provided at no direct charge to viewers" (*Fifth Report and Order* 1997, 13).

Payment of Fees

PTV stations argued that they should be exempt from the 5 percent fee imposed on gross revenues generated from the use of ancillary or supplementary services, so long as those revenues are used to support the stations' "mission-related" activities. The FCC rejected this argument and ruled that PTV stations, like their commercial counterparts, must pay the 5 percent fee (*Fifth Report and Order* 1997, 14–19).

Will Public Television Necessarily "Lose Its Soul"?

The FCC ruling outlined above was met with mixed reactions. PTV stations have applauded the decision because it would give them the flexibility to generate revenue to support the transition to DTV, a process whose costs have been estimated at $1.7 billion. Absent governmental support or other extraordinary injections of new capital, it is not clear how PTV stations will be able to pay for the transition and the ongoing operation of the digital channels. The FCC decision would therefore allow PTV stations to broaden their funding base to support both the digital transition and the operating costs. In reacting to this decision, the president of the Association of America's Public Television Stations said the PTV system would no longer be kept "barefoot and pregnant," apparently by those who somehow oppose the industry's desire to become self-sufficient ("FCC Okays Revenue Services" 2001, 1).

The FCC's decision, however, does raise legitimate concerns, as expressed by its sole dissenter, Commissioner Michael J. Copps. Copps noted that his dissent was not intended to question anyone's commitment to public television and that he was sure that his fellow commissioners would like to see PTV succeed; he simply disagreed with their approach. He was legitimately concerned about a decision that might have the "potential to warp the nation's image of public television and to endanger the identity and even the viability of a national treasure":

> Public broadcasting was to be what commercial broadcasting was not. Commercial television is about appealing to and entertaining the broadest possible market. Public television is about serving the better angels of our nature. It is about sustaining the virtues of education, civic involvement and American democracy. It in no way denigrates commercial television to say that public television is supposed to be, and is, different. When it begins to lose this different identity, it begins to lose its soul. (Dissenting Statement 2001, 1)

Will it be possible for public television to engage in revenue-generating ventures, even advertisements, without losing its soul? The answer is that, given the changing face of the American population, public broadcasting not only can do so, it must do so.

Demographics

America's demographics are changing at an unprecedented pace. According to the U.S. Census Bureau's projections, the combined population of ethnic minority groups will continue to grow more rapidly than that of non-Hispanic whites (U.S. Census Bureau 1996).[2] While the overall U.S. population is expected to grow almost 50 percent, to 394 million in the year 2050, the minority population will account for nearly 90 percent of this increase (U.S. Census Bureau 1996, Table 1). Consider the following projections:

- The non-Hispanic white population will fall steadily from 74 percent in 1995 to 53 percent in 2050.
- By 2030, non-Hispanic whites will account for less than half of the U.S. population under age eighteen.
- Hispanics, Asians, and Pacific Islanders are the fastest growing populations, with a projected increase of 2 percent per year until 2030. (Even at the peak of the baby boom, the total U.S. population never grew by 2 percent a year.)
- By 2010, the Hispanic population will become the second largest race/ethnic group in the United States. After 2020, the Hispanic population will add more people to the United States every year than all other race/ethnic groups combined.

• In 2025, one-fourth of the total U.S. population will live in states where ethnic "minorities" exceed "nonminorities" (U.S. Census Bureau 1996, 1).

If we are serious about public television's mandate, and its survival, the programming that it provides to local communities must reflect this growing diversity. Otherwise, public television will grow out of touch with its constituencies and become irrelevant.

The Changing Face of Politics

Because public television receives a substantial portion of its funding from federal, state, and local governments, it is only natural to worry about the political consequences of the programs it broadcasts. Programs with gay and lesbian content, such as "Tongues Untied," aired on the *P.O.V.* series in 1991, and, more recently, "It's Elementary" have offended some conservative lawmakers, resulting in threats to reduce or even eliminate public broadcasting's funding at the federal and state levels. Undoubtedly, there is a fragile interdependence between public television's programming and its government funding. To state the obvious, this fragility will vary, depending upon the makeup of the political power base at any given time.

While the political pendulum will continue to swing, roughly speaking, between conservative and liberal values, the face of politics will also become more diverse. For example, the percentages of minority politicians serving in Congress have risen substantially in recent years.[3] Dating back to 1967, the year of the Public Broadcasting Act, the number of Hispanics and African-Americans serving in both the House and the Senate has risen from 11 to 62. This is comparable to the increase in the number of women in Congress, which rose from 12 to 67 during the same period.

A similar story seems to be unfolding in the executive branch. While the total number of federal employees dropped between 1990 and 1997, the number of minorities holding senior or executive-level jobs actually increased during this period (*Statistical Abstract* 1998). In fact, the percentage of minorities in policy-making positions has been rising at an appreciably faster rate than that of non-Hispanic whites—109 and 166 percent for African-Americans and Hispanics, respectively, compared to 44 percent for Caucasians.

It may take some time before the makeup of our government truly reflects the demographics of the overall population. But as politics becomes more inclusive, might the unconventional not become more conventional, the marginalized less marginal, and the risqué less risky?

The Emerging Minority Marketplace

Public television receives approximately 37 percent of its funding from individuals and corporations combined. In considering whether to give a voice to traditionally underserved communities, public broadcasting cannot afford to ignore the growing economic power of ethnic minorities.

A recent report prepared by the U.S. Small Business Administration (1999) shows that minority-owned businesses are a rapidly growing segment of the U.S. economy. By 1997, the estimated number of minority-owned businesses had reached 3.25 million, generating approximately $495 million in annual revenues and employing nearly 4 million workers. Consistent with changes in population growth, Hispanic-owned businesses increased more rapidly from 1987 to 1997 than any other types of minority-owned businesses. By 1997, these businesses comprised the most common segment of the minority business community, totaling 1.4 million, followed by Asian-owned businesses at 1.1 million and African-American-owned at 880,000.

This general growth in minority business has translated unevenly into the realm of family income. The Federal Reserve Board found that between 1989 and 1995, "median income rose somewhat for nonwhite and Hispanic families but fell for other families." Previous studies showed an appreciable increase in the median and mean net worth of nonwhite and Hispanic families in 1989 and 1992, although their net worth leveled off in 1995 and still lags behind that of other families (1997, 4, 5).

The Minority Business Development Agency, part of the U.S. Department of Commerce, estimates the current purchasing power of minority groups at approximately $1 trillion. More significantly, it projects that minority buying power "will increase substantially over the next 50 years as the U.S. economy grows, [its] minority population increases and disparities diminish in income between minorities and nonminorities" (U.S. Department of Commerce 1996).

With this rise in the economic power of minority groups, it would behoove public television stations to devote a portion of their "ancillary or supplementary" digital channel capacity to serve the needs of minorities. And if doing so includes the use of advertisements, public television could end up having it both ways: the industry would fulfill its mandate to program for diverse, multicultural audiences while, at the same time, it could obtain much needed funds through subscription fees and advertisements targeted toward minorities.

The Rise of Generation X

The amount of wealth that will be transferred to younger generations over the next fifty years is staggering. Estimates for this intergenerational transfer of wealth range anywhere from $10 trillion over the next twenty years (Johnson 1999) to $136 trillion over the next fifty years (Havens and Schervish 1999). While the accuracy of these estimates is subject to debate, one thing is clear: as the baby boom generation ages over the next few decades, a significant portion of its wealth will be transferred to those born after 1964— Generation Xers. The chief distinguishing attitudinal trait of Generation X, according to marketers, is its tolerance of, and desire for, diversity. J. Walker Smith, a speaker at a recent PBS conference, has written that "diversity in all its forms—cultural, political, sexual, racial, social—is a hallmark of this generation, a diversity, accessible to everyone, that transcends even national borders" (Smith and Clurman 1997, 89).

KQED's Experience

There is anecdotal evidence that public television stations that appeal to diverse audiences can, in fact, attract a whole new set of funders. The recent experience of KQED-TV in San Francisco with the program, "Chinatown" offers a good example of how this can be accomplished. Produced as part of the series *Neighborhood: The Hidden Cities of San Francisco,* this segment on Chinatown told the neighborhood's story from the point of view of those who have lived there. The program used Chinese music, poetry, and oral histories to make Chinatown's history and everyday experience come alive for the viewer.

According to Mary Bitterman, then KQED's president, one-third of the funding for "Chinatown" came from members of the Chinese community in San Francisco, 90 percent of whom had not previously contributed to the station. The remaining amount was funded by corporations and private foundations whose strategic mission, principles, and objectives include furthering the interests of diversity.

Indeed, KQED has a long history of celebrating multiculturalism and recently reaffirmed its commitment to diversity as one of its principal strategic priorities. "Every time we do something to enhance diversity, it is met with such enthusiasm and support from the community," Bitterman said. "If we invite different ethnic groups to participate in our decisions, rather than doing everything behind closed doors, they will help us find the funding we need" (Bitterman 1999).

A Suggested Approach

It is quite possible for public television to make money using its digital spectrum without losing its soul. To do this, the industry must not lose sight of its commitment to diversity and multiculturalism. How will it provide a narrative space for different racial groups to express their hopes and fears, their struggles and triumphs, their successes and failures? How will it allow various ethnic minorities to speak in what one commentator calls the "voice of color" (Johnson 1991)? In short, how will marginalized voices be heard and a wider collection of American stories told?

Attempts to bring perspectives to PTV that are considered "outside the mainstream" have sometimes engendered controversy, both within and outside of the system. In some cases, the industry has been subjected to threats to reduce or even eliminate government funding. In face of these pressures, should PTV shy away from programs that contain unconventional or unpopular views, such as the personal struggles of a black male homosexual? Or does it have the courage to be different? For the purist, the answer is obvious: public television must take risks to reflect America's diversity, even if it means offending the mainstream. But for the pragmatist, the answer is less clear. Because public broadcasting's government funding is highly politicized, programming decisions necessarily require judgments about whether an appreciable number of people in any given community might be offended.

With added income from services based on stations' supplementary digital channel capacity, however, this sort of judgment could be somewhat removed from the province of politics and treated more as a routine financial decision—the kind that most other businesses make every day. A critical challenge for public TV in the next decade will involve striking a delicate balance between the use of digital channels primarily for nonprofit, noncommercial, educational broadcast services and the use of ancillary or supplementary capacity for moneymaking purposes, including the use of advertisements.

How will the public television system develop local and national strategies that foster diversity and multiculturalism while maintaining, or even increasing, its overall financial support? A major part of the answer lies in the need for CPB, PBS, PTV stations, the Minority Consortia, and other stakeholders to develop a system-wide strategy aimed toward that very end. This strategy might include the following concrete goals, which are, in fact, achievable even with the technologies we have today.

Expand the National Schedule to Allow More Room for Innovative Programs and Unique Perspectives

While *P.O.V.* and *Independent Lens* have taken steps in the right direction, only a small percentage of works by independent and minority producers is selected for these series. By expanding its national schedule or creating additional series, PBS could offer independent and minority producers greater access to national distribution. This would encourage innovation in other genres, such as dance, theater, and other performing arts. It would also create a larger pool of diverse, multicultural programming from which member stations could choose, either for broadcast within their respective communities or for distribution to subscribers.

Create One or More Packaged Feeds Devoted to Minority Programming

PBS could package entire channels that are targeted to specific minority or ethnic groups. The availability of one or more packaged feeds of minority programming would also give stations additional options for using their ancillary or supplementary channels. Such packaged feeds could include not only the best of *P.O.V., Independent Lens,* and other series, but also foreign-language movies and the winners of international film festivals, for example. As an added twist, "mainstream" audiences might be required to activate special channels in order to get the English-language version of these programs.

Develop Internet and Other Broadband Strategies to Further Engage Racial and Ethnic Minorities

Media companies have only just begun to explore how best to use the Internet and broadband delivery to connect with audiences and to allow them to connect with one another. Public TV needs to develop a comprehensive Internet and broadband strategy to engage people of *all* colors and to create a whole network of diverse cybercommunities. As the number of users increases, such a network becomes exponentially more valuable, a phenomenon many scholars call a "positive network externality" (Lee, McKnight, and Bailey 1997). Further, the interactivity that takes place within such a network could result in the creation of new forms of content, thereby expanding public broadcasting's diverse library of programs—some of which could be supported with advertising or by means of subscription channels.

Conclusion

In the end, only history can judge how well public television will fulfill its mandate of furthering diversity and multiculturalism while also finding ways to make money on ancillary or supplementary services. Will some people get offended in the process? Perhaps. Will the tides change? Yes. Is it worth the challenge? Absolutely, for serving diversity is what public broadcasting is all about.

PBS has the opportunity to help the entire public television system seize the market for minority programming right now, before cable or any other service does; it could do so by using the cable industry model of combining subscription fees with advertising revenue. This window of opportunity is a limited one, however—for if PBS doesn't do it, *someone else will.* It is therefore incumbent upon PBS, its member stations, and others entrusted with this national treasure to utilize their intelligence, foresight, and courage to fulfill public broadcasting's bold vision throughout the new millennium. In the words of the late Robert Saudek, an independent producer and member of the first Carnegie Commission, public television "must be satisfied with nothing short of first rate thoughts, boundless energy, professional competence and the thrill of the chase" (Saudek 1966).

Notes

1. 47 U.S.C. § 399B (emphasis added).
2. The U.S. Census Bureau defines "minority" as "the combined population of people who are Black, American Indian, Eskimo, Aleut, Asian, Pacific Islander, or of Hispanic origin (who may be of any race)."
3. Based on statistics kept by the Legislative Resource Center in the U.S. House of Representatives, faxed to the author on October 19, 1999.

References

Bitterman, M. 1999. Telephone conversation with the author, October 19 (quotes used with permission).

Bullert, B. 1997. *Public Television: Politics and the Battle over Documentary Film.* New Brunswick, NJ: Rutgers University Press.

Carnegie Commission on Educational Television. 1967. *Public Television: A Program for Action.* New York: Bantam Books.

Dissenting Statement of Commissioner Michael J. Copps Re: *Report and Order* in MM Docket No. 98–203, In the Matter of the Ancillary or Supplementary Use of Digital Television Capacity by Noncommercial Licensees. 2001. FCC Web site ftp.fcc.gov/Speeches/Copps/Statements/2001/stmjc116.html (August 13, 2002).

"FCC Okays Revenue Services in DTV Bitstream." 2001. *Current,* October 22, 1.

Federal Reserve Board. 1997. "Family Finances in the U.S.: Recent Evidence from the Survey of Consumer Finances." *Federal Reserve Bulletin* (January): 4.

Fifth Report and Order. 1997. In MM Docket No. 87–268, In the Matter of Advanced Television Systems and Their Impact upon the Existing Television Broadcast Service, 12 FCC Red 12809.

Havens, J., and P. Schervish. 1999. "Millionaires and the Millennium: New Estimates of the Forthcoming Wealth Transfer and the Prospects for a Golden Age of Philanthropy." October 19. www.bc.edu/swri/m&m.html.

Johnson, A. 1991. "The New Voice of Color." *Yale Law Journal* 100: 2007, 2061.

Johnson, D. 1999. "A Larger Legacy May Await Generations X, Y and Z." *New York Times,* October 20, C2.

Ledbetter, J. 1997. *Made Possible By . . . The Death of Public Broadcasting in the United States.* London: Verso.

Lee W., L. McKnight, and J. Bailey. 1997. "An Introduction to Internet Economics." In *Internet Economics,* ed. L. McKnight and J. Bailey. Boston: MIT Press.

Report and Order in MM Docket No. 98–203. 2001, In the Matter of Ancillary or Supplemental Use of Digital Television Capacity by Noncommercial Licensees. FCC Web site hraunfoss.fcc.gov/edocs_public/attachmatch/FCC-01—306A1.doc (August 13, 2002).

Saudek, Robert. 1966. "The Role of ETV and Its Relation to Programs." Memorandum on some thoughts expressed at breakfast on June 15 with Messrs. Land, Weeks and White.

Smith, J. W., and A. Clurman. 1997. *Rocking the Ages: The Yankelovich Report on Generational Marketing.* New York: Harper Business.

Statistical Abstract of the United States. 1998. September 30.

U.S. Census Bureau. 1996. *Population Projections of the United States by Age, Sex, Race, and Hispanic Origin: 1995 to 2050, Current Population Reports,* P25–1130. Washington, DC: Government Printing Office.

U.S. Department of Commerce. 1996. *The Emerging Minority Marketplace: Minority Population Growth: 1995–2050.* Washington, DC: Minority Business Development Agency.

U.S. Small Business Administration. 1999. *Minorities in Business.* SBA Web site www.sba.gov/advo/stats/min.pdf (August 13, 2002).

Part III

Global Perspectives

13

Introduction

Michael P. McCauley

Two major forces now impinge upon public service broadcasting systems the world over: the global spread of commercial media and the technological changes wrought by the digital revolution. The traditional public service broadcasters of Western Europe have been wont to mention that among industrialized nations, only the United States created a broadcasting system that was advertiser-supported virtually from the start. Ironically, these same broadcasters now find themselves grappling with problems they once thought confined to America. The consolidation of global media industries into fewer and fewer hands exerts pressure on all media systems—public and private—to partake in a steady diet of cheaply produced content of mass appeal. What's more, young people gravitate eagerly toward these programs; it seems public service broadcasting brings with it a need to do the sort of intellectual decoding that many of them find unpalatable.

The changes described above actually began well before the digital revolution or the height of global media consolidation. When cable systems threatened the dominance of traditional television networks, a bevy of niche channels sprang up on systems throughout the world, rendering good imitations, in the process, of artistic and informational content once thought to be solely the province of noncommercial television. This trend will only strengthen with time as national systems (with the U.S. public broadcasting system lagging well behind pace) forsake their analog signals in favor of the binary impulses that form the basis of digital broadcasting. Digital radio and television already deliver content that is largely free from interference, and signal compression technologies have also moved the proverbial 500-channel cable system off the drawing board and into practice in some places. Thus, public service broadcasters can expect a future in which they will be further assailed by tightly formatted niche services, each of them aimed at a fraction of the overall audience once coveted by state-sponsored systems.

Working within this new programming environment, public service broadcasters will no longer be able to maintain their expansive roles as national purveyors of "something for kids of all ages." Broadcasters whose focus is too diffuse will become easy targets for niche-marketed services. Furthermore, those that maintain the lofty aesthetic once embodied by most national systems will be stuck with aging audiences and little in the way of access to younger people, who simply don't care to be uplifted or lectured to any longer. In fact, some observers argue that the British Broadcasting Corporation (BBC), the most venerable of the world's noncommercial systems, has always been programmed for someone other than ordinary people.

Public service broadcasters who are now making their way into the digital age face the prospect of balancing two opposing forces in a way that would make most normative media theorists cringe: that is, they must balance the dictates of both market and culture. They must ensure that their programs are relevant within the artistic and political environments of their native lands, without straying too far from the realm of that which is easily viewed by younger and nonelite audiences. This rapprochement is necessary for mainstream public broadcasters, since this branch of the noncommercial industry seems incapable, by itself, of generating enough income and political support to maintain its former position of primacy (small-scale community media stand a better chance of maintaining authentic public service missions —more on that below). The task is made even more difficult by the fact that many of these broadcasters have no idea how to adapt their content to changing economic and technological circumstances. Indeed, many would be hard-pressed to explain what their roles and missions have been throughout the era of traditional analog broadcasting.

The four authors whose chapters form this part of the book have wrestled with the dilemmas outlined above and have, each in their own way, tried to envision strategies through which noncommercial broadcasters can survive without completely mortgaging their core values. Ira Basen of the Canadian Broadcasting Corporation (CBC) chronicles the adventures and misadventures of his employer when it comes to crafting an overall mission and then funding the enterprise in a way that protects content producers from undue market influences. In Basen's view, CBC Television has drifted perilously close to the point of irrelevance by depending too heavily on income from advertising. This heavy reliance on ad revenue, in his view, generates greater pressures to run cheaply produced content, some of it American, at the expense of programs that are uniquely Canadian. Since other Canadian networks already provide much of that sort of programming, it is easy to see how the CBC has diminished in importance in the eyes of those in Parliament who pay the bills. Basen sees the beginnings of a renaissance at CBC TV, as some producers now sense the incompatibility between advertising support and the production of high-quality programs that are consistently relevant to Canadian citizens. Whether this part of the national broadcaster's operations can be salvaged or not is still an open question.

CBC Radio, on the other hand, is seen as a media outlet that would still be pleasing to those visionaries who crafted Canadian broadcasting policy in the 1920s and 1930s. With a mandate that is intensely Canadian—even regional—CBC Radio remains the kind of service that audience members would also fight to preserve. Basen, who has pursued a career in the production of radio programs, is proud of the status quo, yet he feels that CBC Radio is still vulnerable to attack by conservative pundits who are suspicious of any public organizations that don't bow and genuflect to the wisdom of the market. In the end, he argues, public service broadcasters must always resist the pressure to let advertisers or political critics of any one stripe dictate which kinds of content are permissible to air.

Many broadcasting organizations, public and private, are busy establishing a presence on the Internet, the electronic medium that is touted most often for its supposedly automatic powers of mass democratization. In his chapter, Amit Schejter writes about the Internet sites of public broadcasters around the world. He suggests that publicly funded broadcasting organizations must use the Internet to create new niches for themselves if they're to avoid the major damage and displacement that may come from increased commercial competition. Public broadcasting organizations are, of course, notoriously slow to change; that said, Schejter sees the Internet as one vehicle through which these broadcasters might quickly and effectively reposition themselves for the new multichannel era.

In surveying and theorizing about dozens of Web sites, Schejter finds that public service broadcasters are clearly aiming to have a presence on the Web, but are not, in the end, fully sure *why* they want to be there. Much has been written about the great opportunity for interactivity the Internet will present for us all. At present, though, public broadcasting managers and audiences share misconceptions about both the novelty and extent of possible interaction. The Internet truly does offer links to huge amounts of data. That said, the "interactivity" this medium offers actually amounts to little more than millions of opportunities per day to examine single pages of content that might have appeared in a newspaper or magazine not that long ago. Increased bandwidth, better connectivity, and further development of streaming audio and video might one day allow for true interaction, but for now, Schejter says, public service broadcasters are simply using their Internet sites as vehicles for maintaining their existing identities. Regrettably, survival seems a more important goal than democratization for public broadcasters who enter cyberspace. This observation may be tied to the sheer novelty of the Internet. On the other hand, it might offer another example of the ways in which all public broadcasters have historically responded to changes in technology and market conditions: by sidestepping the necessary redefinition of their social roles and, in the process, continuing to offer the same old content, wrapped up in shiny new packages.

Lyombe Eko describes the whirlwind of globalization and commercialization that has swept through public broadcasting organizations in Africa recently. Pressures from global media conglomerates to carry foreign, mass appeal programs are bad enough, but another problem makes the situation even more complex. Historically, African broadcasters have tended to be tools of the colonial powers that formerly controlled each country in question. Ironically, the wave of democratization that swept through Africa following the end of the Cold War has created another kind of pressure: the pressure to accept commercial stations and networks as an antidote to the perceived flaws of state-sponsored broadcasters. With populations that are deeply skeptical of any industry with vestiges of colonial ties, this movement toward commercialization is often seen as a means of gaining more press freedom for citizens—a real marketplace of ideas. The challenge for many African broadcasters, then, is to accept the contours of a part-public, part-private system while trying, at the same time, to craft a body of media that is truly African in tone and content.

Eko finds that some broadcasters have, in fact, made substantial progress in "Africanizing" their content. Innovations in this regard include multilingual programming, talk shows that foster intense audience participation, and artistic fare that is, in many cases, significant to local audiences. A prime example is the advent of *juju* videos, a popular cult/horror film genre in Nigeria. The spread of new African programming has also been enhanced by the ways in which local broadcasters have adapted satellite and microwave transmission technologies to their own particular needs. Like their counterparts on other continents, African broadcasters continue to feel pressure from multinational media firms that wish to spread their highly Westernized products throughout the developing world. Though the continuance of funding for African public service broadcasting is far from certain, Eko believes that some systems on the continent will do what it takes to preserve places on the spectrum for content that serves local audiences and demands their participation as well.

Finally, Vanda Rideout's chapter examines Canada's experience with the

Internet in a way that speaks to the noblest aspects of public service broadcasting, including its goals of universal access and programs that are fundamentally relevant to people in the communities served. Specifically, she examines Community Learning Networks (CLNs) and Community Access Programs (CAPs), two efforts initiated and sponsored by Canadian government agencies. CAPs provide nonprofit institutions in local communities with funding for Internet connectivity in the form of computers, access to Internet service providers (ISPs), and hands-on training. The virtual communities fostered by the CLN program are designed to facilitate learning, training, networking, community development, and community control at the local level. Simply put, CAPs focus on access to the Internet while CLNs build new communities of interest (or enhance existing ones) at the local, regional, national, and international levels. Examples of successful CLNs include programs to improve skills and upgrade training for workers, marine research centers, youth-at-risk centers, and women's centers. The Canadian government has contemplated thousands of locations where citizens, including indigenous and other marginalized populations, might benefit from these programs. Rideout contends that it is too early to tell whether these initiatives are making a difference in the lives of ordinary Canadians. With future funding uncertain, she also wonders what would happen if the well went dry and some communities were forced to "unplug."

If public service broadcasters hope to survive in the digital era, they will clearly have to reinvent themselves. In particular, it may be useful for these systems to marshal at least part of their resources in service of social development—an ethic that market-based broadcasters will likely never embrace. Specifically, public broadcasters might develop operations that are much more decentralized, focusing more tightly on the real human needs of people who live in specific regions and localities. Efforts are under way in the United States to develop "many public broadcastings" through innovative fund-raising strategies and the use of digitally compressed channels that allow for multiple program streams in any one location. Promising as these may seem, broadcasters such as National Public Radio and the Public Broadcasting Service must go even further to ensure their future relevance.

Taking a lesson from their counterparts in Britain and Canada, these networks would do well to make at least some room for the deployment of more community-scale, low-powered media—the kind that focus intensely on local concerns and needs while causing little in the way of competition or interference for existing broadcasters. A true social development model of broadcasting would move beyond the traditional Western concept of "development," in which prosperous, all-knowing broadcast experts construct media systems that show poor people how to "modernize" through industrialization and the increased use of consumer products. The broadcasting model that I have in mind would avoid these crass impulses toward capitalism. Instead, I would argue that the managers of many public radio and TV stations should put their ratings research back into the file cabinet and seek, instead, to broadcast in ways that help local people realize their goals and aspirations as citizens of healthy democracies.

To date, the mainstream public broadcasting industry in the United States has shunned these sorts of proposals, including the microradio movement that is aptly chronicled in the final chapter of this book. Instead, American public broadcasters argue—sometimes openly, other times not—that any opportunity to put more voices on the airwaves is an opportunity that they alone should control. The logic behind this position is painfully wanting, since the audiences for public broadcasting in the United States, upscale as they may be, are quite small when compared to the universe of potential viewers and listeners. This being the case, public broadcasters in the United States and other Western countries would do well to learn a few lessons from their counterparts in less-developed parts of the world. For that matter, they could learn much from the public access and community-building programs now under way in Canada, programs aimed at helping all citizens to enjoy the benefits of the Internet. If mainstream public broadcasting organizations do make room for more radio and TV services that invite broad community access and bottom-up programming, they may stand a better chance of maintaining legitimacy in an age when high-quality, tightly targeted commercial programs are eroding the space these organizations assumed they would always occupy in people's hearts and on the electromagnetic spectrum.

14

The CBC and the Public Interest

Maintaining the Mission in an Era of Media Concentration

Ira Basen

In my previous life, I was trained as a historian at the University of Wisconsin. For most of the past eighteen years, I have worked as a current affairs journalist at CBC Radio. What these two seemingly disparate worlds have in common is that they both understand the importance of context in telling a story. And so I want to begin with some historical context because without that, it is impossible to understand how the CBC got to where it is today, why its future, at this particular moment, seems so precarious, and where I believe it needs to position itself in this current era of media concentration.

First, the history. The Canadian Broadcasting Corporation (CBC) that we know today is a very different beast than the one envisioned by its founders more than sixty years ago. And yet the media and cultural context that led to its creation is, I believe, remarkably similar to that which exists today.

Conceived in the depths of the Great Depression by an extraordinary group of forward-thinking men and women, and officially established in 1936 by the Conservative government of the day, the CBC was infused from the beginning with two overriding ideas. Supporters of Canadian public broadcasting used them to define the public interest sixty years ago, and they continue to do so today. The first of these ideas was Canadian nationalism or, as that sentiment is so often expressed in Canada, a fear of domination by the American cultural giant to the south.

If we were to enter a time machine and go back to a typical Canadian home circa 1930, and make believe we are typical Canadian radio listeners, what would we find? We would find very little that was distinctively Canadian. With the exception of Saturday night hockey, which began on radio in

1923, the same stars and programs that were captivating audiences south of the border—Jack Benny, Fred Allen, *Amos 'n' Andy, Edgar Bergen and Charlie McCarthy*—were attracting listeners north of the forty-ninth parallel as well. What little Canadian programming there was, was inaccessible to most listeners outside of Toronto and Montreal. In 1930, 80 percent of Canadian listeners were listening to American programs, either on American stations whose signals reached into Canada or on Canadian stations affiliated with American networks.

To Canadian cultural nationalists of the day, the threat was obvious. They formed an organization called the Canadian Radio League, led by a true broadcasting visionary named Graham Spry, to lobby for the creation of a Canadian public broadcaster. "Britannia rules the waves," Spry noted, "shall CBS rule the wavelengths?" In 1932, Spry made his case before a parliamentary committee in this way:

> The American chains have regarded Canada as part of their field, and consider Canada is in a state of radio tutelage. . . . The question before the Committee is whether Canada is to establish a chain that is owned and operated and controlled by organizations associated or controlled by American interests. The question is the State or the United States. Here is a great and happy opportunity for expressing, for achieving, that which is Canada. It is here and now; it may never come again. (quoted in Nash 1995, 85)

"The question is the State, or the United States." Never has this idea been expressed more cogently or more accurately. And it remains as true today as it was seventy years ago.

The second important idea behind the creation of public broadcasting in Canada was a profoundly democratic one. The founders of the CBC truly believed that public broadcasting existed to provide a voice for the voiceless, to counteract the monopolization of the airwaves by the forces of wealth and power. And that is precisely the kind of language they used back then. Leonard Brockington, the first chairman of the CBC told a parliamentary committee in 1938:

> We believe we should be false to our trust as custodians of part of the public domain, if we did not resist . . . any attempt to place free air under the domination of the power of wealth. Either all of us have a right to speak over the air, or none of us has any right to speak over the air. (quoted in Peers 1969, 262)

I can assure you it been a long time since a CBC executive has used that kind of language. It's probably been a long time since a CBC executive has even thought about this. But, as I will argue later, the issue that Leonard Brockington raised in that address—the domination of the power of wealth over the airwaves—is as important a reason for the strengthening of public broadcasting in Canada today as it was in 1938.

But before we get there, I want to talk about the state of Canada's public broadcaster today. It is a truly extraordinary organization, containing within it all that is great and all that is problematic about the country it reflects. It operates full local and national television and radio services in both English and French. It provides French-language broadcasting to those small pockets of Francophones that struggle to maintain their language and culture in the Canadian west. It provides English-language broadcasts to small islands of English speakers in Quebec City and around Quebec's Eastern Townships. In New Brunswick, population 760,000, we offer, on the English radio side, five hours of local programming five days a week in Moncton, St. John, and Fredericton, not to mention full service in French radio and English and French television.

If you've ever been fortunate enough to visit Canada's north, you'll know that there aren't very many people of any kind there—fewer than 100,000 people spread across that enormous land mass. But the CBC offers full radio and television service in both official languages and in eight aboriginal languages.

The point I am making is that trying to be all things to all people in a country as big and as sparsely populated as Canada, with two official languages and many aboriginal peoples, is an enormously difficult and expensive proposition. And yet that is what the CBC is mandated by Parliament to do, and that is what Canadians have come to expect from us. Just try suggesting to New Brunswickers that they are perhaps a bit overserved by the CBC and that perhaps a little consolidation might be in order, and you had better duck for cover.

And how do we pay for all this? The fact is, we no longer can. I don't want to get bogged down in the minutiae of CBC funding, but the broad strokes are important in understanding why, a couple of years ago, our president went before a parliamentary committee to tell them that the CBC is virtually bankrupt and on life support.

There are a couple of things you need to know. First, the CBC has two sources of revenue—an annual appropriation from the Parliament of Canada, which now amounts to roughly $750 million a year, and revenue from TV advertising, which now amounts to more than $300 million a year. Canadians get a lot for their money. On the TV side, $500 million a year gets them two national TV networks, including twenty-five regional stations and a national distribution system. On the radio side, $250 million a year gets them four national commercial-free networks, including seventy-three regional stations.

Unlike public broadcasting in the United States, we receive no money from private donors or sponsors. Unlike most other public broadcasters in the world, we levy no license fees on Canadian television owners. In the United Kingdom, for example, the owner of a color television set is assessed a license fee of about a hundred pounds a year, and that money goes directly to finance the various operations of the British Broadcasting Corporation (BBC). As a result, the BBC does not have to depend on advertising revenue. Nor does it have to depend on how well the government of the day is predisposed toward the organization. Nor does it have to be worried about becoming yet another casualty in a war against the deficit.

Comparisons with other countries yield some interesting results. According to a study done in 1999 by the firm McKinsey and Company, public broadcasting in the UK costs the average Brit $79 a year. In Germany the figure is $136; Italy, $69; Denmark, $195. But Canadians get all that the CBC has to offer—English, French, and aboriginal languages, radio, television, and new media, across a large and sparsely populated country—for only $50 a person. On a per capita basis, that puts us twelfth out of the nineteen public broadcasters studied by the McKinsey group.

And yet there are some Canadians who believe the CBC still gets too much of the taxpayers' money. We will never be able to please everyone. The critical question is how close we are to achieving the dreams of our founders. If Graham Spry were alive today, what would he think? If he happened to find CBC Radio on the dial, I think he would probably be pleased with what he heard. We are not perfect; we do some great things and some not so great things. But we are resolutely, proudly, and totally Canadian. In fact, *Saturday Afternoon at the Metropolitan Opera* is the only non-Canadian program we broadcast on a regular basis.

We are noncommercial. We have not had a commercial on CBC Radio since 1974. Nor do we accept corporate sponsorships or commercial underwriting of programs; nor do we solicit or accept funds from listeners or organizations. We receive all of our money, roughly $150 million a year for English radio, from the parliamentary appropriation to the CBC. And every week, 3.6 million Canadians tune us in, and our audience is smart and loyal and fiercely protective of us. They feel they own us, which of course they do, and that can be our blessing or our curse, depending on what kind of mood they are in.

The situation with CBC television, unfortunately, is quite different. Many years ago, this service chose a different path and is now living with the consequences of that decision. CBC TV has been running commercials since the 1950s. Advertising revenue now accounts for roughly a third of the CBC's annual budget. But there has been a price to pay for chasing those advertising dollars, and it is a price that Graham Spry and the other founders of public broadcasting in Canada would undoubtedly consider far too high.

There is much that is great about CBC television—in news, sports, and current affairs programming, we rank among the best in the world. But for too long, our prime-time schedule consisted of American programming purchased from U.S. networks or bad Canadian imitations of that programming. Scheduling decisions were made to suit advertisers. We forgot what a public broadcaster was supposed to do. We carry professional sports such as Blue Jays baseball, even though lots of other broadcasters are happy to carry Blue Jays baseball. But we desperately need the advertising revenue it generates, and so we do it.

And part of the price we pay for this is that audiences don't care about CBC TV in the passionate way they care about CBC radio. And they don't watch it much either. To many, it's just another station in a big multichannel universe. CBC television has about a 10 percent market share, compared to 42 percent for BBC television, 49 percent for Italian public broadcasting, 39 percent in Germany, 41 percent in France. The programming tastes of Canadians have not changed much since the 1930s. Back then, people were listening to *Amos 'n' Andy* and Jack Benny and Edgar Bergen. Now, we're watching *Friends, The West Wing,* and *Law and Order.*

These and other American shows are consistently the most watched programs in Canada. Most privately owned Canadian stations carry them. The vast majority of Canadians can access American stations over cable or satellite. Cable penetration in Canada is over 75 percent, compared to 68 percent in the United States. A few years ago, I was in Iqaluit, the capital of Nunuvut, way up on Baffin Island. I did some channel surfing in my hotel and discovered local stations from Detroit and Los Angeles.

The McKinsey report looked at how public broadcasters around the world were faring in an age of increased competition from cable, satellite, and digital television. The main conclusion was that the way public broadcasters were funded had profound implications for their ability to compete. In particular, the report concluded that relying on advertising revenues was a dangerous policy, arguing that "an increased dependence on advertising has led inexorably to a more populist and less distinctive schedule" ("Public Service Broadcasters" 1999, 5). In other words, advertising made public broadcasters look and think more like private broadcasters, but invariably, they didn't do it as well.

So audiences stay away, and so do advertisers. And the result is a public broadcaster increasingly at risk—at risk of its budget being treated like a political football to be kicked around every year, and at risk of its audience caring less and less about its future. After all, if the public broadcaster is looking more and more like a pale imitation of the privates, it gets harder and harder to convince taxpayers that it's worth throwing money at. In public broadcasting, being irrelevant is perhaps an even greater sin than being bad.

And that, I'm afraid, is where CBC television finds itself today. Over the past seven or eight years, federal government officials have reduced the CBC's operating budget by approximately a third, more than $400 million, with predictable results in terms of job losses and deterioration of service. There are a number of reasons, both political and fiscal, why they did this, but the important point for our purposes today is that they did it because they knew they could do it and get away with it. They knew the bond between the Canadian people and their public broadcaster had weakened to the point that it was possible to inflict cuts of that magnitude and not have to worry about paying a political price for it.

And they were right—they didn't pay a price. In fact, it is becoming fashionable in conservative political circles in Canada to advocate privatizing the CBC. That is the stated position of our official opposition party. It is also an idea supported by the governments of Ontario and Alberta, though fortunately they are not in a position to do anything about it.

Some good news: CBC television has seen the error of its ways. But here's the bad news: it may be too late. By the mid-1990s, most of the people responsible for the disastrous decision to maximize advertising revenues at the expense of what a public broadcaster should be doing had left the CBC. Many of them, not surprisingly, went into private television, where they are now happily enriching themselves and their shareholders by buying cheap American programs and producing generic Canadian schlock geared to an international audience.

Meanwhile, back at CBC TV, a new "old" vision has emerged. It is Graham Spry's vision of a public broadcaster that is resolutely and unapologetically Canadian and largely commercial-free. And over the past few years, CBC management has made impressive strides toward Canadianizing the schedule and reducing our dependence on advertising revenue. But fewer ads mean less money coming in. And the government has restored very little of the $440 million that was cut. The McKinsey study concluded that the healthiest public broadcasters are those funded through license fees, like the BBC. The most vulnerable are those, like the CBC, that depend on the largesse of advertisers and governments.

And there, in a nutshell, is where the CBC finds itself at the dawn of the twenty-first century. At long last, we seem to have people in charge who actually understand what public broadcasting means, believe in what it is supposed to do, and have a strategy to get us there. But we may not make it. So much good will has been squandered. So much money has been cut that we are no longer able to deliver the services that Canadians want and expect us to deliver. And because of the way we are funded, we continue to be held hostage by our political masters. When our new president declared us to be bankrupt and on life support, the government responded with a one-time infusion of cash, but no increase to our base budget.

Does this turn of events matter? Ultimately, this is the only important question, because if the CBC has no useful role to play, then its survival is really important only to those of us who work there. And to be honest, there are a growing number of people, including some of our traditional friends, who are prepared to answer the question "Does it matter?" with a resounding "no." They will argue that we are on the verge of a digital radio revolution, where your choices of music and information in your home or car will no longer be limited to what you can pick up on your local AM or FM band. Virtually any radio station in the world will be accessible over the Internet or by purchasing a satellite-ready receiver for your car.

On the TV side, they will argue that a public broadcaster, no matter how good, will be swamped in a multichannel universe, that private broadcasters can do programming just as well and more cheaply than the CBC. They say that in a globalized world, national boundaries are less important, and so are national broadcasters. And they will argue that the Internet is more accessible and more democratic than any conventional public broadcaster can ever hope to be.

I don't necessarily disagree with any of that. I believe the CBC, or any public broadcaster, for that matter, needs to move aggressively into new media and meet the challenges posed by the new technologies. But I am also prepared to make the argument that although the broadcasting world has changed enormously over the past sixty years, the parallels between the year 2002 and the year 1936, when the CBC was born, are far greater than they might appear on the surface. And for that reason, the CBC's role as Canada's public broadcaster is just as critical now as it was then.

So let's go back to those two founding ideas behind the creation of the CBC. I have already covered the first one—the need to counterbalance the invasion of American radio and television signals. Our private broadcasters have proved repeatedly that they are not able to resist the lure of cheap American programs, and no amount of government bribery or regulation will change that. And while Canadian viewers and listeners have clearly demonstrated their affection for American programming, there is ample evidence that when presented with a Canadian perspective on news and current affairs, and high-quality Canadian comedy, sports, drama, and music, Canadians will watch. Not, it is true, in numbers that will rival *Who Wants to Be a Millionaire,* but enough to demonstrate the need for a viable, distinctive, noncommercial public broadcaster. At a time when culture and cultural values are America's biggest exports, it is more important than ever to have a place on our airwaves that reminds us what it is about Canada and Canadians that differentiates us from our neighbors across the border. The choice remains the same—"the State, or the United States."

And what about that second great impulse behind the creation of the CBC—Leonard Brockington's insistence that we resist the temptation to place "the free air under the domination of the power of wealth"? As I said earlier, it is no longer fashionable to hear this kind of talk around the CBC; nonetheless, a quick glance around the Canadian media landscape yields one of the most compelling reasons you will find in support of a Canadian public broadcaster.

Let's look first at newspapers. Canada currently has a degree of print media concentration unparalleled in the Western world. In Canada, four large companies own virtually 100 percent of our 104 daily newspapers. But it doesn't stop there. We live in an age of "convergence"; after all, Bell Globemedia, which owns our oldest national newspaper, the *Globe and Mail,* also owns CTV, our largest private television network. CanWest Global, which owns our other national newspaper, the *National Post,* also owns fifteen other daily papers and eleven television stations. The result of all this media concentration, I believe, is that at no time in recent history has there been a narrower range of voices, or a more restricted spectrum of opinion, than we as viewers, listeners, and readers are offered today.

Not everyone agrees with this, of course. This is supposed to be the "information age," and the digital revolution brings with it the potential for enormous diversity. It seems almost perverse to be talking about scarcity at a time like this. As one columnist wrote recently in the *National Post,*

> In the Information Age—where digital technology and the Internet have pushed free market pluralism to the point of cluttered anarchy—the scarcity rationale is no longer regarded as legitimate. The only conceivable counter-claim is a crypto-Marxist conspiracy theory, according to which Time-Warner, Disney, MTV and Hollywood are pursuing a mono-culture strategy of merciless, global domination, including the World Wide Web. (Fraser 2001, B2)

At the risk of being considered a crypto-Marxist conspiracy theorist, I believe the scarcity rationale remains very legitimate today. I do not think we can look to the Internet to get us out of this box. In the first place, it will be a long time, if ever, before we see a majority of people relying on the Web rather than newspapers, magazines, radio, and television as their primary source of news and information.

Second, the future of the Internet is beginning to look a lot like the world that already exists in newspapers, TV, and radio. Thanks to their marketing muscle, the same small number of big players owns the most popular Web sites and search engines. Through their telephone wires and cables, they can control what comes into your house and how much you will have to pay for it. And for all its potential for diversity and for breaking down borders, the Web is still primarily an extension of the dominant American culture. It is not, and I think never will be, a vehicle for telling Canadian stories and re-flecting a Canadian identity.

But public broadcasting can be. It strikes me that at a time when the range of voices on the mainstream commercial media is increasingly re-stricted, the role of a public broadcaster is to broaden that range. This does not mean aligning ourselves with a particular ideology or point of view. We must continue to maintain the highest journalistic standards regarding bal-ance, accuracy, and fairness. But when, for example, people are bombarded with editorials and columnists arguing that our taxes are too high and that government is bad and free markets are good, I believe it is an appropriate role for us as public broadcasters to ensure that we occasionally present a voice that says "no."

But there are risks involved. I once had an interesting exchange of letters with a listener in Vancouver about an interview we did on our national morn-ing show. The interview was with a prominent tax lawyer from a leading Canadian law school who was arguing against proposals to lower the capital gains tax. He believed the capital gains tax was a fair and equitable form of taxation and that we should be suspicious of people who favor its reduction or elimination. The listener wrote to the CBC Ombudsman complaining that our interview was yet another example of the CBC's persistent left-wing bias.[1]

> I expect more from my public broadcaster. I expect to leave a program informed. At the same time, I resent funding an organization through taxes that is consistently abusing its mandate to promote Canadian public opin-ion. Rather, the CBC is an organization that consistently attempts to lead public opinion.

I replied to the listener, saying that I did not believe we were leading pub-lic opinion, but simply reflecting points of view that were not commonly heard in the *Globe and Mail* and the *National Post*. The listener wrote back with what I thought was an interesting perspective on the role of the public broadcaster.

> Face it, the CBC wants to be the voice that counters the opinions expressed in the private media like the *National Post*, to ensure that the other side gets

presented. And that's the mistake you are making because if I don't like what I read in the *Post* or the *Globe*, I cancel my subscriptions. But if I don't like what I hear on the CBC, I tune out, but I keep paying. It is for this reason that I am not sympathetic to complaints about CBC budget cuts. . . .

I strongly feel that a public broadcaster has got to take the high road and not editorialize. The best way for individuals to get unbiased news is to ensure that they have multiple sources for news and formulate their own opinion. . . . Like many Canadians, I turn on CBC radio or TV for Canadian content and perspective. I don't agree that a public broadcaster should pick a side or strategy. The risk to CBC in picking sides is that they back a losing argument and lose support.

I think the fundamental mistake that this listener makes is that he doesn't sufficiently appreciate the impact of market forces on journalism. Or perhaps he just doesn't care. But when journalists or writers begin to concern themselves with wondering what advertisers might say, or corporate sponsors, or even individual donors, the first thing that disappears is the willingness to take chances. And neither great journalism nor great art can happen without risk.

As the media giants pursue their various convergence strategies, the marketplace of ideas will invariably continue to shrink. And it is the responsibility of public broadcasters to do what we can to keep that marketplace open. It is a risky strategy. As the listener pointed out, it can cost us the support of our audience. But the friends we win by behaving otherwise tend to be false allies anyway—fair-weather friends who will abandon us the next time we make a false step or face a financial crunch. In the end, we can do no better than remain true to the words of Leonard Brockington, spoken in 1938.

We believe we should be false to our trust as custodians of part of the public domain, if we did not resist . . . any attempt to place a free air under the domination of the power of wealth. Either all of us have a right to speak over the air, or none of us has a right to speak over the air. (quoted in Peers 1969, 262)

Note

1. The author wishes to protect the identity of the listener whose views appear in the next two quotes. The first quote is from his letter of complaint to the CBC Ombudsman on April 26, 2000. Subsequent to that, we had a lively and interesting exchange of letters. The first paragraph of the second quote is from his letter to me on April 28, 2000. The second paragraph is from his letter to me on May 3, 2000.

References

Fraser, M. 2001. "We're About to Find Out If Big Really Is Beautiful." *National Post*, April 2, B2.

Nash, K. 1995. *The Microphone Wars: A History of Triumph and Betrayal at the CBC*. Toronto: McClelland and Stewart.

Nolan, M. 1986. *Foundations: Alan Plaunt and the Early Days of CBC Radio*. Toronto: CBC Enterprises.

Peers, F. 1969. *The Politics of Canadian Broadcasting 1920–1951*. Toronto: University of Toronto Press.

"Public Service Broadcasters Around the World: A McKinsey Report for the BBC." 1999. McKinsey and Company, January.

15

Public Broadcasting, the Information Society, and the Internet

A Paradigm Shift?

Amit M. Schejter

The information society is dawning upon all industrialized nations. It carries with it great promise, as well as an unknown social challenge. It could make known social institutions obsolete, while maintaining old social orders. In economic terms, it signifies a move away from an industrial economy to a services-oriented economy (Bell 1973) where information has become a key commodity. In technological terms it is usually associated with the convergence of traditional technologies and the introduction of new ones such as the Internet and digital broadcasting. This chapter takes a new look at public broadcasting and describes what its practitioners have done so far on the Internet. Public broadcasters' appearances on the Internet are then measured against their operational roles, as defined and understood with respect to the preinformation society technologies, radio and television.

The role that public broadcasting has assumed in the early stages of the information society is linked to the importance of information in the new economy and new social structure that the information society represents. For many, the information society is not much more than a parade of new technologies (Schement and Curtis 1995, 103), while for many others it expresses the idea of a novel phase in the development of advanced societies (Lyon 1988, 142). The concept of public broadcasting, an institution owned by the public, for which information is the main product, seems to require a bit of redefinition in this time of social change.

This chapter describes the four major traditional models of public broadcasting and their theoretical roots. The guidelines that surrounded the creation of public broadcasting, as this chapter demonstrates, were designed by policy-makers in all four models, mostly in the form of what Tatalovich and Daynes have dubbed "social regulatory policies" (1988, 1998). These are policies designed for the preservation of social values, usually the ones shared by ruling elites. The information society is, for some, a phenomenon that carries the potential for democratization; still, some of the policies that would be required to implement this form of democracy are top-down in nature (Brants, Huizenga, and van Meerten 1996). The attempt to conflate the information society's technological wonders with the notion of a new concept of democracy has already been criticized as an effort by an existing elite to secure its own means of democratic communication (Calabrese and Borchert 1996).

The pages that follow contain a description of public broadcasting on "old" media in four separate models: the American, the Western European, the Developmental, and the post-Communist. This section is followed by a description of the ways in which public broadcasters have chosen to present themselves on the Internet. Specifically, this study describes the state of the home pages of public broadcasters representing the four models, as presented in February and July 2000. The home page was chosen as the unit of analysis since it represents the *gate* through which one enters the Internet site and, thus, the *face* with which the broadcasting organization has chosen to present itself. We find that the look of the home page alone provides much insight concerning the sponsoring organization. An additional link was made to an "index" page if the home page was no more than a logo or some other means of basic identification. Like any other study of broadcasting, the ephemeral nature of content in this study is a given. The home page, just as much as the programming schedule, may change with short notice or no notice at all. For this reason, the study was conducted twice over a period of six months; indeed, significant changes were noted during this time.

Public Broadcasting: The History of an Interventionist Policy

Public broadcasting has developed differently in different parts of the world. Still, today, more than ever before, public media institutions find themselves facing similar challenges. For some, this is due to the emergence of advanced forms of information economies and information technologies; for others, it is due to the potential for such development. In order to identify the crisis of public broadcasting in the context of the information society, the origins and design of existing policy need to be briefly identified. Again, four different models were chosen for this study: the United States, in which public broad-casting emerged as an alternative to a commercially dominated market, thus offering a niche service; Western Europe, where public service monopolies and duopolies existed prior to the introduction of commercial television, and whose fare was based on a broad mandate; the developing world, in which public broadcasting served national needs and goals dictated by government, rather than broad public goals; and the post-Communist arena, in which the party-oriented broadcaster underwent adjustments to a market-based public interest regime. Though the origins and designs of these systems are differ-ent, Williams (1974, 1992, 77) notes that the similarities in program fare between public television stations in different countries are larger than those between commercial and public broadcasters in any given country. It is not surprising, then, that the crises experienced by broadcasters of all four types have similarities. It is even less surprising that most of these broadcasters have done little to change, even when new media have provided them with an opportunity to do so.

The tensions and challenges public broadcasters face are similar because even though national systems have emerged differently, they have all emerged within the context of social regulatory policies. They have all reached the same crossroads, and their decisions are based on the same dilemmas: Should public broadcasting aspire to be an alternative to commercial broadcasting or a gener-alist voice on its own? Should public broadcasting stress its public service side or its role in participatory democracy? And most important, is there room for a public broadcaster in the world of hundreds of available channels?

United States: Public Broadcasting As Niche

Three elements have characterized American public broadcasting from the start: it was to provide some undefined measure of "quality," to serve as a provider of content that the market cannot provide, and to be differentiated from "instructional" media (Carnegie Commission 1967). A later attempt to redefine public broadcasting identified the "functional characteristics and goals of American public broadcasting" as noncommercial, independent, public, and consistently excellent (Carnegie Commission 1979, 25). Oulette (1999) argues that the Public Broadcasting Service (PBS) has put forward a model of "enlightened democracy" in its public affairs coverage that comple-ments commercial television's hegemonic orientation with a different, "gov-ernmental" logic. Engelman (1996) and Hoynes (1994) lament American public broadcasting's overcorporatization, at least in terms of funding. The U.S. Supreme Court in *Arkansas Educational Television Commission v. Forbes* (523 U.S. 666, 1997) found that political debates on public television are not to be considered a "public forum." This decision reflects the marginal role public broadcasting plays in American political discourse.

Western Europe: Public Service Broadcasting

Whether a unified Western European model of public broadcasting exists is debatable (Humphreys 1996, 116), though Blumler (1992) has created a generalized model based on the different national experiences of Western European nations. His model includes six elements: a comprehensive coverage remit; a generalized, "broadly worded" mandate; pluralism; a cultural mission; a central place in politics, both in terms of highly politicized broadcasting organizations and as reporters of the political process; and noncommercialism. According to Barendt, the principal features of public service broadcasting in Europe are general geographic availability; concern for national identity and culture; independence from both state and commercial interests; impartiality; range and variety; and substantial financing by a charge on users (1995, 52).

The European Broadcasting Union (EBU), an organization whose membership is limited to public service broadcasters, requires members to fulfill four conditions: they are under obligation to cover the entire national population, they are under obligation to provide varied and balanced programming, they must actually produce a substantial proportion of the programs they broadcast, and they cannot be linked to a sports rights agency that is in competition with the EBU (EBU 1998). The model that arises in Europe, therefore, is significantly different than the American model, most notably in its broad mandate for programming, its focus on national character, and its general scheme of funding.

The Developing Model: Public Television As National Television

The developing nations can be described as those that remained mostly under colonial control until World War II. Many of their borders were drawn along colonial agreement lines rather than along ethnic, cultural, or geographic lines. The concept of self-rule and "Western-style" democracy was introduced (or enforced) by the colonial powers on the eve of their withdrawal, while technology, especially fully functional broadcasting technology, appeared late relative to the West.

Three common goals, or premises, were behind the introduction of broadcasting in the developing countries (or "third world") according to Katz and Wedell (1977): a contribution to national integration, relative to the new formation of nation-states (171); a role in the modernization and socioeconomic development of the state (181); and a balance between cultural continuity and change (191). The first and third goals are definitely at odds with each other. Further, the process for creating broadcasting systems was based on a foreign model. The adoption of foreign systems resulted from political decisions, although Katz and Wedell attribute this process mainly to technological development (67). Technology, or form, was followed by programming, or content.[1]

Frequently, developing nations ended up with media that served the needs of the rulers rather than the principles of free speech and democracy—that is, to the extent that we can identify a universal desire on behalf of governments to control access to, and the content of, state television's news and current affairs programs (French and Richards 1996, 53).

Post-Communist Public Broadcasting: A Model in Process

Broadcasting in the post-Communist world cannot remain unaccounted for in any comparative international study, especially because of its newly found prominence in the "cyber" world. First of all, the Eastern bloc was not part of the "developing world" as conceptualized in the West. Eastern bloc media were dubbed "Soviet-Communist" and described as totalitarian in the seminal book titled *Four Theories of the Press* (Siebert, Peterson, and Schramm 1956), but that description has long been seen as flawed due to its ideological bias (Nordenstreng 1998). Whatever this model stood for in the past, it bears no resemblance to the media models that emerged following the collapse of Communist rule in much of the Eastern bloc and the rise of a local version of democracy and capitalism.

These changes resulted in media infrastructures that are diverse. Most observers agree that public broadcasting systems in the Eastern bloc countries have remained closely tied to their respective political structures, as adjustments to "democratic" reform have been difficult (Sparks 1997). Developing and post-Communist broadcasters thus resemble each other in their lengthy unichannel phase, their strong organizational ties to government, and their ties to the national—some would say "nationalist"—goals of government-related programming.

Public Broadcasting on the Internet

In order to observe what public broadcasters are doing with and on the Internet, my research assistant and I attempted to reach the Internet sites of as many public broadcasters as possible. In all, we visited seventy-three sites. Forty-six of these sites were not in English; thirty sites were found relevant for the study, since the content of their home page was in English or otherwise understandable. Of these, ten sites were visited a minimum of four times during February 2000 and again in July 2000, while the remaining twenty were visited less frequently, in most cases because there was no change in their content. The sites visited and documented represent public broadcasters that fall into the four models described above. Again, I chose the home page as the object to be studied, as this gate provides the identity of the organization for which the site was designed. Within the home page's projection of identity, I identified two basic elements: the address of the home page and the design. We tried to group the sites according to these elements and by the content and location of the "news" section of the site.

Presence on the Internet

First, it is wise to identify which broadcasters were not present on the Internet at all in July 2000, itself an indication of their status, identity, centrality in public life, and role in democratic participation. The list of the "missing" is deduced from the membership lists of the international broadcasting organizations, the European Broadcasting Union and the Asian Pacific Broadcasting Union. At least two dozen countries that have active broadcasting apparatuses had yet to gain presence on the Internet. This is not an insignificant finding, given the advent of the information society and its effect on the world information order. The developing nations on the list included Afghanistan, Algeria, Bangladesh, Bhutan, Egypt, Fiji, Iraq, Kiribati, Laos, Libya, Micronesia, Morocco, Pakistan, Papua New Guinea, Qatar, and the Kingdom of Saudi Arabia. Post-Communist broadcasters without a Web presence included Albania, Belarus, Bulgaria, Kyrgyzstan, the former Yugoslav Republic of Macedonia, Moldova, and Uzbekistan. The Western European broadcasters falling into this category were the princedoms of Luxembourg and San Marino. During the course of the study, Mongolian Radio and Television[2] and the Israel Broadcasting Authority[3] (of the developing model), Greek Television[4] and Radio Monte Carlo of Monaco[5] (of the Western model) set up new Web sites. Ukrainian Radio and Television's (post-Communist) site was under construction during the entire six-month period.

Domain Names

Internet addresses are designed with an internal hierarchy. The last two letters state the country in which the site is situated; the previous two or three letters, known as the "top-level domain," determine the organizational identity of the site. Thus, ".gov" stands for government, ."org" for nonprofit organizations, and ".co" or ".com" for a commercial enterprise. Top-level domains can provide clues about the delicate relationship between government, the commercial world, and public broadcasters in any given country. Of the sites we visited, the most common feature was the lack of an "organizational" top-level domain altogether. Such sites included broadcasters from all four models. In terms of broadcasters that embrace the Western European model, we identified the Canadian Broadcasting Corporation,[6] Ireland's National Broadcaster,[7] and Italy's RAI.[8] Among the non-English Western sites we found Austria's ORF,[9] Belgium's VRT and RTBF,[10] Denmark Radio,[11] Finland's YLE,[12] the French public television stations France 2 and France 3,[13] Radio France,[14] Germany's ARD[15] and ZDF,[16] the Greek ERT,[17] Iceland's RUV,[18] the Dutch NOS,[19] Norway's NRK,[20] Portuguese Radio and Portuguese Television,[21] Spanish Radio Television,[22] and Swedish Television and Swedish Radio.[23]

Eliminating an organizational affiliation was also popular among post-Communist broadcasters, including Lithuanian Radio and Television,[24] Bosnia's RTVBH,[25] Croatia's HRT,[26] Czech Television,[27] Estonia's Eesti Television and Radio,[28] Hungary's MTV and Magyar Radio,[29] Kazakhstan's national broadcaster,[30] Romanian television,[31] Russian Ostankino,[32] Slovak Television and Slovak Radio,[33] and Slovenian Radio Television.[34]

A common feature among broadcasters from developing nations was the elimination of any country identification. Sites falling into this category include those of China Central Television,[35] Islamic Republic of Iran Broadcasting,[36] Radio Nepal Online,[37] Jordanian Radio Television,[38] Doordarshan of India,[39] and Tunisian Radio and Television.[40]

Organizations were rarely placed under the governmental top-level domain; the only such site in our English language sample was that of Radio Television Brunei.[41] Sri Lanka's international radio system is also accessed through the government's network,[42] as is Mongolian Radio and Television,[43] though their top-level domains do not demonstrate it.

The list of broadcasters who chose (or were assigned) the commercial top-level domain is not limited to the developing nations mentioned above that shed their national-level domain altogether. Among Western broadcasters, this phenomenon is seen in Britain's BBC,[44] TVNZ of New Zealand,[45] and the Malta Public Broadcasting Service.[46] Radio Television Malaysia[47] and the Cyprus Broadcasting Corporation[48] are "developing" broadcasters who chose a commercial identification, albeit tied to a national one. This same phenomenon was seen among non-English sites such as the Korean Broadcasting System[49] and the post-Communist Polish Television and Polish Radio.[50]

A rarer usage is found of the top-level domain ".net," indicating that the site represents a network of sites. Among developing nations it is used by a few broadcasters including Doordarshan of India and Sri Lankan Radio (where the ".net" is the government's); among the Western sites included were those of the Australian Broadcasting Corporation[51] and Turkish Radio and Television.[52] The top-level domain ".org," is used by very few public broadcasters, most of them adhering to the American model: the Public Broadcasting Service, its parent corporation, the Corporation for Public Broadcasting, and the American public radio stations.[53] Japan's NHK,[54] patterned after the Western European model, and systems from developing countries such as Vietnam[55] and Israel[56] rounded out the list.

Design

Unlike the "design" of television stations, a process with a documented intellectual history, the designs of Internet sites operated by broadcasters have yet to be studied. This being the case, I have attempted to create a first, if somewhat rough, typology of broadcasters' home pages, one that reflects similar typologies used for the broadcasting media themselves. I was able to identify two major types of broadcasters' sites: the first is called the *informative* and the second the *representative*. Informative home pages contain a plethora of information, including an abundance of links to other pages within the Web site. Representative pages, on the other hand, remind the viewer of a cover page for a book or report. They contain official symbols and emblems and a limited list of links to other pages on the site. An important difference between the two types is that informative sites are dynamic, changing on a daily basis, while representative sites remained the same, at least during the period of this study.

Public broadcasting sites from most Western countries are of the informative type (the overall media "model" they represent notwithstanding), including the PBS site in the United States and those operated by broadcasters in the United Kingdom,[57] Canada, Australia, and Ireland. But within this group, two subgroups emerge. The "informative-news" subgroup is typified by the Canadian Broadcasting Corporation's site. Its main feature, and its main difference from the other "informative" sites, is that when the home page is opened, the day's top news stories are at its center. At other sites, including those of the BBC and PBS, the home page focuses on "soft" information, mostly the promotion of television programs.

What characterizes the "representative" sites is that they are based mostly in developing countries or countries with a colonial past. These sites can also be divided into two subgroups. The "national-representative" is a group of sites that carry national symbols next to a limited list of links, usually including links such as "About Us." These sites include Iran's IRIB, Jordanian Radio and Television, and Tele Liban of Lebanon.[58] Of special interest in this category is the Tunisian Radio and Television (ERTT) site, which boasts presidential speeches as the first link on its ceremonial "national-representative" home page.[59] The other "representative" model sites refrain from using national symbols, but rather present information-poor gates when compared to the "informative" home pages. These included the Cyprus Broadcasting Corporation and the Swiss Radio and Television sites,[60] along with that of India's Doordarshan.

News

I could not find an English-language Web site that did not have a link to a page defined as "news." Moreover, some countries whose sites are not in English had links to English-language news (three examples are China's CCTV, Iran's IRIB, and Vietnam's VOV). As the different models of public broadcasting may have predicted, the actual definition of "news" differs in different countries. In fact, the category of news may well provide the best validation of the choice to assess public broadcasting Web sites with models originally designed for the study of broadcasting.

At first, the Web site of America's Public Broadcasting Service seems to indicate that this organization has shed its niche-broadcasting mentality in favor of a more general conception of broadcasting content. Indeed, the PBS site features links to a variety of topics, ranging from the arts to business and news; in the latter category, I noted a link to the online version of the *NewsHour with Jim Lehrer,* the nationally televised daily news program. But faithful to its tradition, PBS remains a niche information supplier, disregarding generalist issues such as sports or weather forecasts. I proceeded to investigate the news pages and found that between February and July 2000, PBS developed a link called "News Summary," which contained a "RealAudio" (recorded sound only) version of the *NewsHour with Jim Lehrer* along with round-the-clock news updates and video clips.

This description of the PBS site is significant when compared with the sites of those organizations that are patterned after the more general broadcasting services offered in Western Europe. Canada's CBC offers an example of a Web site in which news headlines appear on the home page, unlike the PBS site with its aforementioned focus on television programs at the center of the page. But this does not reflect the whole philosophical difference between the two models. The Australian Broadcasting Corporation, a "Western" broadcaster, touts news stories on top of its home page as well. Ireland's national broadcaster offers a list of links on its site, of which news is the first link after the organization's e-mail service.[61] On the PBS site, the news link, which had been situated in alphabetical order right between "Nature" and "Science" in February, moved to the bottom left-hand corner of the home page by July. Thus, a major determinant of difference between the American and Western models is in the centrality of news on the Web site.

The appropriateness of analyzing these Web pages with the same models that have been used for the study of broadcasting systems is also maintained when considering the sites operated by broadcasters in developing countries. During the period of this study, the Jordan Radio and Television site linked the surfer to a news page in which the daily headlines were devoted to the whereabouts and actions of the reigning monarch, while on China's Central Television site the news page reflected the sort of "positive" news expected in a developing and strongly regulated environment. Similar patterns can be seen in Iran.

What is not common to broadcasters belonging to similar models is the format in which they choose to present the news. Thus, the American PBS site has a combination of print information and archived video, just like India's Doordarshan. Lebanese Television (Tele-Liban) has a "RealVideo" full version of its newscast, while China Central has an independent news site featuring headlines and stories in text only. In other words, the technological form of news presentation on a Web site is not significantly related to the model of public broadcasting the organization adheres to or to the type of news service the organization delivers.

Discussion: New Medium = New Paradigm?

Three stages characterize the development of broadcasting in the United States (Noam 1996), and these stages can be identified in Western Europe, the post-Communist countries, and many developing nations as well: the limited channel stage, the multichannel stage, and the "cyber" stage. The transition from the first to the second stage was characterized by the fact that each broadcasting system tried to survive its crisis of change by offering more of the services it always had while centering its efforts in the meantime on the procurement of more funding.

The critique of public broadcasting in the United States has been that public broadcasters have not yet offered a true alternative to the fare that Americans have come to expect from commercial networks. The role of "alternative programmer" was eventually taken by new commercial services that audiences have learned to use since the adoption of the Public Broadcasting Act (Shooshan and Arnheim 1988, 10). Some of these commercial ventures have started providing types of programming previously associated with public television. In other words, the "niche" mentality of public broadcasting has found a competitor in other services that believe these niches have commercial potential as well. On the other hand, some of the specialized programs for which public broadcasting seemed the right place raised public opposition, since they seemed to undermine conservative concepts of the ideal American society. Public broadcasting's answer has been to seek new sources of income, independent of precarious government funds, as a means of continuing to supply the same kind of service it has always provided for the American people. According to Hoynes (1994), the resulting increase in support from businesses and listeners has, in effect, "privatized" public broadcasting. In the process, the essential character of noncommercial broadcasting in America—including its niche-marketing mentality—remained unchanged.

European broadcasters, on the other hand, have made efforts to stay general in their missions and to receive protection for both their financial bases and programming philosophies. Thus, political efforts have been made to secure the existence of public broadcasters. These efforts have led to some success, both on the national and pan-European levels, the high point being a protocol to the 1977 European Union Treaty that considers the system of public broadcasting in member states to be "directly related to the democratic, social and cultural needs of each society and to the need to preserve media pluralism." As a result, the Council of the European Union decided in January 1999 that "public service broadcasting must be able to continue to provide a wide range of programming . . . [and to] seek to reach wide audiences" (*Official Journal* 1999/C 30/01, 1). Following the collapse of the Iron Curtain in the late 1980s, public broadcasters in the former Eastern bloc joined hands with their Western bloc counterparts and dissolved their union into the European Broadcasting Union.

It is not hard to understand why some public broadcasters had a hard time changing their ways, so long as their efforts centered on traditional radio and TV transmissions. As Ang (1991) has noted, the decision-making processes in public service organizations are slow, and the capability to change is limited. It is a different story when a new medium arrives, one which incorporates basic characteristics different from the media through which the organization developed. In this case, one might argue, the organization has an opportunity to reconsider its positioning. This is especially true with the Internet for a number of reasons.

First, there is no regulatory framework to govern any organization's presence on the Internet. No licenses or other forms of permission to use the digital infrastructure are needed in most countries. Thus, an organization's presence on the Internet has no inherent justification or connection to the original role played by broadcasters, in the sense that the right to broadcast was awarded to a chosen few and was based on a certain promise of performance or on a legally binding remit. Second, as a result of this regulatory landscape, the Internet is a platform on which presence is not limited to organizations that define themselves as "broadcasters." As a result, nonbroadcasters can also communicate over the Internet. Traditional broadcasters compete for the attention of Internet users, an experience that is truly novel for all concerned. Third, there are still no set traditions regarding an organization's presence on the Internet; in fact, the Internet is characterized by ingenuity and originality, often the direct opposite of the characterization one would offer about public broadcasters. Fourth, the Internet allows for input on behalf of the audience, especially immediate input or feedback. This particular characteristic, often called *interactivity*, is often overestimated or misunderstood. In fact, the interactivity offered by the Internet (especially the World Wide Web, the place where broadcasters' activity takes place) is only as "immediate" as using the telephone for call-in radio and television programs.

The uniqueness of Internet surfing, as opposed to television viewing or radio listening, is not a result of the ability to send feedback to the original communicator. The unique activity associated with the Internet has more to do with the limitations of the technology, and of human nature, than anything else. We perceive the activity of browsing through ready-made content as being "interactive," while in essence it amounts to nothing more than flipping through a large number of pages, stations, or channels of "old" media. When streaming video reaches the quality of television, and streaming audio the quality of radio, the Internet may become primarily a carrier of radio and television content—though with much more choice than present-day broadcasting offers. Thus, the true difference between the Internet and traditional broadcasting is the wealth of information an audience member can expect to encounter when visiting the broadcaster's site at a particular moment, and the ability to reach that information instantaneously. While traditional television offers the viewer a single program at any given moment, it is possible to surf the Web as a means of finding and selecting content that is available from many different content providers—all at the same time. This variety may well encourage new forms of audience activity, especially when video and audio capabilities on the Internet match those of television and radio. The result of this active "choice" by the audience is that the Internet communicator, unlike the traditional broadcaster, cannot dictate a content-based agenda any longer. The notion of programming "flow" developed by Williams (1974–1992) and others will either become obsolete in the new realm of cybercasting or need to be interpreted differently, at the very least. The imperative to match new conceptions of flow with new conceptions of audience choice is important for broadcasters making the transition to the Internet since, in the process, these broadcasters lose their traditional power over audience agendas. This in itself is not a unique feature of the Internet, but rather a common feature of all digital infrastructures of the "information society."

A fifth and final point: continuing technological innovation means the Internet experience for today's surfer is not certain to last long. This state of affairs will also add to the uncertainty that today's public service broadcasters face.

These five differences—no spectrum scarcity, competition with nonbroadcasters, a lack of tradition, a wealth of information, and an uncertain future—lead us to conclude that a broadcasting organization's presence on the Internet, and in particular on the Web, has very little to do with "broadcasting" in the traditional sense. The provision of content on the Web happens under totally different circumstances than broadcasting, in terms of the reasoning behind the activity and the relationship between the content provider and the end user. On the other hand, broadcasters are in the business of communicating, and as much as one can expect any other business to maintain its identity over this new medium, there is no reason why broadcasters should be expected to behave differently. Under these circumstances, public service broadcasters in particular are seeking ways to establish themselves on the Internet as part of their general effort to create "a massive bridgehead" into the world of new media and digital activities (Winsbury 1999, 17).

What We Can Learn About Public Broadcasting and the Internet

The Internet evokes in many the feeling that it is a "free" medium—free of regulation and free of central control. One could have expected that the patterns of organizational identity emerging on the Internet would be varied and, to a certain extent, surprising. As this study reveals, this is not the case for public broadcasters, and it doesn't matter whether they emerged in the American, Western, developmental, or post-Communist worlds. Public broadcasters aim to be on the Internet, specifically on the Web, although they are not yet fully sure why.

The original differences between public broadcasters that emerged as a result of the regime in which they operate are broadly maintained when considering their operations on the Web. These broadcasters have reacted to the emergence of the new multichannel environment by largely maintaining their existing identities. These organizations have not yet chosen the civic or organizational identity they profess to desire for their online operations. There is a distinct difference between what these sites *are* and what they *claim to be,* based on their choice of certain top-level domain names. Perhaps the most important conclusion is that public broadcasters have not risen yet to the challenge of the information society as demonstrated by the emergence of the Internet. The Internet is for public broadcasters simply another medium in which they aspire to survive. Its potential for the democratization of society and thus for a redefinition of the role of public broadcasting has not been achieved. Perhaps it is too early to judge. Or perhaps we might say that old paradigms don't die—they just fade away.

Notes

I wish to acknowledge and give thanks for the contribution of the dedicated, loyal, insightful, and diligent Yair Mendelson, a recent graduate of the communication program at Tel Aviv University, who served as a devoted assistant to this study.

1. For Katz and Wedell, the content of broadcasting was merely a natural follow-up to the introduction of technology, but for other scholars, this content relationship has become the central matter of the developmental theory. Schiller (1969) calls it media imperialism and sees in it part of the process of American cultural imperialism over the third world. This process, he contends, is based on the economic inequality between the first and third worlds and the unidirectional flow of television content from the former to the latter. Lee (1979) describes two competing schools of thought on media imperialism: the Marxist approach, which sees it as a direct and unfavorable consequence of global economic patterns of imperialism; and the non-Marxist approach, which analyzes the flow of communication in terms of diffusion and sees it as part of a more natural acceptance of media products by open societies.
2. www.mol.mn/mrtv
3. www.iba.org.il
4. www.ert.gr
5. www.rmc.mc/indexie.htm
6. www.cbc.ca
7. www.rte.ie
8. www.rai.it
9. www.orf.at/home.htm
10. www.vrt.be and www.rtbf.be
11. www.dr.dk
12. www.yle.fi
13. www.france2.fr and www.france3.fr
14. www.radio-france.fr
15. www.ard.de
16. www.zdf.de
17. www.ert.gr
18. www.ruv.is

19. www.omroep.nl
20. www.nrk.no
21. www.rdp.pt and www.rtp.pt
22. www.rtve.es
23. www.svt.se and www.sr.se
24. www.lrtv.lt
25. http://rtvbh.ba
26. www.hrt.hr//frames.html
27. www.czech-tv.cz
28. www.etv.ee and http://er.ee
29. www.mtv.hu and www.radio.hr
30. www.khabar.kz/
31. www.tvr.ro
32. www.ortv.ru/index.htm
33. www.stv.sk and www.slovakradio.sk
34. www.rtvslo.si
35. www.cctv.com
36. www.irib.com
37. www.catmando.com
38. www.jrtv.com
39. http://ddindia.net
40. www.tunisiatv.com
41. www.brunei.bn/gov/rtb/rtbutama.htm
42. www.lanka.net
43. www.mol.mn/mrtv
44. www.bbc.co.uk
45. www.tvnz.co.nz
46. www.pbs.com.mt
47. www.asiaconnect.com.my
48. www.cybc.com.cy
49. www.kbs.co.kr
50. www.tvp.com.pl and www.radio.com.pl
51. www.abc.net.au
52. www.trt.net.tr
53. www.pbs.org, www.cpb.org, and www.npr.org. Due to the regional nature of the American system, we refer here only to the national sites and not to the sites of the hundreds of public radio and television stations in the United States that have their own Web sites, many times carrying a ".com" suffix to their call letters (such as public radio station WBUR of Boston www.wbur.com, public television station WETA of Washington, D.C. www.weta.com, and others).
54. www.nhk.org.jp
55. www.vov.org.vn
56. www.iba.org.il
57. Concerning the BBC, we refer here to www.bbc.co.uk. It is important to note that the BBC's commercial arm, BBC Enterprises, runs its own Web site www.beeb.com, which is a center for electronic commerce featuring, but not limited to, BBC-related merchandise.
58. www.tele-liban.com/opening.htm

59. www.tunisiatv.com/index1.html
60. http://tora.sri.ch/gd/
61. It was first in February, then moved to second by July.

References

Ang, I. 1991. *Desperately Seeking the Audience.* London: Routledge.
Arkansas Educational Television Commission v. *Forbes*, 523 U.S. 666 (1997).
Barendt, E. 1995. *Broadcasting Law: A Comparative Analysis.* Oxford: Clarendon Press.
Bell, D. 1973. *The Coming of the Post-industrial Society.* New York: Basic Books.
Blumler, J., and T. Nossiter. 1991. "Broadcasting Finance in Transition: An International Comparison." In *Broadcasting Finance in Transition: A Comparative Handbook*, ed. J. Blumler and T. Nossiter. New York: Oxford University Press, 405–426.
Brants, K., M. Huizenga, and R. van Meerten. 1996. "New Canals of Amsterdam: An Exercise in Local Electronic Democracy." *Media, Culture and Society* 18, no. 2: 233–248.
Calabrese, A., and M. Borchert. 1996. "Prospects for Electronic Democracy in the United States: Rethinking Communication and Social Policy." *Media, Culture and Society* 18, no. 2: 249–268.
Carnegie Commission on Educational Television. 1967. *Public Television: A Program for Action.* New York: Harper and Row.
Carnegie Commission on the Future of Public Broadcasting. 1979. *A Public Trust.* New York: Bantam Books.
Engelman, R. 1996. *Public Radio and Television in America: A Political History.* Thousand Oaks, CA: Sage.
European Broadcasting Union. 1998. *Statutes.* Geneva: European Broadcasting Union.
French, D., and M. Richards, eds. 1996. *Contemporary Television: Eastern Perspectives.* London: Sage.
Hoynes, W. 1994. *Public Television for Sale: Media, the Market and the Public Sphere.* Boulder, CO: Westview Press.
Humphreys, P. 1996. *Mass Media and Media Policy in Western Europe.* Manchester, UK: Manchester University Press.
Katz, E., and G. Wedell. 1977. *Broadcasting in the Third World: Promise and Performance.* London: Macmillan Press.
Lee, C. 1979. *Media Imperialism Reconsidered: The Homogenizing of Television Culture.* Beverly Hills: Sage.
Lyon, D. 1988. *The Information Society.* Oxford: Polity Press.
Noam, E. 1996. "Media Concentration in the United States: Industry Trends and Regulatory Responses." http://www.vii.org/papers/medconc.htm.
Nordenstreng, K. 1998. "Beyond the Four Theories of the Press." In *Media and Politics in Transition*, ed. J. Servaes and R. Lie. Leuvan, Belgium: Acco, 97–109.
Official Journal of the European Communities. 1999. Resolution of the Council and of the Representatives of the Governments of the Member States, Meeting Within the Council of 25 January 1999 concerning public service broadcasting (1999/C 30/01). *Official Journal* Web site http://europa.eu.int/eur-lex/pri/en/oj/dat/1999/c_030/c_03019990205en00010001.pdf (August 15, 2002).

Ouellete, L. 1999. "TV Viewing as Good Citizenship? Political Rationality, Enlightened Democracy and PBS." *Cultural Studies* 13, no. 1: 62–90.

Schement, J., and T. Curtis. 1995. *Tendencies and Tensions of the Information Age: Production and Distribution of Information in the United States.* New Brunswick, NJ: Transaction.

Schiller, H. 1969. *Mass Communication and American Empire.* New York: Augustus M. Kelly.

Shooshan, H., and L. Arnheim. 1988. *Public Broadcasting.* Washington, DC: Benton Foundation.

Siebert, F., T. Peterson, and W. Schramm. 1956. *Four Theories of the Press.* Urbana: University of Illinois Press.

Sparks, C. 1997. "Post-Communist Media in Transition." In *International Media Research: A Critical Survey*, ed. J. Corner, P. Schlesinger, and R. Silverstone. London: Routledge, 96–122.

Tatalovich, R., and B. Daynes. 1988. "Introduction: What Is Social Regulatory Policy?" In *Social Regulatory Policy: Moral Controversies in American Politics*, ed. R. Tatalovich and B. Daynes. Boulder, CO: Westview Press, 1–4.

———. 1998. *Moral Controversies in American Politics.* Armonk, NY: M.E. Sharpe.

Williams, R.1974, 1992. *Television: Technology and Cultural Form.* Hanover, NH: University Press of New England.

Winsbury, R. 1999. "Public Space on the Internet: An On-line Search for a PSB Portal into the Twenty-first Century." *Intermedia* 27, no. 3: 4–20.

16

Between Globalization and Democratization

Governmental Public Broadcasting in Africa

Lyombe S. Eko

In view of the diverse models and objectives of public broadcasting, one can say as a general rule that the terms "public broadcasting" and "public service broadcasting" refer to electronic media that are characterized by public ownership, are noncommercial in most countries, and rely on governments, foundations, corporate underwriting, and/or listener support for funding (Hiebert and Gibbons 2000). These media are the home of high-quality, if sometimes elitist and esoteric fare—programming that can, nevertheless, serve as a model for commercial network television (Dizard 2000). Broadcasting in Africa is as diverse as the continent's fifty-three countries. The public broadcasting systems that obtain on the continent are made up of several shades, hues, and degrees of freedom. This diversity reflects the different political, sociocultural, and linguistic environments. It also reflects the diverse relationships between governments and broadcasters in the different countries and regions of Africa. The single most important factor that has influenced the development of broadcasting in Africa is the continent's diverse colonial heritage. Most broadcasting traditions were inherited from the monopolistic traditions left by European colonial powers. The wave of democratization that swept through the African continent in the early 1990s led to the liberalization of the airwaves. Governmental public broadcasters, once virtual monopolies, soon faced stiff competition from private commercial stations and the "surrogate" rebroadcast allies of international broadcasters. Today, Africa's governmental public broadcasters are caught in the crosswinds of globalization, commercialization, and democratization.

The aim of this chapter is to survey contemporary public service broadcasting in Africa and to show what African public service broadcasters are doing in the face of globalization and the internal pressures of democratization. This study was carried out within the framework of the diffusion of innovation perspective, which holds that the world is in a perpetual state of innovation and change, and that this change requires the penetration of inventions and innovations. Inventions diffuse or spread through a process of imitation. As new innovations are introduced, certain factors enable some of them to be widely diffused and adopted while others fail and do not spread beyond the areas in which they were invented or introduced. The diffusion of innovation perspective also holds that when innovations spread, certain communication processes enable them to follow empirically observable and measurable patterns, so-called curves of diffusion. These S-shaped curves represent the initial small numbers of adopters of innovations. As circumstances change, the rate of adoption accelerates; then, after reaching a maximum rate over time, diffusion slows down and stabilizes (Lowery and DeFleur 1995).

The diffusion of innovation perspective was pioneered by a French sociologist, Gabriel Tarde (1903), and tested by Pemberton (1936), Ryan and Gross (1943), and Rogers (1983), among others. According to Tarde, inventions usually diffuse from their geometrical center as waves or concentric circles, like those created by a drop of water in a quiet pool. Each innovation has a center from which it is spread to other areas. Furthermore, innovations are often modified or reinvented in the course of the diffusion process so they fit each existing culture or environment they come into contact with (Kinnunen 1996). Thus, the diffusion process starts with an invention—the development of a solution to a perceived problem or shortcoming (Schumpeter 1939). The invention moves from the invention or innovation center, spreads to sub-innovation centers, and finally into the periphery. Diffusion of innovation theory also holds that countries in the political and economic "periphery" of the world usually adopt innovations at a late stage. These countries learn from the experiences of the innovation centers and sub-innovation centers, thus leapfrogging decades of evaluation, experimentation, and testing of specific innovations. These countries on the fringes of the global economy can be described as late adopters who, manifesting an accelerated diffusion rate over a short span of time, arrive at the same approximate stage in technological innovation as the innovation and sub-innovation centers (Grubler 1996).

The modern media of mass communication have recently been conceptualized as a series of successive and cumulative innovations that ultimately converge on the Internet, itself the innovation of innovations (DeFleur and

Dennis 2002). In the 1990s, Africa saw the arrival and diffusion of a series of communication innovations: private enterprise commercial broadcasting, cable, direct broadcast (subscription) satellite, and microwave multipoint distribution (MMDS) or wireless cable, as well as radio and television rebroadcasters that distribute programming material from other parts of the world. What was the impetus for institutional and technological innovation in Africa's broadcasting services? What was the adoption process of these innovations in Africa? What was the impact of these structural, institutional, and technological innovations on state-run public broadcasting systems? Have African countries showed signs of modifying or reinventing these innovations to suit their national, political, and cultural realities? This chapter aims to answer these questions by surveying the political, social, and economic forces that triggered the spread of electronic media innovations in the post–Cold War era.

The History of Public Service Broadcasting in Africa

State-operated public service broadcasting has been the norm in Africa, both north and south of the Sahara, since independence. When African nations became self-governing in the late 1950s and early 1960s, after long and often bitter struggles against colonial governments, most countries inherited the media setup of the colonial administrations. As a result, their first challenge was to give radio and television (where it existed) an African identity, culture, and accent. Countries set out to "Africanize" or domesticate radio and television (Mazrui 1996). In order to do so, many countries initially tried to selectively use Western techniques, materials, ideas, and forms to produce original, creative, and culturally relevant programming (Hassan 1996). This was no easy task, considering that post-independence broadcasting in Africa was a mishmash of models inherited from European colonial governments. In the 1920s and 1930s, the British colonial administration decided to develop radio as a public service in its African colonies, forming statutory public broadcasting corporations along the lines of the British Broadcasting Corporation (BBC) in virtually all of them. These stations were basically aimed at keeping European settlers in Africa in touch with the rest of the British Empire, though in certain colonies the management permitted local African-language drama to develop (Kerr 1995). Adequate funding for these stations could not be raised from license fees, however, due to the limited number of radio sets in the colonies. Africans could not afford the expensive imported radio receivers. Even when a British company produced a cheaper, battery-powered radio set, the "Saucepan Special" (which became a status symbol among Africans), colonial broadcasting stations could not run on license fees alone (Kerr 1995). Funding ultimately came from a combination of government grants and advertising. Thus, in the early 1960s, broadcasting stations in the former British colonies of East and West Africa were described as a "brood of more or less dutiful offspring" of the BBC (Ainslie 1966, 158).

Broadcast stations in the French-speaking countries were organized along the lines of the French government broadcaster, the Office de Radiodiffusion Télévision de France (ORTF). These stations had even less autonomy than those in the British colonies. They were highly centralized and run strictly according to directives issued by the colonial office in Paris. The French colonial administration introduced African-language broadcasts on African stations for the first time during World War II, when, in the face of the on-slaught of Hitler's armies, France faced military collapse. Broadcasts in African languages were used to rally Africans to the French cause and to facilitate the recruitment of African soldiers for French army campaigns in North Africa and Europe (Silla 1994). At independence, the French-speaking countries inherited these overcentralized, highly politicized bureaucracies, operated and funded as government departments. A small percentage of funding came from advertising.

This mixed public/private system was the economic model inherited by most African countries when they became independent from Britain, France, Portugal, and Spain in the 1960s. The policy framework for postindependence public service broadcasting in Africa was set by American mass communication scholars working under the auspices of UNESCO (United Nations Educational, Scientific and Cultural Organization). As early as 1958, when virtually all African countries were still under colonial rule, the General Assembly of the United Nations called for the building of mass media facilities in countries that were in the process of economic and social development (United Nations 1958). In 1962, the General Assembly passed a resolution stating that the information media had an important role to play in education and in social and economic progress. This led to the formulation, by the United Nations, of the controversial development communication paradigm that dominated broadcasting in Africa for more than forty years.

As formulated in its early stages by Schramm (1964) and other Western experts, the development communication perspective postulated that developing countries do not have the resources to indulge in the luxury of the liberal, watchdog journalistic model of the Western countries. As a result, all media were to concentrate on the task of disseminating information and messages that would improve agricultural production, health, education, national security, and other vital areas. The strategic use of information would lead to nation building and provide a "climate" for national development. The idea that the mass media in general, and informational media in particular, would play an important role in the development of the emerging countries of the third world was based on the assumption that the mass media had very powerful, direct, and immediate effects on listeners and viewers.

This perspective was embraced by virtually all the countries of Africa except South Africa, which used its mass media as an instrument for the promotion of apartheid, its policy of racial segregation. Developmental communication was based on the principle that African countries were fragile, fledgling societies with many internal and external threats. Striving for national unity and cohesion was considered more important than freedom of the press. The tightly controlled mass media, usually government newspapers and broadcasting facilities, were used to promote the values and developmental objectives of the government of the day. Most politicians argued that in situations of abject poverty, where the bare necessities were absent, having mass media that concentrated on criticizing and checking government action was a misuse of resources. Some African countries dusted off the old colonial laws that had been used to muzzle the press, modified them, and quickly imposed them on their own press. Nevertheless, due to differing economic, political, sociocultural, and ideological realities, the application of development communication was never uniform throughout Africa. In that era, statutory public service broadcasters in multiparty democracies like Senegal, Gambia, and Botswana led the way in providing public service programming. Ultimately, with a few exceptions, African countries did not succeed in using Western techniques, materials, ideas, and forms to produce original, creative, and culturally relevant programming.

Radio Programming

Though public broadcasting in the age of development communication was generally tightly controlled, highly centralized, clearly politicized, and used as the personal megaphone of a number of authoritarian leaders, some countries had a good record of producing effective public service and educational programming within the "development communication" framework. For example, Ghana Broadcasting Corporation (GBC) radio had one of the most effective distance education programs on the continent.

One of the hallmarks of public broadcasting is localism—that is, broadcasting that serves as an instrument for the promotion of local cultures, identities, and languages. Some countries placed more emphasis on localism than others. Nigeria and Cameroon, which did not have political plurality for the greater part of their independence, still had regional radio stations that had a wide degree of autonomy in local public service programming. Nigeria, which probably has the most extensive public and private broadcasting networks in

Africa, "domesticated" radio and television and gave it an African accent. Between federal and state broadcasters, diverse national and local programming was produced in the 250 languages and dialects spoken in that country. In Cameroon, the creation of regional stations led to some creative local public service programming. An example is *Meet the Patient,* a "reverse therapy" program in which a reporter visited patients in local hospitals, giving them an opportunity to tell stories, recite traditional poems and proverbs, or sing for the radio audience. Other local radio programs had titles like *Young Farmers' Club, Young Writers' Forum, Safe Journey, Women's Corner,* and *Children's Half Hour.* None of these programs had commercial sponsors.

In Malawi, where "President for Life" (he later lost power in an election) Hastings Kamuza Banda led a cult of personality, the national broadcaster was known for its popular, award-winning dramas on social and community subjects. In Tanzania, under the socialist government of Mwalimu Julius Nyerere, Radio Tanzania, Dar-es-Salaam, became the standard-bearer and promoter of Swahili language and culture in East Africa as early as 1962. Indeed, by actively encouraging almost exclusive broadcasting in Swahili, Nyerere single-handedly transformed the language into the lingua franca of East and Central Africa and made it one of the most widely spoken languages on the African continent. In Benin, where a Marxist government had tight control over radio and television, the government-owned and -controlled broadcaster, Office de Radiodiffusion et Télévision du Benin (ORTB), produced a series of successful African puppet theater programs that were translated and widely distributed around the continent. The most unusual experiment was a Burkina Faso community radio station called Radio Entrez Parler (literally, Radio Come In and Speak Your Mind). The leftist and populist government of the late President Thomas Sankara supported this radio station, which literally opened its doors to anyone who wanted to come in and sound off. The owners of the radio station soon realized, however, that it was too risky and too expensive to keep the doors open—from a political and defamation point of view—and the station quietly went off the air.

Television

At independence, television was viewed as a luxury by most African countries. It was the "poor cousin" of the mass media because of its limited reach and lack of funding. When television was introduced in a number of countries, it was also viewed as an instrument of development. Priority was given to educational programs for schools, teacher training, literacy programs, and the promotion of national development projects. Many countries from Senegal to Kenya created community viewing centers in schools and villages. In areas where there was no electricity, solar television sets were installed. The solar-powered community television set in the village of Deni Biram-Ndao, Senegal, became the model for community education through television.

Democratization, Liberalization, and the Diffusion of New Technologies and Broadcasting Economies

The end of the Cold War triggered a hurricane of political instability in Africa. Popular uprisings, strikes, sit-ins, and demands for political freedom and better standards of living broke out all over the African map. In response, political leaders throughout the continent, seeing that European and American benefactors would no longer protect them from their own people, legalized opposition parties and allowed the press more freedom. The anemic, much suppressed private press was in the thick of the struggle for freedom, often spearheading demands for justice, transparency, and accountability. The political counterdiscourses, rumors, and vitriolic sentiments that had been forced underground by development communication suddenly burst forth like molten magma over the African intellectual landscape, rooting out hypocrisy, corruption, and repression and leaving cowed dictators, bureaucrats, and their intellectual apologists in their wake. An African intellectual and World Bank official, Celestin Monga, captures the heady days of political revolt in his aptly titled book, *The Anthropology of Anger*, which recounts attempts by oppressive African governments to resist or co-opt the anger of the voiceless people on the street (Monga 1996). Country after country legalized opposition parties and civil society organizations (Ihonvbere 1997). Broadcasting was also affected by these political upheavals. Government broadcasting stations, intimately associated with vilified regimes, were attacked by mobs. In the Democratic Republic of Congo (formerly Zaire), journalists of the Zairian Radio and Television Corporation (OZRT), the mouthpiece for the authoritarian regime of Mobutu Sese Seko, were attacked on the streets of Kinshasa, the capital. In Libreville, Gabon, studios of the Gabonese Radio and Television Corporation (RTG) were attacked, as were the studios of Africa No. 1, a French- and Gabonese-owned pan-African radio station viewed as being too close to the Gabonese government.

As a result of the democratic changes and pressure from pirate stations, press laws were liberalized across the continent. Private radio stations (both legal and pirate) broadcasting in several African and European languages sprouted like anthills on the African savanna. Regulatory agencies, unheard of prior to 1990, were created in many countries. These included the Conseil National de Communication (CNC) in Gabon, the National Broadcasting Commission in Nigeria, and the Conseil National de la Communication in

Cameroon. These agencies were given the tasks of managing the electro-magnetic spectrum, delivering licenses to new public and private stations, and acting as referees in case of disputes. However, in many countries, these agencies were either toothless or never given the funding they needed to carry out their mandates. As a result, the privatization of broadcasting in many African countries was done behind closed doors, with powerful corporations, international organizations, and individuals wielding much more power in the process than other interested parties (Silla 1994; Ogundimu 1996).

Many governmental public broadcasters opted for a mixed economic model. Many went into partnerships with private international companies in a bid to shore up their dwindling funds, obtain cheap programming, and hold onto their audiences. In Ghana, the government broadcaster joined forces with a Malaysian company to create *Metro TV* in Accra, while in Cameroon and Gabon, public television organizations joined forces with private com-panies to start subscription television ventures.

To date, virtually all African countries have licensed independent or alter-native broadcasting facilities of one form or another. This new group of broad-casters is a mixed bag of private, commercial, and community broadcasters (including religious broadcasters) whose mission, in most cases, blends pub-lic service broadcasting with the pursuit of profit. The arrival of independent stations has blurred the lines between commercial and public broadcasting in the traditional sense. For example, the French-speaking countries of West Africa have a category of private broadcasters called *association radio*. These nonprofit stations are owned by community groups or associations. They are not forbidden from making profits as long as the profits are not distributed to individual members of the association (Senghor 1996). Finally, on Africa No. 1, the continent's premier commercial radio service, it is not unusual to hear a throaty commercial for Marlboro or Benson and Hedges cigarettes follow a serious ethnographic or historical documentary on the rainforest Pygmies or the Bantu peoples of Central Africa.

Globalization and Its Impacts on African Broadcasting

In addition to commercial pressure from private broadcasters at home, Afri-can public service broadcasters are buffeted by the forces of globalization. The term "globalization" is a catch-all expression, an organizing principle whose wide umbrella covers disparate ideological principles like environ-mentalism, voluntary economic, scientific, political, and cultural associa-tions between countries and regions, codependencies, religious and faith-based relationships, transport, communications infrastructures, and trade (Bamyeh 2000, 64). The phenomenon of globalization has also been defined as cultural politics and cultural economics that presuppose a common knowledge system, transmitted across vast distances by the transnational media and mass travel (Bamyeh 2000, 89). The most visible manifestations of cultural globalization are American. They include the ubiquitous Western information and communication technologies— films, television programs, video games, and other cultural products. Additionally, multinational mass media conglomerates like Disney and AOL Time Warner increasingly practice what Juan Somavia of the International Labor Organization (ILO) has called "the industrialization of cultures . . . through the absorption of smaller players, the weakening of national and local cultures and enterprises . . . and a growing standardization of media products and performances sold around the world" (Buhrer 2000, 1).

In Africa, American and European cultural products like films and television programs are distributed cheaply through new digital technologies for the purpose of making a little extra profit for movie companies, distributors, and advertising agencies. Under pressure from the World Bank and International Monetary Fund (IMF), some African governments privatize their telecommunications and broadcast infrastructure to European or American companies thereby becoming the unwitting vectors of globalization. This situation is compounded by the fact that a lot of the privatizations have taken place under conditions that lack public input and other forms of accountability. The most effective promoter of the globalization of telecommunications and mass media content has been the International Telecommunications Union (ITU). The ITU's most recent plan for Africa is aimed at facilitating the delivery of direct satellite TV broadcasting to all countries on the continent. Each country is granted one orbital position from which up to ten analog channels can be delivered (ITU 2000). The problem is that, with the possible exception of South Africa, none of the fifty-three African countries has the legal framework, infrastructure, resources, and economic base to support such satellite broadcasting. The main beneficiaries of this change have been international direct broadcast satellite companies.

State-owned radio stations had to adjust to this new competitive environment or become irrelevant. Some tightly controlled government broadcasting stations, which had been stuck in the development communication model for three decades, began to take on some of the characteristics of public service radio and television stations (Senghor 1996). As a result of democratization and of IMF- and World Bank-imposed structural adjustment programs, governments across the continent gave state-controlled broadcasters more autonomy—and reduced their already inadequate funding accordingly. This forced the broadcasters to sacrifice some public service programming for advertiser-sponsored specials, underwriting, and mass appeal musical formats favored by advertisers. Additionally, some governmental public broadcasters leased their studios, transmitters, and other equipment to private enterprise broadcasters. Liberalization of the African airwaves as a result of political pressure from within, and of intense pressure to privatize and commercialize from the forces of globalization, resulted in stiff competition for African public broadcasters. Private, commercial radio and TV stations soon surpassed state-controlled stations in the creation and distribution of programming and popular culture. These stations were both the catalysts for, and the results of, democratization. African entrepreneurs tapped financial resources that had been considered nonexistent in Africa, created profitable private enterprise broadcasting, and revolutionized television—albeit with mostly imported content (Ogundimu 1996).

New delivery systems, such as encrypted low-power terrestrial broadcasting, microwave multipoint distribution, and direct broadcast satellites (DBS), were first introduced in Africa in 1992 (Silla 1994). Soon, there was a virtual explosion of television signals from multiple delivery systems to direct-to-home satellite reception via small parabolic antennae. Today, there are more than 150 separate television program distributors on the African continent (Paterson 1998). The lightning speed with which television exploded in Africa has had many unforeseen cultural consequences. The sudden overcommercialization of African broadcasting, under pressure from the American government as well as American and European media conglomerates, has transformed African television into an outlet for all kinds of cheap imported programs, ranging from Jerry Springer to Mexican and Brazilian telenovelas. The flood of commercial entertainment programming into Africa has eroded traditional cultures and is in the process of ushering in an era of mass consumerism (Paterson 1998). Though indigenous private enterprise broadcasting in Africa has succeeded and thrived beyond all expectations, it has, to a large extent, been unable to put an African imprint on broadcasting. This industry is largely dependent on cheap imported or free programming to fill ambitious broadcast schedules. These broadcasters also have relatively high commercial loads; studies show that advertising makes up between 10 and 13 percent of all program fare. This trend has exacerbated Africa's dependence on broadcast programming and hardware (Ogundimu 1994).

International and "Surrogate Broadcasting"

Since the "liberalization" of the mass media got under way in Africa, several of the international broadcasters who used to send only shortwave signals have been allowed to broadcast directly to African audiences on the FM band. In order to support the "Radio Democracy for Africa" project of the Voice of

America (VOA), aimed at creating "surrogate" or affiliate radio operations throughout Africa to promote democracy, the U.S. House of Representatives passed the Promoting Independent Broadcasting in Africa Act (1998). The bill, based on the premise that the promotion of independent radio in Africa is a useful tool for advancing democracy and human rights, provides the VOA's African affiliates the means to relay or rebroadcast American government-funded programming. The VOA simulcasts on FM in a number of African countries and, in some cases, several cities within the same country. Other international broadcasters that have affiliates on the African continent include Cable News Network International (CNNI), BBC World Service and BBC World Service TV, Radio France Internationale, Canal France International, Canal Horizon, Deutsche Welle TV, Radio Television Portuguès International (RTPI), and others. As a result of the activities of these international organizations, African broadcasting is no longer dominated by state-run public service broadcasters.

Reinvention of Broadcast Innovations in Africa

The diffusion of innovation perspective holds that innovations are often modified or reinvented in the course of their diffusion, such that they fit the cultures or environments they come into contact with. The question, then, is whether the innovations introduced into African broadcasting in the early 1990s—private broadcasting stations, commercialization, imported commercialized entertainment, new distribution technologies like MMDS and direct broadcast satellites—have been reinvented, given an African "accent," and put to the service of Africans. These developments are just a decade old, but ten years is a very long time in this age of revolutionary change in information and communication technology. Therefore, it is not premature to look for signs of the reinvention and adaptation of these innovations to African realities.

Putting an African Touch on "New" Distribution Technologies

With the liberalization of telecommunications and mass communication, African entrepreneurs introduced new technologies to the continent. Indeed, African entrepreneurs, sometimes with the assistance of non-African partners, have pioneered novel program delivery systems that have seen little or no use anywhere else in the world. Again, these "new" technologies include the encrypted low-power terrestrial broadcasting and microwave multipoint distribution systems that have been introduced in several African cities (Paterson 1998). MMDS, sometimes mistakenly called "wireless cable," uses special high-frequency transmitters to broadcast several television channels to subscribers. This technology goes back to the first subscription television service (STV) that was started in the United States in 1966. Multipoint distribution systems were authorized in the United States in 1983; however, MMDS suffered a precipitous decline as cable penetration soon exploded there (Straubhaar and LaRose 2000). In Africa, where cable is virtually nonexistent, this older and cheaper technology is now the rage. Thanks to digital compression technology, it is used by many private commercial broadcasters. While some multipoint distribution services operate on a subscription basis, many others opt not to encrypt this traditional pay-per-view content in order to sell commercial time to local and international advertisers (Paterson 1998). This novel combination of technology and business strategy provides some evidence that Africa is in the process of putting its own stamp on the television distribution industry.

Commercial Entertainment Content Production

At first glance, one cannot escape the impression that African viewers are inundated by imported programming of all kinds. Indeed, the television explosion in Africa has led to some interesting forms of broadcasting. The postapartheid South African Broadcasting Corporation (SABC) is a statutory corporation that operates radio stations at the national, regional, and ethnic or tribal levels. The SABC is the largest statutory public service broadcaster in Africa. It is an interesting public/private "mixed media economy" organization. It has a high degree of autonomy and earns three-quarters of its revenue from advertising and corporate underwriting. The rest of its revenue comes from license fees on radio and television sets, as well as government subsidies. The radio stations of the SABC provide national, regional, and local programming in English, Afrikaans, and many local African languages. Indeed, the Independent Broadcast Authority, which oversees the SABC, is considering local content quotas on its radio stations. Unlike most public service broadcasters around the world, however, the stations of the SABC are fueled by advertising. The corporation also rebroadcasts the pay-TV programming of M-NET, a private news and entertainment company that broadcasts mostly foreign programming and runs a direct broadcast satellite subscription service. The SABC has clearly helped reinvent public service broadcasting; indeed, a number of other African public service broadcasters now own subscription broadcasting companies. In Zimbabwe, for example, the state-owned public service broadcaster, the Zimbabwe Broadcasting Corporation, leases three of four government channels during prime time to private commercial broadcasters for a monthly fee (Paterson 1998).

Local Program Production: "Juju" Video in Nigeria

Since imported commercial entertainment has flooded Africa's television screens, it is necessary to explore the state of local TV programming. For decades, Africa's public service broadcasters produced and exchanged only a modest amount of African programming—even though African programs have always been more popular with African audiences than imported shows (Eko 2001). This illustrates the so-called cultural proximity perspective, which holds that television viewers prefer, whenever possible, to watch programming that reflects their language, culture, and values (Straubhaar and LaRose 2000). An interesting experience that took place in Nairobi, Kenya, in the 1980s reinforces this point. The film *Love Brewed in an African Pot,* by Ghanian producer Kwaw Ansah, was so popular that 20th Century Fox, a competing vendor, requested that it be withdrawn from exhibition for some time in order to allow Africans to see the James Bond movie *For Your Eyes Only* (Silla 1994). Other African films—including one about the life of Ugandan dictator Idi Amin Dada—easily outdrew American, European, Indian, and Chinese films in African movie theaters. This pattern of preference for African films (few as they may be) over imported films has been exploited very successfully in Nigeria. There, a new cultural form has evolved, taking advantage of cultural proximity as well as newer, cheaper video production, digital graphics, special effects, and editing technologies. Indeed, Nigeria has given the world a new TV horror genre cult, "juju video" (the word *juju* means "magic" or "supernatural" in Yoruba, a West African language). Based on a strong foundation of early African theater pioneered by the Nigerian Television Authority, juju video is the quintessential example of the Africanization of television content. Small-scale video producers, seeking to fill the void that existed in Nigeria's handful of movie theaters and television stations, started the genre. Over the years, juju video has developed into a booming homegrown video production industry that has, with the support of local entrepreneurs and sponsors, drawn from Nigeria's rich African oral culture and village theater tradition. The stock-in-trade of juju video is computer-generated special effects that highlight stories of evil sects, black magic, witchcraft, African gods and goddesses, disappearing sexual organs, ritual sacrifice, bad children being transformed into animals, greed, corruption, and spiritual punishment (Servant 2001).

Juju video, which is mostly produced in Pidgin English, is also produced in African languages like Igbo, Yourba, and Hausa, and subtitled in English, French, or Pidgin. The typical movie, a mélange of computer graphics, Western cult horror film traditions, and the African occult, is almost always accompanied by the danceable, polyrhythmic juju music pioneered by King

Sunny Ade and other Nigerian musicians. According to the Nigerian Film and Video Censors Board, 1,080 video productions have been produced and submitted to the board since 1997. In the year 2000 alone, 650 movies were produced in Nigeria; some of them sold more than 300,000 copies on video-cassette. Production costs for each movie range from $10,000 to $50,000. Members of the Independent Television Producers' Association of Nigeria seek out local investors for video projects and distribute productions across Africa through formal and informal trading channels (Servant 2001). Indeed, Nigeria is a notable exception to the general domination of African television by imported commercial entertainment. Private enterprise broadcasters in that country carry far less imported programming than elsewhere on the continent (Ogundimu 1996).

Public Service Radio As the New "Palaver Tree of the Air"

Public service broadcasting has also been reinvented in Africa. With the advent of private commercial and noncommercial independent stations, radio shows signs of being Africanized and localized anew. Some stations have been very successful with local programming that is both consistent with traditional cultural practices and relevant to contemporary audiences. Many private radio stations are going back to their local communities and taking over the role of the traditional palaver tree, under which villagers discussed issues and settled disputes. Some radio stations serve as open forums in which villagers gather to discuss issues of interest and participate in storytelling (Mhlophe 1996). Some West African palaver radio shows replicate real-life village situations; for example, hosts and guests use multiple languages and switch dialects in the course of the program. Sometimes, language itself becomes the topic of discussion (Senghor 1996). The "palaver tree of the air" is Africa's answer to talk radio. Through local "culturetainment," radio promotes cultural diversity, records and enriches African cultures, and increases ratings. This is a case of commercial radio doing what was never thought possible or feasible—giving voice to the voiceless segment of African societies. Not surprisingly, this type of local grassroots programming is shunned by some newly launched urban commercial broadcasting stations, which increasingly opt for easy Western and African pop music formats (Zulu 1996).

Conclusion

African broadcasting is at the crossroads. In the face of fierce competition, state-owned and statutory public service broadcasters must decide whether to continue being of service to all citizens by producing and broadcasting commercially nonviable programming or to become "niche" broadcasters who specialize themselves into oblivion. As a result of the dramatic political changes that have taken place since the 1990s, African broadcasting is in a state of flux characterized by a complex combination of funding, ownership, and content parameters. In most African countries, public service broadcasting has become an interesting mix of commercial and noncommercial enterprise that produces commercial entertainment programs as well as traditional public interest fare. The key ingredients in this mix are freedom and independence. If public service broadcasters have freedom from undue political and commercial pressures, as well as the independence necessary to make tough decisions, their industry could well be a winning proposition.

The diffusion of commercial broadcasting in Africa has not followed the normal curve of adoption; indeed, the rapid spread of commercial broadcasting has compressed and abbreviated normal adoption patterns and processes. As a result, African countries have been obliged by the forces of globalization to liberalize and/or privatize their broadcasting systems. They have often done so without the luxury of adequate time to conceptualize, define, adopt, and evaluate policies that spell out the role of commercial broadcasting within their political, economic, cultural, and social systems. What does this state of affairs portend for the future of African public service broadcasters? In short, they face the same major challenge that public service broadcasters now struggle with around the world. They have to reinvent themselves and adapt to the changing broadcast environment or risk becoming irrelevant. As managers of extensive networks that none of the new commercial broadcasters can match, they should welcome healthy competition as a force that keeps them from sinking into complacency.

References

Ainslie, R. 1966. *The Press in Africa: Communications Past and Present*. London: Victor Gollancz.

Bamyeh, M. 2000. *The Ends of Globalization*. Minneapolis: University of Minnesota Press.

Buhrer, J-C. 2000. "Le BIT souligne l'enjeu d'internet pour les pays en développement" (The ILO stresses the Internet challenge for developing countries). *Le Monde*, March 1, 1.

Defleur, M., and E. Dennis. 2002. *Understanding Mass Communication: A Liberal Arts Perspective*. Boston: Houghton Mifflin.

Dizard, W. 2000. Old Media, *New Media: Mass Communication in the Information Age*. New York: Addison Wesley Longman.

Eko, L. 2001. "Steps Toward Pan-African Exchange, Translation and Distribution of Television Programs Across Africa's Linguistic Regions." *Journal of Black Studies* 31: 365–379.

Giffard, C., A. De Beer, and E. Steyn. 1997. "New Media for the New South Africa." In *Press Freedom and Communication in Africa*, ed. F. Eribo and W. Jong-Ebot. Trenton, NJ: Africa World Press, 75–99.

Grubler, A. 1996. "Time for a Change: On the Patterns of Diffusion of Innovation." *Daedalus* 125: 19–43.

Hassan, S. 1996. "The Modernist Experience in African Art: Toward a Critical Understanding." In *The Muse of Modernity: Essays on Culture As Development in Africa*, ed. P.G. Altbach and S. Hassan. Trenton, NJ: Africa World Press, 37–61.

Hiebert, R., and S. Gibbons. 2000. *Exploring Mass Media for a Changing World.* Mahwah, NJ: Lawrence Erlbaum.

Ihonvbere, J. 1997. "Democratization in Africa." *Peace Review* 9: 371–378.

ITU. 2000. "World Radiocommunication Conference Concludes on Series of Far-Reaching Agreements." www.Itu.int/Newsroom/Press/Releases/2000/13.html (October 10, 2001).

Kerr, D. 1995. "African Broadcasting Pioneers and the Origins of Radio Drama in Central African Broadcasting Services." *Critical Arts* 9: 30–42.

Kinnunen, J. 1996. "Gabriel Tarde as a Founding Father of Innovation Diffusion Research." *Acta Sociologica* 39, 430–442.

Lowery, S., and D. Defleur. 1995. *Milestones in Mass Communication Research.* 3d ed. White Plains, NY: Longman.

Mazrui, A. 1996. "Perspective: The Muse of Modernity and the Quest for Development." In *The Muse of Modernity: Essays on Culture as Development in Africa*, ed. P.G. Altbach and S. Hassan. Trenton, NJ: Africa World Press, 1–18.

Mhlophe, G. 1996. "Storytelling, A Part of Our Heritage." In *The Muse of Modernity: Essays on Culture as Development in Africa*, ed. P.G. Altbach and S. Hassan. Trenton, NJ: Africa World Press, 109–115.

Monga, C. 1996. *The Anthropology of Anger: Civil Society and Democracy in Africa.* Boulder, CO: Lynne Rienner.

Ogundimu, F. 1996. "Private-Enterprise Broadcasting and Accelerating Dependency: Case Studies from Nigeria and Uganda." *Gazette* 58: 159–172.

Paterson, C. 1998. "Reform or Re-Colonization? The Overhaul of African Television." *Review of African Political Economy* 2: 571–584.

Pemberton, H. 1936. "The Curve of Cultural Diffusion Rate." *American Sociological Review* 1: 547.

Promoting Independent Broadcasting in Africa Act. 1998. H. Res. 415, 105th Cong., 2d sess., 144 Cong. Rec. H7655.

Rogers, E. 1983. *Diffusion of Innovations*, 3d ed. New York: Free Press.

Ryan, B., and N. Gross. 1943. "The Diffusion of Hybrid Seed Corn in Two Iowa Communities." *Rural Sociology* 8: 15.

Schramm, W. 1964. *The Mass Media and National Development.* Stanford, CA: Stanford University Press.

Schumpeter, J. 1939. *Business Cycles: A Theoretical, Historical, and Statistical Analysis of the Capitalist Process.* New York: McGraw-Hill.

Senghor, D. 1996. "Radio Stations in Africa, Issues of Democracy and Culture." In *The Muse of Modernity: Essays on Culture as Development in Africa*, ed. P.G. Altbach and S. Hassan. Trenton, NJ: Africa World Press, 79–108.

Servant, J.-C. 2001. "Boom de Vidéo domestique au Nigeria" (Home video boom in Nigeria). *Le Monde Diplomatique* (February): 6.

Silla, M. 1994. *Le paria du village planetaire ou l'Afrique à l?Heure de la télévision mondiale* (The pariah of the planetary village or Africa in the era of global television). Dakar, Senegal: Nouvelles Editions Africaines du Senegal, 1994.

Straubhaar, J., and R. LaRose. 2000. *Media Now: Communications Media in the Information Age.* Belmont, CA: Wadsworth.

Tarde, G. [1903] 1962. *The Laws of Imitation.* Gloucester, MA: Peter Smith/Holt.

United Nations. 1958. General Assembly Committee on Information from Non-Self-governing Territories: Social Conditions in Non-Self-governing Territories A/AC/35/SR.180.

Zulu, B. 1996. "Rebuilding Africa Through Film Video and Television." In *The Muse of Modernity: Essays on Culture as Development in Africa*, ed. P.G. Altbach and S. Hassan. Trenton, NJ: Africa World Press, 63–78.

17

Canadians Connected and Unplugged

Public Access to the Internet and the Digital Divide

Vanda Rideout

This chapter focuses on Canadian public interest in, and access to, the Internet. The first section provides an overview of the federal government's role in creating an information society. Section two discusses inequalities arising out of the information society, or what is commonly referred to as the *digital divide*. The final section examines two government programs that provide public access to the Internet as a bridging solution for the digital divide.

Building the Information Society

From the 1970s through the 1990s, the Canadian federal government reformed the legislative, policy, and regulatory framework for telecommunications and broadcasting within a neoliberal policy framework. Those steps facilitated the introduction of new communication services and paved the way for the convergence of cable, telecommunications, and other media systems. It was in the 1990s, however, that the government of Canada extended these initiatives by furthering the neoliberal policy model to lay the groundwork for an information society and a knowledge economy.

The general theme guiding the information society policy framework and programs can be found in the 1997 government's Speech from the Throne. In that speech, the government promised, "to make Canada the most connected country in the world" and a "world leader in development and use of advanced information and communication technologies" (Speech from the

Throne 1997). This commitment was seen as an important move to help realize economic growth and competitiveness, both domestically and internationally (Industry Canada 1996, 2).

The federal government had previously discussed the need to develop and implement a strategy for an information highway. This strategy—the outcome of interdepartmental activity involving the Departments of Industry Canada, Canadian Heritage, and Human Resources Development Canada, as well as other federal departments and agencies—was spelled out in the report *Building the Information Society: Moving Canada into the 21st Century* (Industry Canada 1996). Essentially, the report points out the initiatives and policy recommendations needed to facilitate the country's transition to an information/knowledge economy. According to the report, more jobs would be created as a result of increased innovation. Cultural identity and sovereignty would also be reinforced, and universal access to the new information highway, a "network of networks," would be available to all Canadians at a reasonable cost.

Under the lead of the Department of Industry Canada, the information highway initiative took shape when the Information Highway Advisory Council (IHAC) was created. The framework guiding IHAC and the other federal departments centered on issues such as access, lifelong learning, the linking of jobs to innovation, government services online, and increased competitiveness and economic growth. The first IHAC report, *Connection, Community, Content: The Challenge of the Information Highway* (1995), was criticized because of the elite makeup of the advisory board and its recommendation that the development and operation of the information highway be left to the private sector. With a need to address unresolved issues and to accommodate the exclusionary aspect of the first IHAC report, the council was reconvened. The initial IHAC process was exclusionary because consumer groups, community representatives, and public interest organizations were not invited to participate. The second and final IHAC (II) report, *Preparing Canada for a Digital World* (1997), responded to the previous criticisms by including a number of organizations and groups representing the public interest, consumers, communities, and other activists. This final IHAC report discusses the importance of developing an electronic network for all Canadians, promising "to meet their individual and collective goals—whether these be economic, social or cultural". According to the report, the best way to achieve these goals would be to embrace the latest communication and information technologies, a view that is also held by proponents of the information society revolution (Castells 1996; Carincross 1997; Pool 1983; Negroponte 1995; Rheingold 1993).

Together, both IHAC reports advance the idea of a utopian, wired future that would eliminate geographic obstacles and help in the renewal of local communities and regional economies. Dan Schiller skeptically describes this idea as the "Internet as salvation" viewpoint (1999, xiii). Nonetheless, IHAC II recommendations do reflect the outcome of a broader consultation process that included some community and public interest groups and organizations. These recommendations include government funding for community access initiatives, including libraries, schools and not-for-profit community networks and sites; government funding to develop public and noncommercial content; and the availability of government information and services in both electronic and traditional formats (IHAC 1997). An interview with a federal civil servant who wanted to remain anonymous revealed the presence of three competing strategies (Personal interview 2000). The first was to establish the more public IHAC Council. The second was a National Access Strategy spearheaded by Industry Canada and the Department of Heritage. The third was the Connecting Canadians Strategy that Industry Canada had been working on at the same time that IHAC was under way. The Connecting Canadians agenda offers an extensive menu that ranges from electronic commerce (e-commerce) and government online (e-government) to access to the Internet from public schools, libraries, and communities. In other words, Canadians would benefit from better jobs and educational improvements by taking part in an integrated wired society. Having access to the Internet would also eliminate geographical barriers regardless of where in the country one lives.

Support for the Connecting Canadians agenda has been widespread among communities, public interest groups, nongovernment organizations, and academics because of the hope and belief that being wired to the Internet provides a window of opportunity for democratic and progressive input. It is important to keep in mind, however, that this so-called new society and economy bears a strong resemblance to the old industrial one. Other perspectives on the information society see what is taking place as a deepening and extension of global capitalism, including the production of information, communication, and media goods and services (Mosco 1999; Robins and Webster 1999; H. Schiller 1986; D. Schiller 1999). This further extension of capitalist relations exacerbates existing inequalities while also creating additional ones.

The Canadian Digital Divide

There is little doubt that the information society offers a cornucopia of new information, entertainment, and financial and economic services through wire-based, terrestrial wireless, and satellite technologies, home communication services, and Internet access. Access, equality, and universality are important requirements for full citizen participation in an information society. But these services are not available to everyone. The use of these new technologies and services, and the developing patterns of awareness, indicate that many Canadians are not, and will not be, able to fully participate in an information society.

Information society inequalities at the national level in Canada are being tracked by Statistics Canada, Ekos Research Associates, and the Public Interest Advocacy Center, among others. Their findings are similar to those in the *Falling Through the Net* series from the U.S. Department of Commerce (U.S. Department of Commerce 1995, 1998, 1999). For example, research conducted by Statistics Canada and Ekos Research Associates (1998, 2000) shows differences in household access to the Internet, which demonstrate inequality that is based on income, education, geography, gender, and age. It is important to keep in mind, however, that these differences in access are not unique to the Internet. Beyond household computers and Internet service, differences in levels of access and availability also exist in other communication technologies, such as cable television and telephone services. Increasingly, those Canadians who have cable television and telephone services do not necessarily find them affordable. Many Canadians on fixed and low incomes take great pains to keep telephone services because they consider them necessary and essential (Rideout, forthcoming 2003).

These class differences come to the fore when we realize that higher-income households are three times more likely than lower- and lower-middle-income households to have home Internet access. *The Information Highway and Canadian Communication Household* (Ekos Research Associates 1998) research indicates that although overall access to the Internet from home has significantly increased, most of the growth has occurred in the upper-middle- and upper-income groups. Lower-income (83 percent) and lower-middle-income (79 percent) households still have no access from home and continue to lag in the digital divide (Reddick 2000, 18). Technological inequality also affects disabled people, women, and aboriginal peoples. Moreover, people who live in upscale urban areas have access to better information highway and communications services than do rural or inner-city core dwellers, revealing that geography still matters as well (Mosco 1999, 40).

Statistics Canada research documents a growing gap between information "haves" and "have nots." Research in the United States by National Telecommunications and Information Administration (NTIA), Ekos Research Associates, and the Public Interest Advocacy Centre describe these inequalities as a *digital divide*. Although Internet penetration rates in Canada have increased across income quartiles, education levels, geographic locations, and age groups, the gap between the top and bottom income groups widened by 7 percent from 1996 to 1997 (Ekos Research Associates 1998).

The Dual Digital Divide: The Information Highway in Canada by Andrew Reddick sheds more light on the digital divide, explaining it as a complex phenomenon that is widening in scope. According to Reddick, the terms
"haves" and "have nots" represent "a pejorative view of first and second
class information society citizens" (2000, 7). Statistics Canada, Ekos Research Associates, and Reddick all agree that the first divide occurs between
users and nonusers. But according to Reddick, a second divide is evident in
the nonusers. For example, when households were asked why they did not
have home Internet access, a split occurred between people who said they
couldn't afford access, on the one hand, and an equal number of people who
saw no value or purpose in the Internet. This explanation of the emerging
pattern of Internet access and use is what Reddick calls a "dual digital divide" (2000, 44). It is this second group of nonusers that raises major policy
concerns regarding barriers to access, diversity in the means of access, literacy, the capacity to use the technology, and cost. Members of this subgroup also demonstrate a lack of understanding or appreciation regarding
the potential benefits and possible uses of the Internet by promoters and elite
information users, such as academics, governments, and industries.

A profile of Internet users based on a number of demographic characteristics provides a more detailed picture of who is lagging behind in the digital
divide. From June 1998 to July 1999, the growth rate of Internet use among
women was almost twice as large as among men. Higher rates of Internet use
are evident in those who are twenty-five years of age or less, earn an income
of $60,000 or more, and have a university education. Yet, despite the in-
creases in Internet use in the past two years, the digital divide still affects
people who are female, have low income, are over the age of sixty-five, have
lower levels of education, or live in rural and remote areas (Figure 17.1).

Public Internet Access Programs

While, in varying degrees, all federal government departments are involved
in the achievement of public Internet access, the two departments that have
been most active in addressing social information highway use are Industry
Canada (IC) and Human Resources Development Canada (HRDC). HRDC's
major access program, which operates through its Office of Learning Technology, is called the Community Learning Network (CLN). The aim of the
CLN is to provide multipoint access within and across communities to foster
formal and informal technology-based learning content. As such, the program targets HRDC equity groups, including aboriginals, the disabled, seniors, and marginalized communities.

Industry Canada undertakes a number of initiatives through the Informa-

Figure 17.1 **Percentage of Canadians Using the Internet in the Past Three Months**

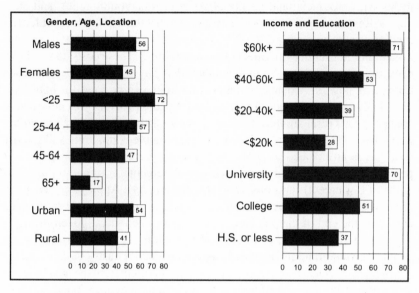

Source: Ekos Research Associates, Inc., June 1998.

tion Highway Application Branch to address different dimensions of the information highway agenda. These initiatives include the Community Access Program (CAP), SchoolNet, First Nations SchoolNet, Computers in the Schools, and VolNet, which are all part of the larger Connecting Canadians program. The Community Access Program is the one that is most centrally concerned with local public access to the information highway via the Internet. The program's mandate is to establish 10,000 access sites to the Internet in both rural and urban areas throughout the country. It is interesting to note that, originally, CAP was to be a joint HRDC/IC program. However, it was the Department of Industry that once again seized the day by introducing an access program before any other department, which, it could be argued, led to a splintering of departmental initiatives on public access within the federal government.

Community Access Program

Created in 1995, CAP provides not-for-profit organizations such as educational institutions, public libraries, community centers, community freenets, and municipal and territorial governments with funding for Internet connectivity (Industry Canada 1996, 2000, 2002). Maximum funding can reach $30,000, but is usually less as a result of the program's partnership arrangements with provincial and territorial governments, communities, and businesses. Responses from CAPs to date indicate that the average level of federal funding is approximately $25,000. The program covers the cost of computers, an Internet service provider (ISP), and training. These costs do not, however, take into account volunteer labor that has been provided to teach Canadians how electronic communication links can be used for both individual and community development. Initially, the program was designed to connect 1,000 rural and remote sites; in point of fact, it has established approximately 5,000 centers in 3,200 rural and remote communities. Primarily rural CAPs are located in public libraries (46 percent), public schools (28 percent), municipal government facilities (8 percent), community-based facilities (13 percent), and business sites (5 percent). Approximately 3,800 urban sites were also established in similar public locations (Industry Canada 2002). At the end of the public access program, the federal government anticipates that it will have invested $196 million in these sites. The program requires a Memorandum of Understanding between Industry Canada and the relevant provincial and territorial governments. Partners from the private sector also provide in-kind contributions, such as telecommunication services or donated equipment. It is important to point out, however, that private contributions at the community level have been minor, with the lion's share of CAP funding coming from government sources (Rideout 2001).

Organizations representing seniors and low-income, rural, and consumer organizations, such as the Public Interest Advocacy Center (PIAC), have recommended that the federal government provide one-half of the overall cost for integrated services in each community. PIAC estimated that the cost would be $31 million, or $125,000 for each community, using a base of 250 integrated community access organizations. It is estimated that the average cost for an integrated advanced community service would be $250,000 per year, with exceptions for rural and remote services requiring separate funding. Recommendations have been made for federal support that could be delivered in the form of a yearly contract, with a specific set of deliverables (Reddick 1998, 61–67).

Being able to access the Internet from a number of public sites such as a CAP, a school, a library, or any other public service location is particularly important for low-income Canadians, as Figure 17.2 indicates. Reddick's research indicates that the greatest divide on the information highway is class- or income-based (2000, 47). Cost barriers to accessing the Internet are multidimensional. Moreover, cost barriers need to be considered in a context wider than that of online services. The most obvious costs for individual

Figure 17. 2 **Where Did You Use an Internet Account in the Past Three Months?** (N = 1,380)

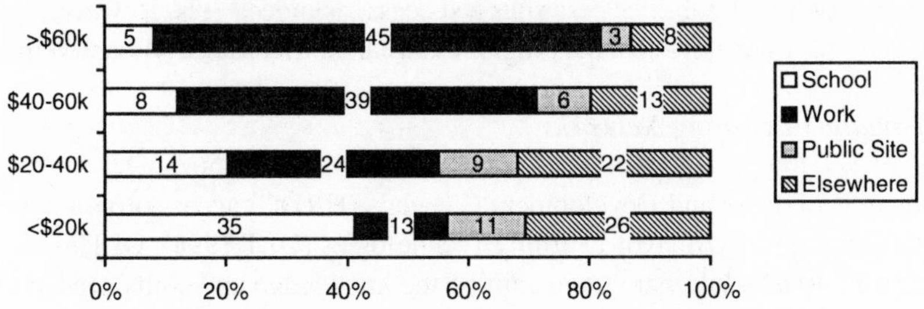

Source: Ekos Research Associates, Inc., 1998.

households include computer hardware, television boxes for Internet/Web connections, software, and monthly ISP charges. Evidence in Ekos Research Associates' *The Information Highway and the Canadian Household* (1998) and *Rethinking Government* (1995) also shows that the cost of a personal computer, when combined with monthly ISP charges, is beyond the budget for many middle- and lower-income households, when compared to upper-income households.

The information that is being searched for on the Internet tells us more about the social needs of low-income Canadians (Ekos 1998). By providing public access to the Internet, CAP does provide a mechanism for eliminating some social barriers for people interested in participating in the information/knowledge society. For example, the 20 percent of low-income users who use these sites do so to conduct job searches and obtain library, education, health, and community information. This indicates the importance of Internet policies that foster technological access and take social context and specific community needs into consideration.

However, a number of problems and uncertainties are evident in the program. The program's focus has been on technical access, computers and connections, to the exclusion of human social needs; for example, job training, useful information, literacy programs, and other community service programs. Another major problem is the limited life of the program. The rural CAP ended March 31, 2000, and was followed by the end of the urban program on March 31, 2001. Without long-term, sustainable funding, CAP may accomplish little more than the raising of expectations and hopes for community access to the Internet. Finally, an independent evaluation of the program has been conducted, but the findings have not been made available to the public. Questions still remain about the public availability of the internal government audit and the number of access sites still in use; considering the cost of the program to Canadian taxpayers, some form of external analysis would be prudent. No doubt, the Department of Industry Canada considers the establishment of 8,800 public access sites a success, as indeed it is. However, the big, looming question about the program's sustainability remains unanswered.

Community Learning Networks

Human Resources and Development Canada's (HRDC) access program operates through its Office of Learning Technologies (OLT 1998). OLT's mandate is to assist adult learners in gaining the knowledge and skills needed to meet the demands of an information-based economy. In 1999, OLT's mandate was expanded to support lifelong learning, with funding valued at $30 million through the Community Learning Network (CLN) pilot project. Individual projects receive $25,000 for the development phase. Successful CLN pilots may receive from 50 percent of the cost of the project up to $250,000 for a three-year effort to develop informal learning or group learning networks (outside of institutional settings). A key element of each CLN is the building of a geographic networked community, or community of interest, that responds to organizational and/or individual learning needs. The program targets youth, literacy, skills and training, and community and individual development—all parts of OLT's lifelong learning philosophy. Community Learning Networks are intended to rely on existing technology and networks at libraries, schools, service agencies, or CAP sites. The CLN program also encourages partnerships with other not-for-profit organizations as long as they serve local, regional, or national communities of interest. Full projects are evaluated by a panel of nongovernment personnel, using the CLN assessment criteria spelled out in the guidelines for application. By the end of December 2001, OLT had approved seventy-nine CLN applications (Mastin 2002).

As previously stated, the primary goal of CLNs is to facilitate learning, training, networking, and community development and control at the local level. Project sponsors are expected to have an established track record in developing or delivering community-based, technology-assisted learning opportunities. Partnerships may be formed with the voluntary sector, cooperatives, sector councils, band or tribal councils, labor or professional associations, provincial governments, municipal governments, libraries, schools, or federal departments or agencies. Emerging community network models reveal that community-based initiatives would probably not have taken place without such established locally based partnerships built around the sharing of resources and common goals. Communities have found it imperative to mobilize and reorganize themselves to respond to changing economic forces and to take advantage of potential opportunities resulting from information highway technologies. In many cases, this urgency to "be connected" can be found in the interest generated in Canadian rural and remote communities as they organize to develop economic options. It can also be found in the social and cultural criteria that permit citizens to continue to live and work in their home communities (Rideout 2000, 15–17). Many of these communities have relied on a single industry for their economic and social existence, such as forestry, mining, fishing, or agriculture. As these industries move or downsize, or their resources become depleted, many local citizens have few options, aside from moving to larger urban centers in search of work.

Often, community learning networks place importance on locally produced content and information. People want access to public service and community information that is free or, at the very least, affordable. Essential information that meets citizen and community needs may not have any commercial value, but it does have social and cultural value. As previously discussed, the cost for use can be an impediment for irregular users. Other impediments are evident for those people who have literacy problems or low education levels or who simply fear the technology. While there has been growth in Internet access from home, particularly for upper-income Canadians, the digital divide is widening at the same time for lower-income Canadians. In June 1998, for example, there was a 5 percent difference in the incidence of Internet access between lower- and lower-middle-income households; by January 2000, the difference had grown to 14 percent. Furthermore, the spread between upper- and lower-income households increased from 27 percent to 44 percent. This indicates the importance of public access sites in bridging the digital divide for those who currently desire access but can't afford it, and also for those who do not have home access, but might become occasional users in the future.

One of the major differences between CLN and CAP is that the former is social needs-based, while the latter focuses on access to technology and a network. Also, community stakeholders are more involved in the development and control of CLNs. Despite these benefits, however, the CLN program is not without its problems and uncertainties. The strong emphasis on community partnering requires the cooperation of a number of community groups and organizations that may not have similar views on the development and direction of a CLN. Second, the CLN application form requires a high level of expertise and sophistication to complete. Consequently, some of the marginal communities the program is attempting to reach may not bother to apply, due to a lack of human and community resources. Unlike the CAP, however, it appears that the CLN pilot program does not have a specific end date. What we do know is that initial funding for the first three years of the pilot was budgeted at $30 million.

Conclusion

At this stage, it is still too early to tell whether public access programs will bridge the Canadian digital divide. Both programs for public access to the Internet (CAP and CLN) may be inadvertently creating demand and reliance, along with a sense of urgency to be connected to the Internet. Important questions need to be addressed about these public access programs: What happens if sustainable funding is impossible to achieve at the community level? What will happen to the connected communities if long-term sustainable government funding does not occur? What will happen to communities that have to unplug? The major drawback with the national research conducted by Ekos Research Associates, the Public Interest Advocacy Centre, and Statistics Canada is the focus on individual household access to the Internet. In order to understand what is happening in communities, further in-depth research and analysis should be done to evaluate the costs and benefits of public access to the Internet. This will require a research approach that takes into consideration the political, economic, and social relations of both the region and the community. Research needs to identify community partners and organizations, government programs, community social needs, and the benefits and drawbacks of the information society. Community-specific digital divide problems need to be identified. Finally, government access programs need to be scrutinized to see if they do overcome digital divide problems in the short as well as the long term.

References

Carincross, F. 1997. *The Death of Distance.* Cambridge, MA: Harvard Business School.

Castells, M. 1996. *The Rise of the Network Society.* Vol. 1 of *The Information Age: Economy, Society and Culture.* Oxford, UK: Blackwell.

Ekos Research Associates. 1995. *Rethinking Government.* Ottawa: Ekos Research Associates.

———. 1998. *The Information Highway and the Canadian Household.* Ottawa: Ekos Research Associates, Inc.

———. 2000. *Rethinking the Information Highway: Privacy, Access and the Shifting Market Place.* Ottawa: Ekos Research Associates.

Industry Canada. 1996. *Building the Information Society: Moving Canada into the 21st Century.* Ottawa: Ministry of Supply and Services. info.ic.gc.ca/info-hghway/ih.html.

———. 2002. Information Highway Application Branch, e-mail correspondence with S. Armstrong, February 11.

Information Highway Advisory Council. 1995. *Connection, Community, Content: The Challenge of the Information Highway.* Ottawa: Information Highway Advisory Council.

————. 1997. *Preparing Canada for a Digital World.* The Final Report of The Information Highway Advisory Council. Ottawa: Information Highway Advisory Council.

Mastin, R. 2002. Personal interview by author. Hull, Quebec. January 22.

Mosco, V. 1999. "Place Matters: Citizenship and the New Computer Technopolis." In *The Communication Revolution at Work: The Social, Economic and Political Impacts of Technological Change,* ed. R. Boyce. Montreal and Kingston: McGill-Queen's University Press, 39–56.

Negroponte, N. 1995. *Being Digital.* New York: Knopf.

Office of Learning Technologies. 1998. Community Learning Networks (CLN) Initiative: Guidelines for Application. www.olt-bta.hrdc-drhc.gc.ca/CLN/cinguide_e.html.

Personal interview by author of a federal civil servant who wished to remain anonymous. 2000. Ottawa, Ontario. October.

Pool, I. 1983. *Technologies of Freedom.* Cambridge, MA: Belknap Press.

Reddick, A. 1998. *Community Networking and Access Initiatives in Canada.* Ottawa: Public Interest Advocacy Centre.

————. 2000. *The Dual Digital Divide: The Information Highway in Canada.* Ottawa: Public Interest Advocacy Centre.

Rheingold, H. 1993. *The Virtual Community.* Reading, MA: Addison-Wesley.

Rideout, V. 2000. "Public Access to the Internet and the Canadian Digital Divide." *Canadian Journal of Information and Library Sciences* 25 (nos. 2/3): 1–21.

————. 2001. "Overcoming the Digital Divide in Atlantic Canada Communities." Paper prepared for the Canadian Communication Association Annual Conference, May 27–29.

————. 2003. *Continentalising Canadian Telecommunications: The Politics of Regulatory Reform.* Montreal: McGill-Queen's University Press.

Robins, K., and F. Webster. 1999. *Times of the Technoculture: Information, Communication and the Technological Order.* London and New York: Routledge.

Schiller, D. 1999. *Digital-Capitalism: Networking the Global Market System.* Cambridge, MA: MIT Press.

Schiller, H. 1986. *Information and the Crisis Economy.* New York and Oxford: Oxford University Press.

Speech from the Throne to open the first session of the thirty-sixth Parliament of Canada. 1997. September 23. www.pco-bcp.gc.ca/throne97/throne_e.html.

U.S. Department of Commerce, National Telecommunications and Information Administration (NTIA). 1999. *Falling Through the Net: Defining the Digital Divide.* www.ntia.doc.gov.ntiahome/ftn99/contents.html.

————. 1998. *Falling Through the Net II: New Data on the Digital Divide.* www.ntia.doc.gov/ntiahome/net2/.

————. 1995. *Falling Through the Net: A Survey of "Have Nots" in Rural and Urban America.* http://www.ntia.doc.gov/ntiahome/fallingthru.html.

Part IV

Where Do We Go from Here:
Civic Space, Cyber Market, Public Trust,
or Grassroots Alternatives?

18

Introduction

DeeDee Halleck

The chapters in this section of the book explore five distinct directions for public media. Though each author explores a specific pathway for serving a variety of publics through electronic means, one common thread runs throughout: in a highly competitive market environment, sustaining a space and infrastructure for noncommercial public interest media is a daunting task.

Barry Dornfeld's chapter, Social Capital, Civic Space, and the Digital Revolution, is a case study of WHYY, an organization with public radio and television stations that serve the Philadelphia area, including Camden, New Jersey; Wilmington, Delaware; and the Delaware Valley. WHYY-FM's signature production is *Fresh Air* with Terry Gross, a nationally distributed interview radio show that has remained quite popular for more than a decade. On the television side, WHYY has done little in the way of local production, relying instead on Public Broadcasting Service (PBS) feeds of national series for the bulk of its program schedule. Herein lies the dilemma. Many of the programs historically offered on public television have now inspired competing shows on niche-marketed cable networks; for example, upscale historical dramas are now available on Bravo, financial news on MSNBC, and nature documentaries on the Discovery Channel. As a consequence, WHYY, like other public television stations, is finding that its subscriber base is eroding and that federal funds are increasingly hard to get. Enter the consultants, of which Dornfeld was one.

For decades public television stations have been pushed to carry national programs produced by major stations such as WNET (New York), KQED (San Francisco), WGBH (Boston), and KCET (LA). It is ironic that WHYY's consultants recommended, among other things, that the organization focus more of its attention on local concerns. But this makes sense. The one thing public television has that corporate networks do not is a collection of well-equipped studios in major cities across the nation. These studios and other bits of local infrastructure should be made available for the use of interested citizens who live in those same communities. The scenario suggested by WHYY's consultants also includes the identification of other local organizations that might collaborate in media projects. The groups that first came to mind were, of course, those typically associated with public television's upscale audience: a local opera company and a museum that was showing an Eakins retrospective. The corporate mind-set at WHYY still focuses on the attraction of an elite audience. But what about those citizens who are so often described in the rhetoric of public broadcasters' mission statements, including minorities, women, and ethnic communities? It is a bit of a leap to expect that WHYY, or any PBS affiliate, will become a melting pot of civic space by bringing "the rabble" into the fortress.

Actually this sort of melting pot is already available in many communities through public access cable channels. The many media centers that have been built around the nation through the franchise requirements placed on cable companies create civic space where a wide variety of users can share the benefits of media technology. At present, Philadelphia does not have a public access facility, though several local organizations are trying to establish one. I doubt that this is what WHYY's consultants had in mind, but perhaps an *authentic* civic strategy might take successful public access projects in other cities as its model.

The consultants also suggested an internal reorganization in which WHYY's radio, TV, and Web operations would be brought into the service of one synergistic content-based portal. It is small wonder that this idea has run into resistance from some of WHYY's radio staff; considering the success of *Fresh Air,* these people probably feel that a multimedia portal approach would allow the company's television operations to become too dominant. There is an ocean of difference between the cultures of radio and television, and efforts to bridge the two worlds may prove quite difficult.

The notion of "portals" is tied to the speculative dreams of e-commerce, dreams from which many people have already been rudely awakened. Dreams with Internet themes are sometimes even shared by activists, who have praised the potential of cross-geographic connectivity and rapid information distribution for organizing, especially in the antiglobalization movement. The chapter by Sandra Smeltzer and Leslie Regan Shade, titled Resisting the Market Model of the Information Highway, looks at the state of Internet organizing in Canada. The authors note that the Internet has served as a "libretto" for protests: passing on slogans, mapping routes for demonstrations, and documenting actions. Begun in Seattle, the Independent Media Center movement has demonstrated the usefulness of computers, video, and digital still photography in focusing attention on activism and justice movements. For example, *indymedia.org* is a global Web site with many city-based links, a site that uses photos, text, audio, and video to chronicle resistance activities from Melbourne to Los Angeles. During the April 2001 Free Trade Agreement of the Americas (FTAA) meeting in Montreal, activists used a variety of Internet tools to post background information and rally support for their actions.

But recent antiterrorist legislation in Canada has made some observers skeptical about the ultimate usefulness of Internet technology for resisting the status quo. Specific fears include the potential for authorities to identify and track radical activity electronically. Smeltzer and Shade outline the many bills and regulations that have sprung up to contain radical possibilities in Canada. One bill would criminalize the act of blocking a bus that carries a conference delegate or some other "protected person." Many civil disobedience tactics involve nonviolent sit-downs to block roads or building entrances, but these tactics may now be defined as terrorist activities thanks to legislation that has been hastily drawn up in the post–September 11 atmosphere. In the end, the authors argue that activists who work against globalization and the increasing marketization of electronic media must maintain a presence both online and on the ground in order to ensure effective mobilization.

Jerold M. Starr's Public Television in the Digital Age is a sobering look at public TV in the United States and the pressures that keep it from developing into a democratic public sphere. When radio first appeared in the early 1900s, even Herbert Hoover extolled its educational potential and decried the possibility that it might one day be used for commercial gain. With the evolution of each new electronic media technology, there are brief utopian moments when the public is told that now—*finally*—we will have a medium that serves the public interest. The latest milestone was the opening up of digital TV channels, an occurrence that, in ideal terms, would herald a new era of better educational and cultural programming, not to mention increased public participation. But in one of the biggest giveaways of all time, the FCC ceded new spectrum to all existing TV operators, commercial and noncommercial. Alas, even public television plans to market its digital channels, though technical difficulties and huge conversion expenses have put many specific plans on hold for now. America's recent economic slowdown is also hampering the digital television rollout. It is difficult to convince many people to buy expensive new TV sets when it would be hard to discern major improvements in picture quality without the use of a four-foot screen.

Starr outlines the hypocrisy inherent in PBS's program selection and underwriting policies, which prevent a program on gems funded by DeBeers and a documentary on ceramics funded by Dow-Corning from being perceived as conflicts of interest. On the other hand, a program on gays and lesbians in the workplace with 23 percent of its production costs paid by a union is deemed improper for public television. Corporations prefer programs with innocuous content, not investigative documentaries. The Ken Burns documentaries that have held sway on public TV's prime-time schedule in recent years are not known for their cutting-edge journalism, which is why I suppose that General Motors has been so eager to fund them.

There is also the problem of competition from cable and direct broadcast satellite services. Starr points out that the cooking, exercise, and home and garden shows now available on commercial cable channels are better produced (and get better ratings) than similar PBS programs. He also discusses the window-dressing of local "community advisory boards" and the lack of democracy in the public television system in general. Only two of 350 stations allow subscribers to vote for the board of directors.

Part of the problem with public television can be found in its politically charged funding process. Starr points to a long-standing historical tradition in the United States of extracting fees for use of public resources: oil drillers, lumber companies, and cable operators must all surrender funds in return for their use of public land and infrastructure. Likewise, Starr proposes a trust fund for public media, one that might be funded, in part, by contributions from broadcasting organizations that now pay virtually nothing for their use of the spectrum. Most industrial countries spend more than the United States on public media. In Europe citizens pay between $36 and $136 a year to support public service broadcasting. In the United States we contribute a measly $1 per person per year for public broadcasting. If there was a spectrum fee, proceeds could be put into a trust fund that would generate much larger payouts than those now available through yearly appropriations from Congress. This scenario would also take PBS out of the political arena and thereby allow it to program content that is more controversial and expansive (legislation would also be needed to protect public broadcasting from censorship by state and local politicians). Promising as this idea sounds, I doubt that such a funding scheme would be able to make much of a difference unless fundamental questions of governance are addressed. If PBS affiliates were to renew their commitment to localism, as Barry Dornfeld's chapter suggests, the local governing boards for these stations could become arenas for grassroots reform. Public television board meetings, including most committee meetings, are required by law to be open to the public. Since most people in the United States now feel rather alienated from public television, the prospect of attending meetings may not seem relevant or useful. In the past, however, independent TV producers who were locked out of the public television programming process have, on occasion, made use of these meetings to promote their work. As commercial network fare dumbs down even further and the venues for open expression become fewer, public television boardrooms may once more become active sites of struggle.

If the attention that U.S. citizens pay to public broadcasting has waned, at times, one reason can be found in the development of a lively alternative media sector. In The Grassroots Radio Movement in the United States, Marty Durlin and Cathy Melio provide an insider's view of both grassroots media and the forces that are constantly pressing against them. These pressures sometimes come in the form of consultants like the ones who worked for the Healthy Station Project (HSP), a program funded by the Corporation for Public Broadcasting (CPB). Many community radio stations have been pressured by CPB and its consultants to "professionalize" their often small volunteer staffs. Durlin and Melio view the HSP as an attempt to mainstream and moderate what were often unique, quirky, community-centered stations. The HSP proposed that community radio stations use more content from national sources of program distribution. The authors argue that this suggestion and others have often served to homogenize a station's programming in a way that violates its original commitment to the local community. Many stations were also encouraged to eliminate volunteers, who, ironically, were the lifeblood of many community-based stations. Durlin and Melio strongly support localism and the use of volunteers. They see noncommercial radio stations as ideal training grounds for people who want to produce a diverse collection of programs; not surprisingly, stations that use dedicated volunteers also tend to contribute more powerfully to the civic life of the community. Finally, grassroots stations provide entry-level access to the airwaves for young musicians, who find that radio promotion can generate support for the sale of their cassettes and CDs.

Marty Durlin manages KGNU-FM in Boulder, Colorado, and Cathy Melio works at WERU-FM in East Orland, Maine—the two founding stations of the Grassroots Radio Coalition (GRC). GRC's annual meetings provide a forum for community radio producers, administrators, and volunteers to share experiences and programs. Durlin and Melio speak enthusiastically about the sorts of exchanges that happen at these conferences: dialogue about issues such as community involvement, activism, and accountability. These topics are not usually covered at conferences sponsored by the National Federation of Community Broadcasters, an organization that once persuaded many stations to use the Healthy Station Project to root out local activists and community volunteers.

Grassroots radio people are now at the forefront of one proposal advocated by the WHYY consultants mentioned in Barry Dornfeld's chapter—

the development of synergistic relationships with organizations that use other media technologies. Grassroots stations have been collaborating with Web radio producers and microradio advocates in many parts of the country. Other collaborations have taken place with the alternative press, cable access TV stations, progressive Web sites, and other nonprofit entities. Many stations now stream their programs over the Web from improvised home-built servers. This is the sort of adept technical design that often escapes the abilities of larger, more bureaucratic stations. All of these cooperative efforts have fostered the sort of horizontal distribution that is directly opposed to the top-down hierarchies at National Public Radio (NPR) and PBS. Melio and Durlin demonstrate that consultants from the Healthy Station Project and other like-minded initiatives are miles away from understanding the goals—and appreciating the strengths—of grassroots radio. The audiences that grassroots producers seek are not homogenized masses, but rather collections of people whose voices are often underrepresented or suppressed by mainstream media.

The Pacifica Network is an important model for noncommercial radio. This network, founded after World War II by Lewis Hill, has pioneered many of the programs and formats now popular not only on grassroots radio, but on NPR and commercial radio as well. Pacifica recently experienced a lengthy crisis of governance that was finally resolved in early 2002. Durlin and Melio compare the board and administration that are at the root of many of Pacifica's problems to the staff of the Healthy Station Project. Both tried to clip the wings of radical movements by suggesting program schedules that were decidedly safe and bland. During the recent crisis, grassroots radio stations played a major role in rallying support for banned Pacifica producers, broadcasting their programs and keeping in touch with the larger communities that support the original Pacifica ideal. Many grassroots stations continued to broadcast the popular program, *Democracy Now!* (renamed for the interim, *Democracy Now! in Exile*). The availability of this program by way of satellite, the Internet, and a new televised version—which I helped to produce for cable access stations through Deep Dish Television—was a major factor in forcing Pacifica to resolve the crisis in a democratic mode and return *Democracy Now!* to national distribution. The television version of this program will continue, and this collaboration between community radio and alternative television networks augurs well for the prospect of a revitalized public media sphere in this country.

Finally, Andrea Cano's chapter titled Microradio: A Tool for Community Empowerment details the work of a group of dedicated activists and professionals to take advantage of a Federal Communications Commission (FCC) decision in late 2000 to authorize a nationwide system of low-power FM (LPFM) stations. Designed to foster access to the media system for educational and other community groups, the LPFM authorization paves the way for the start-up of 10- and 100-watt stations that serve the specific needs of certain communities and historically marginalized groups.

The speed with which the LPFM decision was announced forced Cano's Microradio Implementation Project (MIP) into action more quickly than anyone expected. Established by the Office of Communication, United Church of Christ, MIP provides assistance to qualified microradio applicants, as well as help with actually getting stations on the air once construction permits are secured. Difficulties ensued with the application process, as the FCC implemented a lottery system that provided five separate time periods, or "windows" for the filing of LPFM applications. Despite the agency's promise to give a thirty-day notice before the opening of each window, many church and community groups that wanted a microradio license found it difficult to mobilize that quickly. A set of political developments that coincided with the 2000 presidential elections also made the application process more difficult. The election of George W. Bush foreshadowed the installation of a new, more conservative FCC chair—a man who certainly was not a champion of microradio. Finally, President Clinton signed an appropriations bill in the waning days of his term that contained a technical rider that crippled the effort to secure as many LPFM frequencies as possible.

Undaunted, a group of grassroots activists, public media advocates, communications attorneys, and radio professionals pressed ahead to help the first handful of LPFM stations make it to the air. Their efforts also ensured that other stations would secure construction permits and that many would-be microradio operators would take full advantage of the three most recent filing windows for license applications. MIP and other like-minded organizations are clearly fighting an uphill battle in getting the LPFM movement off the ground. Cano and her colleagues continue to face opposition from the commercial broadcasting lobby and National Public Radio, with each of them coveting any extra spectrum space that might become available. National religious networks are also submitting many LPFM applications—in direct contravention of an FCC rule that prohibits their participation in the program. The MIP and other allied organizations plan to file petitions to deny such licenses and will also continue the effort to help qualified applicants take their rightful place on the radio dial.

All of these chapters start from the premise that public media are of major importance in civic life. The airwaves are a public resource that is now being used by market forces that have no accountability to local communities. The commercial media are loyal to only one cause—the bottom line. Commercial broadcasting is spiraling to the lowest common denominator, with programs becoming more and more sensational in a desperate bid to reach larger audiences. Witness the program I saw last week—*The Fear Factor* featuring *Playboy* bunnies. This disgusting exploitation of human emotions is a violation of even the few shreds that remain of American broadcasting's public interest mandate. Until there is a restructuring of the national spectrum infrastructure to empower noncommercial media, it will be important for concerned citizens and advocacy groups to rethink the direction of public television and radio and to support grassroots efforts whenever possible. What progressive broadcasters in the United States now need is something we might call *The Hope Factor.*

19

Social Capital, Civic Space, and the Digital Revolution

Emerging Strategies for Public Broadcasting

Barry Dornfeld

Public broadcasting organizations face an environment of turbulence in the early part of this new millennium unlike any other period in their histories. What seemed to stations, and the system as a whole, to be the great promise of the digital revolution has emerged as a serious threat to their survival. In short, stations face mounting competition from various media outlets—cable, satellite, and Internet-based—and increasing costs from the slower-than-expected shift to the digital broadcast environment. While federal funding for public broadcasting has maintained its level overall, other pieces of the funding pie are in decline, particularly the number of memberships stations can obtain (see Behrens 2001) and, most recently, foundation support. Clearly the shift to digital broadcasting and, eventually, the Internet as a platform for media distribution offers great opportunities in yet-to-be-defined ways; but the cost-benefit ratio for these new media seems to be exploding upward just as the dotcom boom lowers onto the heads of those in the media industry. The digital terrain of Web-based services and multichannel feeds in television and radio offers less promise as a land of abundant bandwidth, enhanced content, and potential income; instead, this terrain poses a quandary for the business strategies being developed by public broadcasting stations and the system as a whole. As public broadcasting consultant Richard Somerset-Ward puts it: "How can an underfunded, underperforming, and somewhat dysfunctional system play any meaningful role in a marketplace that is already overcrowded with aggressive and profitable media?" (Somerset-Ward 2001, 239).

Despite these challenges, public broadcasting organizations now face an equally unprecedented potential for positive transformation. Somerset-Ward and others are optimistic that stations can surmount these challenges with business plans based on new services and venues, some of which hold great promise for public broadcasting to better serve its public interest mission. Much of the ideology behind this drive to revisit the industry's mission falls under the broad rubric of "social capital," an idea that has recently gained currency, in part, because of Robert Putnam's queries about the pitfalls of "bowling alone" (see Putnam 2001).[1] Putnam's metaphorical thesis—that Americans tend, increasingly, to "watch" the goings-on in their communities instead of taking part in bowling leagues or PTA groups—points to an erosion of civic participation over the past fifty years. He further posits that certain public institutions (public broadcasting, for example) can effect change by trying to renew interest in civic engagement. Indeed, this viewpoint suggests a sense of purpose quite different from that of the traditional mission of public broadcasting. Rather than tying concepts of the public interest to an educational mission, Putnam and like-minded thinkers suggest a strategy in which certain "catalysts" act in the name of social good, community integration, and public service provision—creating, in the process, a kind of virtual multimedia glue that might hold together an increasingly torn social fabric.

With the background of this new strategic impulse in play, I focus here on the struggles involved in planning the future of one public broadcasting organization, on some interesting ways in which stations are approaching their new media environments, and, more broadly, on the implications suggested by these new directions. I am interested in the ways in which technological shifts interact with the shifting strategic environment for nonprofit organizations generally—and public broadcasting organizations, more specifically—to create both opportunities and threats for these organizations.[2] My interest stems from work done as part of a team that consulted with WHYY in Philadelphia, which I followed up with a series of later interviews and discussions, and by tracking the progress of the organization's (and the public broadcasting system's) efforts. The exact location of the public service ideal within these shifting forces becomes an interesting question. In the end, these experiences raise further questions about the ideal of public service broadcasting in a national cultural economy dominated by corporate interests, and whether the much-desired notion of public service laid out by public broadcasting commentators like Tracey (1998) and McChesney (1999) represents a realistic goal, given the media ecology of the early twenty-first century.[3]

During our consulting process, the leadership team at WHYY—a large organization without an extensive track record of producing national programming, but with a solid membership base—was concerned about the coming migration to digital distribution of media content and the strategies available to a large public broadcasting station. A clear caveat here is that the broader notion of the "public interest," and the difficult questions about whether and how public broadcasting organizations are serving it, did not drive this strategic effort. Instead, this strategy process was driven by the question of how best to implement WHYY's mission, given the threats and opportunities the organization then faced, both internally and externally. Of course, one can make the argument that an organization like WHYY serves the public interest by definition, but this is an increasingly difficult argument to make, given the shifting roles of public broadcasting stations in recent times.

The station's leadership group concerned itself principally with rethinking the value proposition WHYY would, in the foreseeable future, offer those who fund it and support it. More specifically, we put the following question to management: Given the changing media environment, would WHYY's "theory of the business" (Drucker 1994)—that the organization exists principally as a distributor of national programming produced elsewhere, and that members and regional and national institutions support this service because of their interest in the common good—be adequate to ensure a vital future for the station? Another way to conceptualize WHYY's business model, from management's point of view, was to say that the organization operated principally as a program distributor paid not for the amount of programming delivered to audiences, but in light of a more general sense of its value to the regional community. Since WHYY, at the time of this strategic planning effort, was not producing much original programming—and given the threat from alternative means of program delivery that were already becoming available—WHYY's leadership thought that its theory of the business, outlined above, did not hold much hope for the future.

WHYY's Track Record and Place in the System

WHYY can be grouped with the larger radio and TV stations in the public broadcasting system in terms of its membership numbers, but has historically been ambivalent about its role in producing national programming and limited in the resources available for local programming (this situation is typical of other large public broadcasting organizations, with the exception of those like WNET and WGBH, which produce larger portions of public broadcasting's national program stream). The largest public broadcasting entity in the Delaware Valley, WHYY serves a fairly dense and geographically broad area. It centers on the Philadelphia metropolitan area, but includes urban centers like Camden, New Jersey, and Wilmington, Delaware, as well as large suburban and rural sectors. It is an area overlapped by other stations' footprints, as many of the region's homes, depending upon the reach of their radio receivers and cable television suppliers, receive signals from three or four public television and/or public radio stations. The city of Philadelphia also has another public broadcasting outlet in WYBE-TV. This station, which has always had an uneasy relationship with WHYY, offers an engaging multicultural alternative to the programming options that other stations offer. WHYY's membership and fund-raising levels have remained solid, though fairly flat, over the past ten years—signs of stability on the one hand, but also of potential problems with the station's ability to adapt to change.

WHYY-FM is probably best known for *Fresh Air,* the long-running nationally distributed interview program hosted by Terry Gross. The station is also proud of its news-oriented discussion show called *Radio Times;* together, these two programs foster a decent sense of local identity. WHYY-TV's success, especially on the national front, has been more limited. The ill-fated *Dinosaur* series, a difficult program for the station to manage internally, has been the only memorable program produced for national broadcast over the past two decades. More recently, a few WHYY productions, including Glenn Holsten's *Philadelphia Diary* (1999) and his recent *Thomas Eakins: Scenes from Modern Life* (2001), have made it onto the national schedule.

With this record of program performance in mind, WHYY hired Bill Marrazzo, an industry outsider with no direct experience in public broadcasting, to be its new president in late 1997. Marrazzo had worked in both the public and corporate sectors, having run Philadelphia's Water Department and a large environmental consulting firm. Most importantly, he brought an agenda to remake the organization with a sense of corporate planning and productivity that was stronger than those previously employed inside the station and, indeed, throughout much of the public broadcasting system. Changes quickly took place in WHYY's organizational ethos and overall direction, and they first surfaced in a shift in corporate language. Marrazzo has been adamant about using terms like "the company" to describe the radio and TV operations. While these simple words are commonplace in the corporate world Marrazzo came from, they do not roll easily off the tongues of most public broadcasting professionals. Marrazzo also brought with him a new concern about the station's economic opportunities and, thus, he crafted an organizational focus that was decidedly more entrepreneurial. This shift in language and culture has not been easy for people who work inside the organization; some people bristled at the changes, perceived and otherwise, in 1997—and some still do.

In 1998, the station embarked on a strategic planning initiative that involved the Center for Applied Research (the consulting group where I was working) and the Tierney Group, a large advertising and communications firm that was engaged to help shape the station's new corporate identity and brand. This initiative resulted in the following three major changes at WHYY (along with several other smaller undertakings).

The Civic Space Strategy—A New Direction for WHYY

Perhaps the most significant outcome of the planning initiative was WHYY's embrace of a new "civic space strategy." We suggested to the leadership group that it think of the organization as being in the business of "producing civic space." This notion is not too far removed from Jurgen Habermas's (1962/ 1989) much-discussed "public sphere," though it is more concerned with organized culture and public consumption than with politics and democracy. We used the term "civic space" to mean the physical, social, and psychological space in which people meet one another as members of the Philadelphia/ Delaware Valley community. Our hypothesis was "that communities with vital civic spaces are in the end more productive and richer communities, more capable of solving their own problems through community participation" (Hirschhorn, Gilmore, and Dornfeld 1998). By helping produce this region's civic space, we argued that WHYY would make itself more noticeable and more valuable—even indispensable—to the region's cultural, occupational, and civic life, qualities the organization would have been hard-pressed to claim at the time. By weaving itself into this civic space, WHYY would increase the likelihood that businesses and individuals in the region would be willing to fund its operations; increased support would, in turn, make the organization better able to seize new opportunities available through the use of digital technologies.

The strategy outlined above points to a shift in mission, a different conception of localism or regionalism than the one that WHYY (and many other stations, for that matter) had traditionally embraced. At the same time, it reflects an internal decision to back away from fee-for-service lines of business and other entrepreneurial options that had been discussed. WHYY's leaders tied the concept of civic space to the development of brand identity for the organization. This would be accomplished through the forging of partnerships or alliances with local cultural, educational, and civic organizations. Working in this manner, WHYY would coproduce content for its distribution channels while, at the same time, supporting the missions of its partner organizations. As the station's Web site proclaims in its "Community" section:

> The tri-state area is made richer by its varied tapestry of cultures and neighborhood interests. As WHYY marks the beginning of its fall broadcast

season, we commit ourselves to becoming the common ground where each and every member of our community can meet and weave together a vision for our region. It all begins with WHYY's commitment to create and present more programming for on-air and on-line regional services. (WHYY 2002)

Partnerships already under way included projects with Philadelphia's Fairmont Park Commission (documentaries and short environmental messages for children) and the Opera Company of Philadelphia (live radio broadcasts on Sunday afternoons). Another example was the broadcast of the aforementioned *Thomas Eakins: Scenes from Modern Life,* a well-funded, high-quality documentary coproduced with the Philadelphia Museum of Art (PMA) and the Pennsylvania Academy of the Fine Arts (the broadcast coincided with the PMA's blockbuster exhibit of Eakins's work). By forging partnerships of this kind, WHYY management felt that some "multiplier effect" would take place, wherein supporters of one cultural institution would also support another, related institution. One challenge that WHYY faced in forging these partnerships was the task of producing more TV, radio, and Internet content . . . without adding additional costs for salary and infrastructure.

Embodying the Civic Space—A Redesigned Facility

A second strategic thrust involved the redesign and renovation of the WHYY building, along with a capital campaign to support this construction project. A $15 million renovation resulted in a workspace that was better integrated internally and also more visible to the outside community. The new building embodied the civic space metaphor in some ways, including the redesign of the traditional television studio into the Independence Foundation Civic Space—a multiuse studio in which the station has been hosting events that may or may not be tied to broadcast or Web publication. Marrazzo writes, "In addition to our daily outreach of news coverage in the neighborhoods of our region, we now regularly invite people representing a variety of local constituencies to our Technology Center, to listen to their needs and concerns. And, we know that by joining with some of our area's most respected news agencies, we can enrich our content" (2000).

Glass walls face out onto the area surrounding the station, spilling images, an audio broadcast, an electronic signboard, and a glimpse of public broadcasters at work into what is now, ironically, a fairly barren space on the edges of tourist traffic. Fortunately, this part of the city will be rejuvenated with the redesign of both Independence National Historic Park and the National Constitution Center, large federally funded projects designed to preserve and present American history and to attract additional tourism traffic. (WHYY has set up a Webcam to document the construction of the National Constitution Center, placing its logo and marking its presence on the Constitution Center site.) The more difficult challenge lies in the fact that this part of Philadelphia is not, and probably will never be, an area that residents of the region flock to; thus, WHYY might not be able to realize some of the hopes that the civic space metaphor suggests. With regard to the inside of the building, the organization has made an effort to open its "civic space" for use by community and nonprofit groups. This effort has met with some success, with a variety of broadcast and community events now being hosted in the lobby.

The Reorganization of WHYY's Work-force

The plan to shift WHYY away from its traditional split between radio and TV operations and into what the organization's leaders refer to as a "service area orientation" has been more difficult. For one thing, it has met with a great deal of resistance from staff members. The strategic idea is, of course, to create content that can be used across different media platforms. With this in mind, station managers plan to organize the staff into six service strands: the Wider Horizons service for audiences over age fifty, an Arts and Culture service, a Children's Service, a Home College Service, a Workforce Training service, and the Regional News and Public Affairs service. According to the plan, these services would bring resources to bear across radio, TV, Web, and community platforms in order to develop and deliver programs and other content. Each of these market-oriented service strands would have a leader responsible for developing projects and programming, managing resources, and managing relations with staff members and outside partners.

This reorganization would involve a significant change in the internal culture of WHYY, in which former radio people would soon work next to television people, developing content together for their specific service strands. The organization has only just begun to move toward this structure and, from what I have observed, management has faced some difficulty in effecting the desired changes. It remains to be seen how much production activity this new structure will yield; for now, the possibility that some production will be moved outside the WHYY building is a source of anxiety for staff members.

Implementing the New Strategy in a Changing
Media Environment

The implementation of WHYY's civic space strategy is an evolutionary process, one that has, perhaps, been slower and more difficult than the organization's leaders would have liked. Richard Somerset-Ward has been working with WHYY during the rollout of this strategy, focusing on the transformation of public broadcasting stations into "community partners" through the development of alliances with regional organizations (Somerset-Ward 2001, 239–240). He also sees public broadcasting stations as "community portals" (246–247) that, in conjunction with their partners, will develop a set of digital resources for citizens in the region. A community portal will "provide an entrance point, a gateway, to all these various services that the community can supply."[4] As Somerset-Ward sees it, these portals will include an education center, a health center, a democracy center, a cultural collaborative, a virtual news room, and so on, all based on the availability of broadband access to digital programming.[5] He feels this strategy would be easy to fund—more so than efforts to fund existing stations or the present-day public broadcasting system as a whole. Instead of paying for public broadcasting, stakeholders will put their money into community-based programs, needs, and services, with public broadcasting acting as a catalyst for the delivery of some portion of these services.

Other stations in the system are exploring these ideas as well. For example, Connecticut Public Television is advancing the notion of community alliances through its Mapping the Assets project, a well-funded collaborative survey of cultural institutions in the region, with an eye toward future partnerships. An article in *Current* touts WTTW's Network Chicago project, which "aims to invest heavily in creating local content that can be distributed across traditional and emerging media platforms . . . by targeting an audience engaged in civic life, partnering with other community groups, and marketing multimedia sponsorships to underwriters" (Bedford 2000, 1). Somerset-Ward (2001) cites examples of similar efforts at stations in Indiana and Nebraska.

This broad strategic direction raises a host of questions that generally fall into two categories. First, there are questions of practicality. Does this strategy of portals and alliances really hold significant promise for stations that wish to solidify their places in "civic space"? Does this civic space still exist, given current reports about the decline of social capital in the United States? Do public broadcasting stations have the kinds of competencies and organizational resources necessary for becoming successful catalysts in civic space or for developing successful community portals? What kinds of structural changes will be necessary within stations, or between stations, to accomplish these shifts? We can already see a change in job titles, with new designations such as "chief content officer" replacing the traditional "vice president of programming." Given the public broadcasting industry's history of resistance to change, however, some observers wonder whether present-day stations actually have the kind of organizational flexibility that would help them survive in the digital age—especially when they will be playing on the same turf as highly competitive private sector companies.

This issue of competition raises other practical questions: What kinds of competitors, commercial or public, are already vying for this same virtual space or will be in the near future? Will these companies be local in orientation, or will they be national or transnational companies that offer customized local resources? For example, Philly.com, Knight-Ridder's regional online newspaper operation, recently launched a portal strategy that aspires to some of the same goals the public broadcasting model does—but obviously with much more corporate backing and greater potential for delivering audience members to advertisers. Lastly, the market for participation in broadband technologies, which seemed so promising in the beginning of the digital transformation, has slowed down considerably with the burst of the dotcom bubble and the overall slowdown in the American economy. While new civic space partnerships might not be dependent on high-speed Internet connections, they are certainly enhanced by the ability to move a great deal more digital content into homes, schools, and other institutions by way of telephone or cable systems. If broadband penetration grinds to a halt, these partnerships will seem less viable.

A second set of questions concerns the tension between the public interest concept and public broadcasting's increasingly market-based orientation. Miller describes Habermas's classic formulation of the public sphere as "the site where subjects meet as citizens to discuss topics common to them that require deliberation" (1993: xviii–xix). The civic space WHYY hopes to carve out might turn into a space for the consumption of culture and the arts and the reception of other information, rather than a space for political debate (though management is investigating this opportunity as well). If we accept the premise that the economic climate in the larger broadcast industry and the policy-making ethos of our times have combined to push public broadcasting stations toward a market-based orientation, we need to ask whether this orientation is likely to assure organizational survival. If the answer is "yes," we must also ask how, or if, the surviving organizations will better serve the public interest. New notions of civic space certainly do not match the classic definitions of public service broadcasting,[6] but perhaps our understanding of citizenship is in the process of changing from the commitment to political discourse, participation, and civic values to a new ethos of freedom of choice in lifestyle and consumption. In this sense, WHYY's strategic direction seems more consistent with the view that Americans are largely consumers rather than citizens, a view commonly mentioned as one of the central tenets of neoliberalism.

If all of this theoretical churn results in a new version of public broadcasting that still serves the same constituency, through different media forms and platforms, we will have to wonder whether much has been accomplished beyond the survival of a bureaucratic entity that speaks to some aspect of the overall social good. An optimistic view, like that of Somerset-Ward, sees the maturation of broadband technologies as a means of developing important new roles for public broadcasters and audiences through community-based public service activities and resources. On the other hand, we should not forget that the "portal" metaphor itself comes from an e-commerce business strategy and that Internet search engines serve the economic function of keeping eyeballs glued to monitors, selling products and attracting more advertising dollars to cyberspace. In this arena of consumption, it is far more likely that access to electronic portals will not be shared equally by all and that the public whose interests are served will continue to be the limited slice of the population that public broadcasting has usually served best. However new civic space initiatives evolve, we can take some encouragement from the kinds of changes that organizations like WHYY are attempting. These shifts within institutions that have traditionally not been open to change offer some hope for renewed visions of what public broadcasting and public service media can be, and for fresh opportunities for serving the public interest.

Notes

1. See also the Social Capital Community Benchmark Survey at www.cfsv.org/communitysurvey/index.html. In this survey, three dozen community foundations, other funders, and the Saguaro Seminar of the John F. Kennedy School of Government at Harvard University joined together to "look at how connected we are to family, friends, neighbors and civic institutions on a local and national level. These connections—our Social Capital—are the glue that hold [*sic*] us together and enable us [*sic*] to build bridges to others."

2. I am grateful for the help of Bill Marrazzo, president of WHYY, David Othmer, vice president for content production, and Richard Somerset-Ward, consultant to the station and to Corporation for Public Broadcasting, who each granted me interviews for the research that led to the writing of this chapter. The Center for Applied Research (CFAR) in Philadelphia ran the consulting engagement I was part of, under the direction of principal consultants Larry Hirschhorn and Thomas Gilmore. I am thankful for their collegiality and intelligence during the course of this project.

3. McChesney defines public broadcasting as "a system that is nonprofit and noncommercial, supported by public funds, ultimately accountable in some legally defined way to the citizenry, and aimed at providing a service to the entire population—one which does not apply commercial principles as the primary means to determine its programming" (1999, 226).

4. Interview with Richard Somerset-Ward at WHYY, April 6, 2000.

5. Ibid.

6. See Tracey (1998, 26–32) for an exposition of these tenets of public service.

References

Bedford, K. 2000. "WTTW's Network Chicago: Brand for the Digital Future." *Current,* June 5, A16–A18.

Behrens, S. 2001. "Pledge Woes and Membership Slide." *Current Online,* March 26. www.current.org/funding/funding0106member.html (August 14, 2002).

Drucker, P. 1994. "The Theory of the Business." *Harvard Business Review* (September–October): 95–104.

Habermas, J. 1962/1989 *Structural Transformation of the Public Sphere: An Inquiry into a Category of Bourgeois Society.* Cambridge, MA: MIT Press.

Hirschhorn, L., T. Gilmore, and B. Dornfeld. 1998. "A Theory of the Business for WHYY." Philadelphia: Center for Applied Research. Unpublished report.

Marrazzo, B. 2000. "President's Column." *Applause Magazine,* May. WHYY, Philadelphia.

McChesney, R. 1999. *Rich Media, Poor Democracy: Communication Politics in Dubious Times.* Urbana: University of Illinois Press.

Miller, T. 1993. *The Well-Tempered Self: Citizenship, Culture and the Postmodern Subject.* Baltimore: Johns Hopkins University Press.

Putnam, R. 2001. *Bowling Alone: The Collapse and Revival of American Community.* New York: Touchstone Books.

Somerset-Ward, R. 2001. "Public Television in the Digital Age." In *A Digital Gift to the Nation: Fulfilling the Promise of the Digital and Internet Age,* ed. Lawrence K. Grossman and Newton N. Minnow. New York: Century Foundation, 239–261.

Tracey, M. 1998. *The Decline and Fall of Public Service Broadcasting.* New York: Oxford University Press.

WHYY. 2002. "Community" Web Page. www.whyy.org/community/index.html.

20

Resisting the Market Model of the Information Highway

Sandra Smeltzer and Leslie Regan Shade

We now have over ten years to reflect on the developing culture of the Internet, from its emergence as a research and development (R&D) and educational tool in the early 1990s to its commercialization in the mid-1990s and the ensuing Web-based hypercommodification of today (Raphael 2001). It has become evident that a moral distinction describes the tensions inherent in this development of the Internet: commerce versus commons applications, or as both Walters (2001) and Moll and Shade (2001b) refer to it, "e-commerce vs. e-commons" visions.

Dowding, in discussing the early development of "information highway" policy in the United States and Canada, differentiates between the socio-technical tradition and the newer technoeconomic convergence regime. According to this distinction, the sociotechnical tradition accounts for "concurrently and equitably, the needs and contributions of all society—the market, civil society, the government—and the technology created, controlled, and beneficially experienced by the whole of society." The regime of technoeconomic convergence, on the other hand, "assumes first and foremost that profits realized by the private sector through the nexus of technology and the market should remain in private sector hands" (2001, 12).

This chapter will examine these tensions between commerce versus commons visions, or the technoeconomic versus sociotechnical realms, through several recent examples of events and policy-making in Canada that are centered on technology. Current examples of the market model will be looked at, including legislation under the banner of national security, provoked after September 11 (Bill C-36, the Anti-Terrorism Act; Bill C-35, An Act to Amend the Foreign Missions and International Organizations Act; and Bill C-42, the Public Safety Act), privacy legislation (Bill C-6), and the debate over the National Broadband Task Force. These examples highlight both policy-making that is counter to the public interest and a policy-making process that has explicitly rejected any viable public input.

In opposition to the powerful market model, the Internet has been engaged as a tool for education, awareness, and the mobilization of social issues. Viable and robust examples of this commons model are found in the Internet's use by global civil society groups for promoting human rights, environmental concerns, and antiglobalization activities (Warkentin 2001). Recent Canadian examples of the commons model will be briefly discussed here, including the use of the Internet by the Citizens for Local Democracy (C4LD) group in Toronto, mobilized to protest the amalgamation of the City of Toronto in the late 1990s, and Internet activities surrounding the Free Trade of the Americas (FTAA) meeting in Quebec City in April 2001. In both instances the Internet was used as a tool of resistance to market models in local and global spheres.

However, tensions can be exacerbated when the market model meets the commons model. We see this when legislation aims to criminalize dissent that could place national security at risk. Thus, on-the-ground activism runs the risk of becoming extinct, but does this then mean that online activities are a viable substitute? How effective, then, is the Internet as an oppositional tool?

The Criminalization of Dissent

In August 2001, the *Ottawa Citizen* published a series of articles under the general title "Criminalizing Dissent," in which various authors explored the parameters of the current state of civil liberties and gently challenged the status quo of authority in Canada. Some of these authors suggested that the criminalization of dissent has moved beyond rhetoric and is now ominously seeping its way into policies, programs, and legislation (Pugliese and Bronskill 2001).

In the wake of September 11, a few key pieces of legislation introduced into the Canadian House of Commons confirm that this wariness was not unwarranted. In name, Bill C-36 (the Anti-Terrorism Act), Bill C-35 (An Act to Amend the Foreign Missions and International Organizations Act), and Bill C-42 (the Public Safety Act), appear to support and strengthen our constitutional rights of freedom of speech, freedom of assembly, and freedom of information. However, upon closer inspection it becomes apparent that sec-tions of these bills actually challenge civil liberties, criminalize dissent, and shake the foundations of what is in the public interest.

As part of Canada's new plan to combat terrorism, Bill C-36 has become the object of heated domestic debate. One of the more controversial aspects of this omnibus bill would allow seventy-two-hour preventive arrests of individuals suspected of being involved in a terrorist activity and require them to give testimony before a judge without actually being charged. Bill C-36's quick tour of the House of Commons and Royal Assent on December 18, 2001 (see canada.justice.gc.ca/en/news/nr/2001/doc_28217.html) was predicated upon the supposed willingness of Canadians to concede some or many of their civil rights in exchange for greater security. A Gallup Canada poll conducted in October 2001, right after amendments to soften Bill C-36 were introduced into the House, surveyed (only) 1,011 Canadians on the issue of security versus privacy. The poll found that 72 percent of respondents would "sacrifice" privacy for increased national security. These individuals considered it to be "more important for police to intercept communication between suspected terrorists than for the government to protect the privacy of the public" (Tibbetts and Bronskill 2001). However, the report did not indicate whether these citizens were aware of existing limitations on their privacy or of the ways in which their daily movements were already being monitored. As citizens living in a technologically advanced society, we are watched and tracked throughout our daily lives, from the phone calls and keystrokes that we make to the movies we watch and the books that we borrow from the library. Because of the process of digitization, these activities can now be rendered as easily stored and transferred bits of information (Whitaker 2000), which means that dominant groups now possess more sophisticated mechanisms to "see without being seen"—the very essence of power, according to Michel Foucault (1980). With Bill C-36 now law, security and intelligence organizations will have even greater authority to track and monitor our information and communication technology usage because, as discussed briefly below, the gamut of activities that are considered to be terrorist in nature would be significantly expanded.

On its own, Bill C-35, the "Act to Amend the Foreign Missions and International Organizations Act" (see www.parl.gc.ca), appears innocuous. However, as Naomi Klein notes in a November 2001 article in the *Globe and Mail,* this supposedly benign bill takes on malignant qualities when combined with Bill C-36. Under Bill C-35, the definition of an internationally "protected person" would be expanded to include foreign dignitaries who are granted diplomatic immunity when they come to Canada. Bill C-36 would create a situation wherein "interference" with a "protected person" would be considered a terrorist rather than just a criminal act. Thus, depending on how "interference" is defined or interpreted, it is possible that demonstrations outside of Canadian-hosted international meetings involving foreign dignitaries (such as the G-8, G-20, FTAA, and Multilateral Agreement on Investment protests) could be interpreted as terrorist activity. According to former Canadian federal justice minister Anne McLellan, Bill C-36 was amended to ensure that the definition of "terrorism" refers to neither lawful nor unlawful "legitimate" political activism (Department of Justice Canada 2001). However, Bill C-36 states that "anyone who commits a violent attack on the official premises, private accommodation or means of transport of an internationally protected person that is likely to endanger [that person's] life or liberty" has committed a terrorist act (Klein 2001). Thus, Klein asks the following questions: "Is blocking a road on the way to a summit an attack on the 'means of transportation' of 'internationally protected persons' that restricts their 'liberty?' Was pushing against the chain-link fence that surrounded so much of Quebec City during the Summit of the Americas in April 'a violent attack on the official premises' of a protected conference?" Perhaps Klein's questions will become irrelevant if Canada's Public Safety Act (Bill C-42) also becomes law. As the latest addition to Canada's antiterrorism plan, Bill C-42 would allow the government to create "military security zones"— an excellent method, as many civil libertarians have pointed out, to completely separate protesters from international meetings hosted in Canada.

Online or on the Ground?

We do not wish to suggest, by way of the arguments detailed above, that manifestations of our freedom of speech and assembly be relegated to virtual locales in reaction to the questionable viability of real-life peaceful demonstrations, protests, and other forms of opposition to programs, policies, and laws that may not be in the public interest. As Vincent Mosco has noted, "traditional forms of social mobilization and opposition can still speak louder than messages transmitted in electronic space" (2001, 18). Recent examples of on-the-ground social mobilization in Quebec, Seattle, and Genoa suggest that we cannot pin our hopes to the Internet as the sole or primary means to effect substantial change. However, as an instrument for the dissemination of information or as an organizational tool, the Internet has certainly proved valuable in, for example, the anti-MAI campaign (Clarke and Barlow 2001) and the anti-FTAA movement, as well as in the work undertaken by C4LD against the amalgamation of the City of Toronto.

C4LD was formed in December 1996 by a group of Toronto citizens as a response to what they perceived to be antidemocratic processes of the provincial government. Under the leadership of Mike Harris, the Conservatives came into power in the province of Ontario in 1995 and proclaimed a "Common Sense Revolution" involving deficit reduction, sweeping cuts in government, social, and welfare services, and a new reign of corporate rights. The evisceration of social citizenship rights, however, also ironically created a new combative response in the guise of citizen-based advocacy and activism, including the creation of C4LD. A particular focus of this advocacy group's work was opposition to the Harris government's plans to amalgamate the City of Toronto and its smaller surrounding cities into one giant "megacity." The group also opposed Harris's plans to abolish elected school boards. In addition to the widespread mobilization of citizens through public forums and debates, an electronic strategy was pursued. Led by Liz Rykert and sponsored by Web Networks, an affiliate of the Association for Progressive Communications (APC), this online presence proved to be a valuable and vibrant resource for both online and offline mobilization. The posting of proposed legislation, transcripts from local council and committee hearings, editorials and opinion pieces, notices of meetings, and the creation of mailing lists and Weblists were just a few of the available online resources. In a discussion list on civic networking, Rykert described C4LD's successful strategy as combining both online and on-the-ground activities:

> We have been meeting as a movement—not an organization in the formal sense—since December '96 . . . and the effort has resulted in more participation by regular citizens then I have ever seen. We have a web site, two lists, a 2,500 person phone tree that is activated once a week, a hotline, newsletters that are cool broadsheet black and white single sheets, a [CD] called No Mega-CD :-), a meeting every Monday night and an incredible group of committed citizens. In Feb[ruary] and March we were getting 2000 people at meetings every Monday night. (We go to the legislature together.) At one point there was a 24 hr. filibuster and we kept the seats in the gallery filled much of the time. Last Monday we had about 200. It was our 38th meeting. . . .
>
> So how did we get such participation . . . we have created a community where people find a voice and then they speak up, we get good info out in the face of mainstream media bias, and we use the meetings and the discussion lists as a place for people to learn from each other and support each other to act. In many cases the first thing someone will say when they stand up at the mike at the meeting is: "I have never been politically active in my life but . . .
>
> Our approach to the on-line use of the tools is to shape them and place them in ways that match and enhance the on the ground actions. Part of my job is to pay attention to the different ways we are communicating and the different paces within those venues.

(Forwarded from Liz Rykert to civic-values@civic.net, Subject: Soliciting Opinions, Date: Thu, 21 Aug 1997 21:17:13 –0400, URL: civic.net/
civic-values.archive/199708/msg00325.html)

Mobilization for protests at the FTAA meetings in Quebec City in April
2001 also involved a vigorous on-line strategy, as a diverse range of non-
governmental organizations (NGOs), citizen groups, and spontaneously created affinity groups used Web sites, listservs, and e-mail to coordinate,
strategize (in light of the security perimeter erected to detract protesters),
and then report on both the official government-sponsored meeting, the NGO
People's Summit, and the actual street protest. Sylvia Ostry refers to such
use of the Internet to bring together disparate groups that share a common
theme (in this case, antiglobalization) as "dissent.com"—"a new service industry: the business of dissent . . . that is very effectively operated by a core
group of NGO's headed by a new breed of policy entrepreneurs" (2001, 7).
Not only is dissent.com's function to coordinate and organize on-the-ground
demonstrations; it is also, as Ostry explains, to create "the libretto for the
street operas and the TV sound bites that inevitably accompany the counter-
meetings . . . examples of sound bite versions at Seattle were 'Fix it or nix
it'. . . these slogans circulate on the Internet and one can hear echoes in
newspaper and television interviews, at student meetings, and so on. As soon
as a book or pamphlet is published summaries are circulated and the message
is spread. The Internet clearly is having an unprecedented impact on the
diffusion of information and the process has just begun" (7).
    Dissenting groups involved in the FTAA protest, which utilized the Internet
as an instrument for coordination, included the Montreal-based SalAMI,
WomenAction, the Stop FTAA group, the Convergence des Lutes Anti-
Capitalists (Carnival Against Capitalism), and established NGOs such as the
Council of Canadians and Solidarity Network. The Quebec Indymedia also
posted news, commentaries, digital photographs, and videography. As Castells
specifies, an antiglobalization movement (such as this FTAA protest) is more
than "simply a network, it is an electronic network, it is an Internet-based
movement. And because the Internet is its home it cannot be disorganized or
captured. It swims like fish in the net" (2001, 142).
    Returning to the new climate of criminalizing dissent, we must then ask:
if the Internet helps to coordinate the convergence of citizens outside of an
international meeting such as the FTAA, only to have these citizens turned
away and even possibly charged as terrorists, how effective, then, is the
Internet in its oppositional role? Certainly, the Internet is valuable in facilitating the spread of information about onerous pieces of legislation and threats
to our civil rights. As Nick Dyer-Witheford (1999) and Naomi Klein (1999)

have argued, the Internet has been used to spread information about exploitative labor practices, the plight of domestic and distant workers, gross consumerism at the expense of social concerns, and the criminalization of dissent. However, a vicious circle has emerged. The bills discussed above will give organizations such as the Canadian Security Intelligence Service (CSIS) and the Communications Security Establishment (CSE) increased power to track our Internet usage in order to pinpoint possible security risks to our country (especially considering that the definition of "terrorist" acts has been expanded since September 11). Similarly, under the new Patriot (Provide Appropriate Tools Required to Intercept and Obstruct Terrorism) Act in the United States, intelligence agencies have been given greater authority to track individuals suspected of terrorist activities. In light of recent concerns regarding security in both Canada and the United States, these modifications may not seem unreasonable. However, privacy advocates and civil libertarians are concerned that these new laws will push citizen rights into a precarious situation (see resources at the Center for Democracy and Technology at www.cdt.org/security/usapatriot/analysis.shtml).

Even before the bills were introduced into the House, Canadian citizens have been questioned about their participation in legitimate activities. Tony Hall, a professor at the University of Lethbridge and avid critic of the Mounties, received a visit from the Royal Canadian Mounted Police's (RCMP) National Security Investigations Section to question him about "his writings critical of free trade agreements and their effects on indigenous peoples," as well as his potential role in the anti-FTAA demonstrations in Quebec City (Pugliese and Bronskill 2001). Allison North, a student at Memorial University, told a newspaper in May 2000 that the prime minister of Canada "didn't deserve an honorary degree" from her university "because of his government's cuts to education funding. Shortly after, an RCMP officer questioned her on whether she planned to do anything to threaten [prime minister] Mr. Chrétien or embarrass him when he picked up his degree. At that point, according to Ms. North, her organization, the Canadian Federation of Students, didn't even have plans to hold a demonstration" (Pugliese and Bronskill 2001). Of importance to this discussion, Hall's and North's run-ins with the authorities occurred prior to September 11 and prior to the proposed bills. And, once again, recent efforts to further criminalize dissent have given dominant groups even stronger control over new information and communication technologies. Thus, it is difficult to argue that the Internet can be a viable tool to challenge programs, policies, and laws that are not in the public interest if the technology is increasingly being controlled by the same forces against which people often protest.

The Market Model

The latest pieces of legislature discussed above are predated and supported by a number of other government-led initiatives that ensure that the future of information and communication technologies in Canada follows a model that is not in the best interest of the citizen. In particular, Bill C-6, the Personal Information Protection and Electronic Documents Act, and the Broadband National Task Force are examples of policy-making that have taken place without wide public consultation.

The Personal Information Protection and Electronic Documents Act appears to represent a positive step toward protecting personal information, as it "establishes a right to the protection of personal information collected, used or disclosed in the course of commercial activities" (see www.parl.gc.ca). However, its primary function is to encourage consumer confidence in electronic commerce. As the former federal minister of Industry Canada, John Manley, stated in a speech specifically dedicated to discussing Bill C-6, "Canada will become a leader in electronic commerce only if consumers and business are comfortable with the new technologies. . . . Trust is crucial" (Manley 1999). In order to address citizens' concerns regarding privacy, particularly in the new "information age," the bill requires organizations to gain an individual's permission prior to the release of personal information. However, since the government is also concerned that electronic commerce not be restricted, the bill has been constructed in such a way that businesses can circumvent this permission requirement. As Valerie Steeves explains, organizations need only "imply an individual has consented to the collection of his or her personal information . . . [and] it is unlikely that a consent requirement will protect my individual choice when my employer, bank, insurance company or health clinic asks me for my health history" (2001, 55).

As another example of the market-driven, consumer-oriented future of information and communication technologies in Canada, the National Broadband Task Force (NBTF) was established by the former minister of Industry Canada, Brian Tobin, in the fall of 2000. The mandate of the NBTF is to examine "the best approaches to make high-speed broadband Internet services available to businesses and residents in all Canadian communities by the year 2004" (broadband.gc.ca). Three rationales for the task force were provided: to ensure Canadian competitiveness in a global economy, to address the digital divide, and to create "opportunities for all Canadians."

Presciently, David Johnston, ex-head of Canada's Information Highway Advisory Council (IHAC), was named to lead the thirty-five-member task force, which included twenty-two members with clear corporate connections to the communications industry (including Nortel, Alcatel, Lucent,

IBM, Rogers, and Bell). Only five members were clearly identified with broad public interest issues such as universal access and privacy. As with IHAC, where deliberations took place "behind closed doors" (Clement, Moll, and Shade 2001, 26), the NBTF deliberations were closed to the public—although submissions could be made and were posted online at the NBTF Web site. However, only thirty-four submissions were made, with most of them championing the deployment of broadband services, particularly for remote and rural communities.

Media coverage of the NBTF was scarce, although one opinion piece published in the *Ottawa Citizen* provided a critical perspective on both the composition of the task force and its definition of access:

> The Internet is becoming a critical part of public infrastructure, delivering government services, health information and educational opportunities. The task force mandate mentions access, but access to what, for whom, and who decides these critical questions? The communications industry can hardly be expected to answer these questions without prejudice. "Access" includes not merely access to the technical infrastructure—the pipes, hardware and software—but access to the social infrastructure: literacy, diverse content, vibrant communities, and the ability to create and communicate, not just be the passive recipient of streaming video, flashy graphics, and branded stickiness. Access includes geographic availability in rural, remote and Northern communities. It includes creating public access sites for those Canadians who don't have domestic Internet services, for those who don't want domestic Internet services, and for those that don't have a domicile. Universal usability involves innovative designs that can accommodate a diverse citizenry. (Moll and Shade 2001a, A15)

The NBTF released its report in June 2001, complete with a press conference in Ottawa featuring a live satellite link to Iqaluit communities, Webcasts, and Minister Tobin beamed in from Clarenville, Newfoundland. The task force recommended the deployment of a national broadband network at a cost of between $1.85 billion and $4.5 billion (Cdn). The emphasis was on connecting rural and remote communities and aboriginal settlements, with priority given to providing service to health facilities, libraries, schools, and other public institutions (NBTF 2001). Surprisingly, media coverage was lukewarm (perhaps a reaction to recent dotcom slumps), criticizing both the necessity for and cost of deploying broadband. Instead, the media paid more attention to NBTF recommendations to review foreign investment rules, with the view toward easing federal regulatory measures in order to ensure participation in the project.

In October 2001 it was reported that Tobin was seeking $1.5 billion (Cdn) for the broadband project (Scoffield 2001b), amid criticisms of the project's frivolity because of heightened security concerns following the events of September 11 in New York and Washington, D.C. It was later reported (Scoffield 2001a) that monies allocated in the forthcoming budget were drastically reduced from Tobin's original request. Indeed, the 2001 budget (announced December 10) allocated $110 million (Cdn) for a scaled-down "innovation agenda," with funds being directed to build a kind of super-Internet for schools, universities, and medical researchers.

Although the broadband project has been detoured for the time being due to more pressing national concerns, it has not been derailed. Perhaps this detour will allow for a more thorough examination of some critical questions with respect to broadband. Clement has already questioned whether broadband serves the interests of industry or communities: "High bandwidth applications are pushed by the telecommunications industry to fill up the fibre cable they developed and laid. It's actually a supply-push agenda, not a demand-push agenda. There is no strong public demand pulling for more broadband, rather it's the industry that has developed an oversupply of carriage capacity to sell so they are trying to stimulate demand for it and get the government to underwrite the cost" (May 2001). Indeed, evidence abounds that low-bandwidth services, such as e-mail, chat rooms, and the downloading of documents, are the services most used by consumers. Keith Hampton's research on the users of Netville—a suburban community in Canada where some community members were given, free of charge, high-bandwidth connections and access to a variety of resources—indicated that the resources considered most valuable by Netville community members were low-bandwidth applications such as e-mail, mailing lists, and chat rooms (Hampton and Wellman 1999, 2001). This, of course, is anathema to the visions of telecom leaders who see e-commerce as a priority. As a case in point, Microsoft's Bill Gates recently urged political and corporate leaders to make domestic broadband access a priority in order to encourage the use of the Internet as a mass medium for advertisers (Warner 2001).

Online and on the Ground

At the moment, it would be misleading to conceive of the Internet, or other information and communication technologies, as being particularly useful as a means to challenge activities that are not in the public interest—that is, if these technologies must operate in a political and economic environment that is essentially undemocratic, market-driven, and consumer- rather than citizen-oriented. In order for the Internet to be a true means of public expression, to go beyond the dull scenarios of serving as a mere carrier for e-commerce and pay-per-view videos, we must first make sure that other forms of on-the-ground public expression are democratic. Public expression starts with public input into the design and policy that give initiatives such as the broadband project a "Canadian" character. Meaningful public consultation engages diverse groups of citizens, including nonprofit groups, women, labor, public educators, and youth.

And here is the crux of this chapter—we need such on-the-ground public input to ensure that our online activities can resist the market model. Online activities can also act as instruments in the coordination and dissemination of information that support our on-the-ground social mobilizations. Thus, a fight on behalf of the public interest must occur both online and on the ground.

References

Castells, M. 2001. *The Internet Galaxy: Reflections on the Internet, Business, and Society.* Oxford: Oxford University Press.

Clarke, T., and M. Barlow. 2001. *Global Showdown: Citizen Politics and the WTO.* Toronto: Stoddart.

Clement, A., M. Moll, and L.R. Shade. 2001. "Debating Universal Access in the Canadian Context: The Role of Public Interest Organizations." In *E-Commerce vs. E-Commons: Communications in the Public Interest*, ed. M. Moll and L.R. Shade. Ottawa: Canadian Centre for Policy Alternatives, 23–48.

Department of Justice Canada. 2001. "Strengthening the Safeguards With Amendments to the Proposed Anti-Terrorism Act: Fact Sheet." canada.justice.gc.ca/en/news/nr/2001/doc_27906.html.

Dowding, M.R. 2001. "National Information Infrastructure Development in Canada and the U.S.: (Re)Defining Universal Service and Universal Access in the Age of Techo-economic Convergence." Ph.D. diss., Faculty of Information Studies, University of Toronto.

Dyer-Witheford, N. 1999. *Cyber-Marx: Cycles and Circuits of Struggle in High-Technology Capitalism.* Urbana: University of Illinois Press.

Foucault, M. 1980. *Power/Knowledge: Selected Interviews and Other Writings, 1972–77.* New York: Pantheon Books.

Hampton, K.N., and B. Wellman. 1999. "Netville On-Line and Off-Line: Observing and Surveying a Wired Suburb." *American Behavioral Scientist* 43, no. 3. 475–492.

———. 2001. "Long Distance Community in the Network Society: Contact and Support Beyond Netville." *American Behavioral Scientist* 45, no. 3. 477–496.

Klein, N. 1999. No Logo: Taking Aim at the Brand Bullies. Toronto: Knopf.

———. 2001. "Hate Bill C-36? Wait Until You Meet Its Brother." *Globe and Mail*, November 28, A19.

Manley, J. 1999. Speaking Notes for the Honourable John Manley Minister of Industry, Presentation to the Senate Committee Studying Bill C-6. December 2. e-com.ic.gc.ca/english/speeches/42d8.html.

May, K. 2001. "Government's High-Speed Internet Project Would Pump $1B into Industry." *Ottawa Citizen*, June 18. www.vcn.bc.ca/lists/broadband/200106/msg00022.html

Moll, M., and L.R. Shade. 2001a. "What Do You Want the Net to Be? If You Want It to Serve All Canadians, You'd Better Get Involved." *Ottawa Citizen*, February 15, A15.

Moll, M., and L.R. Shade, eds. 2001a. *E-Commerce vs. E-Commons: Communications in the Public Interest*. Ottawa: Canadian Centre for Policy Alternatives.

Mosco, V. 2001. "Myth-ing Links: Power and Community on the Information Highway." In *E-Commerce vs. E-Commons: Communications in the Public Interest*, ed. M. Moll and L.R. Shade. Ottawa: Canadian Centre for Policy Alternatives, 9–20.

National Broadband Task Force (NBTF). 2001. The New National Dream: Networking the Nation for Broadband Access. broadband.gc.ca/Broadband-document/english/table_content.htm.

Ostry, S. 2001. "Dissent.Com: How NGO's Are Re-making the WTO." *Policy Options/Options Politiques* (June): 6–15.

Pugliese D., and J. Bronskill. 2001. "Keeping the Public in Check"; "How Police Deter Dissent: Government Critics Decry Intimidation," August 18. www.canada.com/ottawa/ottawacitizen/specials/criminal/criminal01.html.

Raphael, C. 2001. "The Web." In *Culture Works: The Political Economy of Culture*, ed. Richard Maxwell. Minneapolis: University of Minnesota Press, 197–224.

Scoffield, H. 2001a. "Tobin's Plan Loses in Budget." *Globe and Mail*, November 28, A1.

———. 2001b. "Tobin to Seek $1.5 Billion for Net." Globe and Mail, October 13, A16.

Steeves, V. 2001. "Privacy Then and Now: Taking Stock Since IHAC." In *E-commerce vs. E-commons: Communications in the Public Interest*, ed. M. Moll and L.R. Shade. Ottawa: Canadian Centre for Policy Alternatives, 49–56.

Tibbetts, J., and J. Bronskill. 2001. "Security Trumps Privacy: Poll 72% Willing to Sacrifice Privacy to Help Police Catch Terrorists." *Ottawa Citizen*, November 22, A1.

Walters, G.J. 2001. *Human Rights in an Information Age: A Philosophical Analysis*. Toronto: University of Toronto Press.

Warkentin, C. 2001. *Reshaping World Politics: NGOs, the Internet, and Global Civil Society. Lanham, MD: Rowman and Littlefield*.

Warner, B. 2001. "Bill Gates: Broadband Woes Hobble Net Advertising." Reuters, December 6. www.washtech.com/news/software/14058-1.html.

Whitaker, R. 2000. *The End of Privacy: How Total Surveillance Is Becoming a Reality*. New York: New Press.

21

Public Television in the Digital Age

Town Hall or Cyber Mall?

Jerold M. Starr

The Telecommunications Act of 1996, passed overwhelmingly by both houses of Congress, provided one of the biggest giveaways in U.S. history. The act provided every television licensee with an additional channel free of charge to develop digital television (DTV) transmission. This technology permits high-definition television (HDTV), which produces a picture six times sharper than the resolution of today's standard definition TV (SDTV). DTV also can handle six-channel, movie-theater quality, Dolby digital surround sound.

Alternatively, the 6Mhz digital channel can be used to offer four or more SDTV program streams and/or video services at the same time. For commercial broadcasters, this might include video-on-demand, games and special-interest programming, targeted news and traffic reports, sports, weather and financial data, addressable and classified advertising, direct marketing, and Internet data transmission. The value of these frequencies has been estimated at $70 billion or more (Center for Media Education 1998; Common Cause 1997).

To achieve the transition, every station will have to spend $1 million to $1.5 million for a new transmitter. A major producing-station seeking to replace all of its production equipment now might also have to spend as much as $5 million to $10 million; however, the cost of the new production equipment is comparable to the old and is dropping in price. Many stations already are replacing worn-out analog equipment with digital as needed, and all have the option to lease.

Public broadcasters have estimated the total cost of the digital transition for them to be $1.7 billion. With roughly 350 stations, this amounts to about $5 million per station. This figure probably is generous, in view of the fact that stations average fewer than 100 hours of local program production a year. Indeed, 300 stations produce nothing for the Public Broadcasting Service (PBS) National Program Service.

In October 1997, public broadcasters submitted a DTV funding proposal to the federal government for $771 million, to be spread over three years. In addition, PBS announced a plan to raise $1 billion. As of November 2001, the federal government had contributed only about $56 million toward the transition costs. However, state governments had provided about $460 million and foundations and corporations another $213 million (Odenwald 2001a).

In recent years, PBS member stations, following the advice of public relations firms have emphasized the cost of digital conversion in their fundraising appeals. Soliciting our contributions, the stations assure us that these additional channels will solve everyone's program needs. They also promise a whole range of communications services for local communities. It is a truism, however, that technology serves those who control it. As long as U.S. public broadcasting is kept in thrall to political officials, corporate underwriters, and affluent subscribers, the vast service potential of the new digital technology will never be realized.

U.S. public broadcasting is at a critical juncture in its thirty-five-year history. Political intimidation, corporate seduction, and financial insecurity have seriously undermined the industry's original mission. With structural change, public broadcasting in the digital age finally can fulfill its mission to become a town hall of the air for the "unserved" and "underserved" constituencies for whom it was created—children, seniors, minorities, the poor, and active citizens. Without structural change, however, public broadcasting will continue its descent into becoming just another cybermall, this one "branded" for more educated and affluent consumers.

The Promise of PBS: Town Hall of the Air

In Europe, public broadcasting traditionally has served as the principal forum that enables the whole nation to talk to itself (Keane 1995). In 1967, the Carnegie Commission on Educational Television (1967) recognized that "all that is of human interest and importance" may not be "available or appropriate for support by advertising" and proposed a system free of commercial constraints. Accordingly, the purpose of U.S. public broadcasting would be "not to sell products" but to "enhance citizenship and public service."

Public broadcasting was to serve as a forum for debate and controversy where we could "hear the voices of groups not normally heard" and "see America whole, in all its diversity." As he signed the bill into law, President Lyndon B. Johnson (1967) proclaimed, "Public television [will] help make our Nation a replica of the old Greek marketplace, where public affairs took place in view of all the citizens."

The new digital technology could facilitate the fulfillment of the PBS mission. The smaller and lighter digital cameras and easy online editing bays provide for mobility and quickness in local production. The multiple program streams make possible a true citizens' channel. *Harper's* editor Lewis Lapham (1993), a former PBS program host himself, suggests that PBS "forget about costly entertainment production values" and take a lesson from C-Span on the art of eavesdropping. He would bring PBS cameras into campus debates, state legislatures and city halls, town meetings, university lecture rooms, and plays and poetry readings.

Larry Daressa (1996, 20), former board chair of the Independent Television Service, calls for a truly social public television that stages "community events in which people could congregate via television to explore shared concerns." The Twentieth-Century Fund Task Force (1993) has suggested that public television adopt the model of the "electronic town square" in which stations "take the lead in attempting to solve community problems by putting their resources at the disposal of community groups and agencies that are addressing these problems."

Media scholar Pat Aufderheide proposes that public broadcasting be "a public project executed through broadcasting . . . using mass communication as a tool of public life" (1991, 170–171). In all of these visions, the audience would be a public, not just a mass; it would participate, not just consume.

The Broken Promise of PBS

Scanning the typical PBS schedule these days, one finds weasels eating snakes, British people talking, and beltway pundits barking, along with a surfeit of how-to shows: how to cook, lose weight, remodel and decorate your house, invest money, and manage your emotions. However, there is nothing on how to dissect propaganda, evaluate policies, choose good leaders, and defend the public interest.

There are nightly and weekly programs about big business and Wall Street, but no regularly scheduled programs addressing workplace, consumer, or environmental concerns. In the final analysis, it comes down to a question of what stories get told and who gets to participate in the telling. While the perspectives of government and corporate leaders are important, they must be balanced by coverage from the bottom up—with an understanding of what is happening to our workers, consumers, taxpayers, and environment. PBS should and could do this. It does not.

Three stations (WBGH in Boston, WNET in New York, and WETA in D.C.) provide more than 60 percent of the PBS program schedule, while more than 300 stations do not contribute anything. Independent producers account for nearly

20 percent of all national programming, but almost all of their productions must be channeled through the same three "presenting" stations.

Worse, as author and filmmaker B.J. Bullert (1997) reports, PBS gatekeepers do not consider public interest advocates to be "journalists," even if they are accomplished filmmakers. In her words, gatekeepers often label advocates' work as "propaganda" and assume that advocates' interests bias reporting. If anything, the trend at PBS is toward more coproduction deals with commercial partners looking for lucrative "back-ends," such as Disney's ABC, Fox, Reader's Digest, Sony Classical, Time-Life Records, Warner Brothers, and the like (Ledbetter 1997; Starr 2001).

While 75 percent of public broadcast funding comes from the public in one form or another, corporations are the single largest source of underwriting for programs.

In 1997, PBS liberalized its underwriting guidelines to allow underwriters' products, slogans, celebrity spokespersons, mascots, theme music, and phone numbers with Web addresses to be shown on the air. "What we have here is the commercialization of PBS," observed Andrew Papalardo of Young and Rubicam (Behrens 1994). PBS now accepts as many as three consecutive fifteen-second underwriting "messages" for a national program. Local stations are allowed thirty-second messages. Even children's shows feature pitches for fast food and theme parks.

This change in underwriting practices has two consequences. One is a paucity of news and public affairs. As WGBH's Victoria Devlin once observed: "Corporations are not big risk-takers when there's perceived controversy" (Weisman 1987). The result, as TV critic Marc Gunther (1993) points out, is an overabundance of "safe" programming" like nature, science and how-to shows, most of which have crossed the line into product merchandising. In 1995, former PBS program director Kathy Quattrone complained, "Many program decisions are being based not on the program value they bring but [on] what kind of [financial] deal it can bring" (Bedford 1995).

The second consequence is that the news and public affairs that do make it onto the PBS schedule tend to be as establishment-biased as one would find on the commercial networks. PBS's flagship nightly news program is *NewsHour with Jim Lehrer*. The show is two-thirds owned by Liberty Media (a former subsidiary of AT&T, now one of the ten biggest media companies in the country) and sponsored by several large corporations, like Archer Daniels Midland and Pepsi-Cola. Lehrer claims: "We try very hard to represent all of the relevant positions on any given issue as best as we can." However, research by Vassar College professor William Hoynes (1994) has found that all public interest group advocates combined accounted for a mere 6 percent of Lehrer's guests. In 1995, Lehrer's former cohost Robert MacNeil, anticipating his retirement, acknowledged, "We [at PBS] are not as provocative, innovative, creative or original as we should be" (Weiskind 1995).

To make matters worse, PBS (1990) systematically bans independent productions that receive even partial support from labor or public interest groups. PBS claims this is necessary to avoid the "perception," however unfounded, that the program content might have been influenced by its funding. Examples of such discrimination are legion, but two should make clear how rigidly this dictum is enforced.

In 1994, PBS refused to air *Defending Our Lives,* winner of the Academy Award for Best Documentary Short. The film critically examines the problem of battered women. PBS turned it down on the grounds that one of the producers was a member of a nine-member prison support group concerned with the issue. The producer neither funded, profited from, nor controlled the film, but PBS said the "perception" that shows are being "created to advance the aims of [a particular] group" is "as important as the fact" (Starr 2001, 95).

In 1997, PBS was scheduled to air *Out at Work,* an award-winning documentary about three lesbian and gay workers' struggles for justice and dignity in the workplace. PBS suddenly canceled, claiming that it had discovered that 23 percent of the film's modest $65,000 budget came from such "problematical" sources as a lesbian action foundation and some labor unions. One of the film's directors, Kelly Anderson, said: "None of the funders in question gave more than $5,000 to the project, and most gave $1,000 or less." PBS official Sandy Heberer insisted: "PBS guidelines prohibit funding that might lead to an assumption that individual underwriters might have exercised editorial control over program content even if, as is clear in this case, those underwriters did not" (Starr 2001, 35). Journalist James Ledbetter (1997b) asked PBS official Barry Chase if this decision meant that a labor union could never fund any program on public television that had to do with issues of the workplace. Chase replied: "Yes, that's exactly what I'm saying."

In contrast, former CBS and ABC news correspondent Jerry Landay (2001) reveals that three conservative foundations—Bradley, Olin, and Scaife—subsidized at least seventeen single programs or series on PBS from 1992 through 2000. All the programs served as a platform for the views of the foundations' grantees and their organizations. These included a program on "scientific creationism," problems in the black community on a lack of self-reliance, an attack on "political correctness" based on alleged "reenactments," a three-part series on the "gender wars" dominated by antifeminist voices, and a debate on "school choice" with thirty-eight of forty-two guests supporting public funding of private schools. Not only did these shows air, but there was no public acknowledgement of PBS's violation of its own "perception" guideline.

Worse, there are numerous examples of serious corporate conflicts of interest that PBS and its member stations have allowed to pass. Some of these conflicts are obvious: for example, programs on gems funded by DeBeers and Tiffany's, on the technology of materials funded by Corning, and on the computer funded by Unisys. Some are subtler, like the *Antiques Roadshow* funded by Chubb, a company that insures antiques (Starr 2001). Some are hidden, like *Wall Street Week* host Louis Rukeyser interviewing analysts who tout certain companies with which they had an undisclosed financial relationship ("Money Talks" 2001).

The corporations themselves have clear political motives for their involvement with PBS. For example, an ad director at General Motors views the PBS target audience as a group of people who influence the thinking of many others in their communities ("More Companies" 1991). Accepting an award from PBS for *Masterpiece Theatre,* a Mobil Oil spokesperson acknowledged, "You are building a constituency for Mobil" (Brennan 1985, 111). In the final analysis, the PBS green light to corporate and conservative foundation underwriting, and its ban on labor and public interest group funding, amounts to a de facto censorship of program content.

Unfortunately, the problem does not end with the PBS National Program Service. Since stations are required to carry only about ten hours a week of the national schedule, there is considerable member station discretion on what to offer local viewers. Nevertheless, promoting civic engagement remains a foreign idea at PBS member stations, where the common language has become one of focus groups, ratings, "cumes" (i.e., cumulative weekly ratings), and branding. The typical station produces a mere 100 hours a year of local programming. Only 16 of 351 stations have a local nightly news presence and the most distinguished of these, *Newsnight Minnesota,* has shut down.

Community advisory boards, mandated by Congress in 1978 to recommend programming addressed to "the specialized educational and cultural needs of the communities," have become little more than black holes of volunteer energy kept on the books only because they are required by law. Governing boards are no better. Only 2 of 351 stations allow subscribers to vote for members. Program philosophy is rarely discussed. In fact, public broadcasting executive Willard Rowland Jr. says that when it comes to programming, station managers are oriented "toward a narrowly defined audience of upscale viewer–check writers" who end up "substituting for the public as a whole"(1976, 118).

Former KQED-San Francisco CEO James Day once observed that "the greatest force for blandness is not the government; it's the stations" (Powledge 1972). Numerous cutting-edge public affairs series have been offered free, via satellite downlink, to PBS member stations over the years, yet only a minority of these programs have been deemed fit to carry. Such programs addressed community issues that are part of the PBS mission, but are typically ignored; for example, issues in the workplace (*We Do the Work* and *Livelihood*), in the gay and lesbian community (*In the Life*), and about human rights around the world (*Rights and Wrongs* and *South Africa Now*). A new show, *Mental Engineering,* dissects broadcast commercials to educate consumers and keep corporations honest. It is carried by only 50 of 351 PBS member stations.

Lewis Lapham has characterized the public television system as "the Holy Roman Empire during the last days of its decaying hegemony—351 petty states and dukedoms, each with its own flag . . . court chamberlain and trumpet fanfare" (1993, 37).

Digital Television: What's the Deal?*

All of the information detailed above provides a necessary context for evaluating the likely future of public broadcasting in the digital age. As we consider this transition, however, we must first take note that it is not just around the corner. Conflicting interests have stalled the digital rollout. According to the relevant legislation, broadcasters are expected to complete the transition to digital transmission by December 31, 2006, at which time they will occupy channels 2 through 51. By the end of that year, they must return their present analog spectrum (channels 60 through 69) to the Federal Communications Commission (FCC). However, there was a loophole in the legislation. The 2006 deadline could be extended indefinitely until 85 percent of viewers in a market are able to receive DTV signals. Many of the nation's 1,500 stations already are claiming hardship and asking for an extension of the deadline.

Among the obstacles are consumer costs. The enhanced resolution of HDTV is apparent only in DTV sets with screens forty-two inches or larger. Sets that big currently sell for up to $7,000 and require separate remote controls for analog and digital programming. Set-top decoders for those with cable or satellites dishes cost less—between $300 and $600—but cable and consumer electronics manufacturers have not been able to agree on a technical standard that will allow digital signals to be passed through to all TV sets. Even when technically feasible, such decoders are not an option for the 20

---

*The details included in the paragraphs below were up to date when this chapter went to press. Changes in DTV policy are unfolding at a rapid pace, however. For the latest developments, see the FCC Web site (www.fcc.gov). Top developments may be found on the site's main page, while more details about digital television may be found at www.fcc.gov/dtv.

percent of homes without cable, most in the poor and rural communities for which public broadcasting was dedicated.

There also are intellectual property disputes. Motion pictures already are in HDTV format and would comprise much of the early programming. The distributors want legislation that would require copy-protection instructions to VCRs to not copy any pay-per-view or video-on-demand shows. Other content providers want a standard that would keep digital TV content off the Web. The paucity of high-quality digital content discourages manufacturer and consumer investment in new equipment. There is even a dispute between broadcasters and cable system operators over which channels must be carried.

As a consequence, only about 1 million U.S. homes have DTV sets equipped with over-the-air receivers (maybe 1.6 million sets in all), compared to the 222 million TV sets owned nationwide. The National Association of Broadcasters has asked the Federal Communications Commission (FCC) to relax certain interim rollout deadlines, as have members of Congress on behalf of small market stations. Given the free channels and financial uncertainties, broadcasters have no incentive to build out quickly. By April 2001, only 186 of the nation's 1,500 stations were broadcasting in digital format (Greppi 2001).

In September 2001, the FCC established an incentive for broadcasters to clear their analog channels in advance of the 2006 deadline so they could be auctioned off to wireless carriers. An investment banking company was appointed to negotiate a package deal with bidders to compensate broadcasters and set deadlines. Broadcasters will be permitted to continue analog broadcasting on the new digital channels until a switch to DTV becomes practical.

Despite this substantial carrot, FCC chair Michael Powell has judged the 2006 deadline to be "unrealistic" and has appointed communications attorney Rick Chessen to head a new DTV task force to address the many obstacles to meeting it (Halonen 2001b). In November 2001, Representative Billy Tauzin (R-LA) joined with Representatives Ed Markey (D-MA), John Dingell (D-MI), and Fred Upton (R-MI) to deliver an ultimatum to the television industry to resolve its differences and move forward; if not, Congress would intervene ("Digital Delay" 2001; "House Tells" 2001). This is easier said than done.

Former FCC chair Bill Kennard has noted that it took color TV twenty-two years and the VCR sixteen years to reach the 85 percent level of penetration required by the legislation. In his view, the DTV conversion will take much longer (Halonen 2000). In 1997, a committee headed by David Liroff (1997) of WGBH-TV Boston advised, "It will be ten years before DTV receivers can be found in 30 percent of households." In 1996, the *New York Times* reported, "the full transition from analog to digital broadcasting is expected to last 15–50 years."

Public Broadcasters Get In on the Deal

While member stations were extolling the future benefits of the new technology for their viewers, the industry's trade group—the Association of Public Television Stations (APTS)—sought its own digital deal with the FCC. Claiming it already did enough public service, APTS petitioned the commission to permit members to use their additional digital channels for "revenue generating purposes."

On October 11, 2001, the Republican majority on the FCC ruled that public broadcasters could use some of their new digital channels for subscription video and fee-based services—like paging, data delivery, and videoconferencing — all with advertising. While public broadcasters still must devote a "substantial majority" (unspecified) of their weekly digital capacity to noncommercial, educational broadcasts, the door was opened wide to greater commercialization—along with a 5 percent tax on such revenue (Center for Digital Democracy 2001; FCC 2001a, 2001b; Halonen 2001a; Odenwald 2001b). Michael Copps (2001), the lone Democratic appointee on the Commission, stated in dissent: "The sale of advertising puts on the block one of the very things that makes public television special and different from commercial broadcasting. I believe that permitting advertisements is contrary to statute, contrary to the will of Congress and contrary to the mission of public broadcasting." A bipartisan group of House members urged FCC chair Powell to reconsider the decision, warning of "creeping commercialism" on public TV. Representative Markey suggested that this might undermine public broadcasting's financial support from viewers and from congressional appropriators (Halonen 2001a). Indeed, on the day of the decision, Representative Cliff Stearns (R-FL) proposed cutting $12 million from the Corporation for Public Broadcasting (CPB) digital funding because the stations had a new vehicle for raising such funds. Although soundly defeated, this was only the first such attempt (Odenwald 2001b).

At the same time, PBS has not offered much of a programming vision for the coming digital era. According to Gary D. Poon, formerly executive director of PBS's Digital Television Strategic Planning Office, HDTV will be most commonly used for the usual prime-time series, like *Nova, Nature,* and *Great Performances.* During the day, according to Joel Brinkley's (1997) report in the *New York Times,* we might get as many as four different feeds, "like children's programming on one channel, an adult education show on another, a gardening show on a third and elementary-school course work on the fourth." Former PBS president Ervin Duggan has envisioned a full-time kid's channel, a lifelong learning channel, and a channel that would deliver business and financial information and professional training (Center for Media Education 1998, 9). In short, PBS will offer the same old stuff, only more of it.

Ironically, cable already has rendered these familiar PBS genres redundant. Whole networks present programs around the clock on cooking, exercise, home repair, gardening, investing, nature, history, and the like. Many of these programs are better produced and draw bigger ratings than comparable PBS member station offerings. This situation will be amplified in the digital era.

On the other hand, none of these corporate-owned cable networks can offer the kind of programming for which PBS was created—universally accessible, noncommercial public affairs programs designed to serve the public interest. Not only would this type of programming provide a unique identity or "brand" for PBS; it would also do enormous good for our democracy. Without structural change, however, the public service potential of the new digital technology will be squandered.

Toward a Public Broadcasting Trust

The trouble with PBS starts with funding, the structure of which breeds the insecurity and compromises that undermine its mission. Public broadcasting in other democracies has reliable and often independent sources of funding, like a TV license fee. In Europe, citizens pay between $36 and $136 a year to support public service broadcasting. In Japan they pay $20, in Australia $28, and in Canada $50. Ratings range from 13 percent in Canada up to 44 percent in the UK. In the United States we pay a little more than $1. With so little money for production and promotion, PBS draws only 2 percent of the national audience.

From the first, Carnegie Commission (1967) chair James R. Killian Jr. argued that "a free, innovative, creative public television service" would not be possible if it were to be "ultimately dependent" on Congress for its funding. Carnegie proposed a federal trust fund based on a manufacturers' excise tax on the sale of television sets. Lobbied heavily by the National Association of Broadcasters (NAB), Congress removed the trust fund proposal from the legislation. As a consequence, PBS has forever been in survival mode, always vulnerable to those who control the purse strings (Starr 2001).

For the past thirty years there has been a succession of proposals to address this problem. In 1978, 1987, and 1988, Congress proposed various fees to subsidize public broadcasting—on TV and radio license holders, license transfers, or factory sales of consumer electronics products and broadcast equipment. In each case, industry lobbyists killed the bills. After a while, even the public broadcasters stopped trying.

Interviewed in the trade paper *Current* ("APTS Priority" 2001, 15), APTS President John Lawson hailed the FCC's permission for the commercial use of new digital channels as "a landmark victory for public television, because it enables public-private partnerships that over time could become as important as a trust fund in creating a new revenue source." Not only is this a gross overstatement, it is misleading. The thrust of past proposals for a public broadcasting trust was to liberate the service from its dependence on corporate and government support, so it could fulfill its original mission—*not* to provide the means for closer partnerships with commercial firms.

What is needed is an independently funded Public Broadcasting Trust (PBT), comparable to Little League Baseball, the U.S. Olympic Committee, or the American Red Cross. This would take public broadcasting off the federal dole, remove corporate program sponsorship, and free the service to pursue its mission without chronic censorship pressures. This would give the public at least one place to turn for alternative views and independent analysis, one place dedicated to educating citizens rather than selling eyeballs to advertisers.

It is easy to see why past Congresses felt that commercial broadcasters should pay the bill. They make billions from their free use of the public's airwaves. As former PBS and NBC News president Lawrence Grossman has observed, "Broadcasting is the only industry in America where you can make money off a public resource and not pay a thing for it" (Twentieth-Century Fund 1993, 152). Oil drillers, cattle grazers, cable operators, and cellular phone companies all pay a fee for using a public resource. Why not broadcasters?

Citizens for Independent Public Broadcasting (CIPB) calculates that public broadcasting needs $1 billion a year for all local and national programming on TV and radio. This would be three times the amount of money currently spent, but still less than the amounts that other democracies spend for public media. This goal could be accomplished in several ways: a 5 percent tax on the sale or transfer of TV and radio licenses, a 2 percent tax on broadcast advertising, a 2 percent annual spectrum fee, or a tax on spectrum auctions (Starr 2001). The Congressional Budget Office currently estimates that $18 billion in new spectrum will be auctioned off over the next few years. Dedicating just these proceeds to a PBT endowment would accomplish the goal.

In December 1998, the President's Advisory Committee on the Public Interest Obligations of Digital Television Broadcasters recommended that Congress create a trust fund for public broadcasting, and that if it does, the field should reduce or eliminate "enhanced underwriting," which "closely resembles full commercial advertising." The public agrees. A national poll at the time found that 79 percent of Americans favored a proposal to require commercial broadcasters to pay as much as 5 percent of their revenues into a fund to support noncommercial public broadcast programming (Lake, Snell, Perry 1998).

Of course, a fully developed PBT proposal would have to address much more than just the funding mechanism for public broadcasting. Among other reforms, new measures are needed to protect public broadcasting from censorship by state and local politicians and to ensure that local boards of directors are truly diverse, have a clear sense of mission, and recruit and reward station managers for measurable public service (instead of for their expertise in profit-making ventures). Community advisory boards would have to be empowered to perform their designated function. Greater accountability at the national level would also have to be ensured. A draft of a proposal that contains these features can be found on the CIPB Web site: www.cipbonline.org

In the final analysis, we will find no automatic solution to public broadcasting's problems in new digital technology. This technology certainly could be used to revive and reform a service that has largely abandoned its vital mission. However, it will not happen without structural change in the system itself. All we need is the political will. Our democracy deserves no less.

References

"APTS Priority: Expand Funding Sources as PubTV Gets Its 'Second Chance.'" 2001. Interview with John Lawson. *Current.* December 3, 10, 12–15.

Aufderheide, P. 1991. "Public Television and the Public Sphere." *Critical Studies in Mass Communication* 8: 168–183.

Bedford, K. 1995. "Job Description: Watch Your Step, Make Magic." *Current Online.* November 6. www.current.org/pbs/pbs601.html (August 14, 2001).

Behrens, S. 1994. "How Will PBS Make Underwriting User Friendly?" *Current,* July 4, 1.

———. 1998. "Gore Panel Endorses Adding Educational DTV Channels." *Current,* December 21, 1, 10.

Brennan, T. 1985. "Masterpiece Theater and the Use of Tradition." *Social Text* 12, 102–112.

Brinkley, J. 1997. "PBS Makes Digital Plans." *New York Times,* October 20.

Bullert, B.J. 1997. *Public Television Politics and the Battle over Documentary Film.* New Brunswick, NJ: Rutgers University Press.

Carnegie Commission on Educational Television. 1967. *Public Television: A Program for Action.* New York: Bantam.

Center for Digital Democracy. 2001. "Another Step Down the Slippery Slope: FCC Approves Public Television's Commercial-Revenue Plans." October 23. www.democraticmedia.org/news/washingtonwatch/publictv.html

Center for Media Education. 1998. *Reinventing Public Broadcasting in the Digital Age.* Washington, DC: CME.

Common Cause. 1997. *Channeling Influence: The Broadcast Lobby and the $70 Billion Free Ride.* Washington, DC: Common Cause.

Copps, M. 2001. "Commissioner Copps on the Commercialization of PBS." *Civil Rights Forum Newsletter,* October.

Daressa, L. 1996. "Television for a Change: To Help Us Change Ourselves." *Current,* February 12.

"Digital Delay." 2001. *Broadcasting & Cable,* March 12, 35.

Federal Communications Commission. 2001a. "FCC Clarifies Rules for Noncommercial Television Stations." *Use of Digital Television Channel Capacity.* October 11.

———. 2001b. "In the Matter of Ancillary or Supplementary Use of Digital Television Capacity by Noncommercial Licensees." MM Docket No. 98–203, October 17.

Greppi, M. 2001. "Digital TV for 200 Bucks." *Electronic Media,* November 11.

Gunther, M. 1993. "Public Relations: Are Corporate Sponsors Influencing What PBS Viewers See?" *Detroit Free Press,* July 7.

Halonen, D. 2000. "FCC Fee a Low-power Missile?" *Electronic Media,* October 16, 1, 30.

———. 2001a. "Ads OK for Public DTV." *Electronic Media,* October 15.

———. 2001b."Another Way to Free Up Frequencies." *Electronic Media,* September 24, 20.

"House Tells TV Execs to Resolve DTV Issues." 2001. *Electronic Media,* November 5.

Hoynes, W. 1994. *Public Television for Sale: Media, the Market and the Public Sphere.* Boulder, CO: Westview Press.

Johnson, L.B. 1967. Remarks of President Lyndon B. Johnson upon Signing the Public Broadcasting Act of 1967. CPB Web site. http://www.cpb.org/about/history/johnsonspeech.html (August 14, 2002).

Keane, J. 1995. "Structural Transformations of the Public Sphere." *Communication Review* 1, no. 1: 1–22.

Kennard, W. 2001. *Report to Congress on the Public Interest Obligations of Television Broadcasters As They Transition to Digital Television.* www.fcc.gov/speeches/kennard/statements/2001/stwek106.pdf.

Lake, Snell, Perry, and Associates. 1998. *Television in the Digital Age: A Report to the Project on Media Ownership.* Washington, DC: Benton Foundation, December.

Landay, J. 2001. "Right's Funding Should Flunk PBS's Perception Test." *Current,* June 18.

Lapham, L. 1993. "Adieu Big Bird: On the Terminal Irrelevance of Public Television." *Harper's,* December, 35–38.

Ledbetter, J. 1997a. *Made Possible By: The Death of Public Broadcasting in the United States.* New York: Verso.

———. 1997b. Speech at Media & Democracy Congress II, October, New York.

Liroff, D.B. 1997. "On the Eve of DTV, Public TV Is Not Yet Ready to Cope." *Current* 3, November 20.

"Money Talks." 2001. *Columbia Journalism Review,* March/April: 15.

"More Companies Tune into PBS." 1991. *Fortune,* April 22, 17.

Odenwald, D. 2001a. "Stations to Digital TV Date: Drop Dead!" *Current,* November 5, 1, 20.

———. 2001b. "FCC Okays Revenue Services in DTV Bitstream." *Current,* October 22, A1, A14.

PBS. 1990. *PBS National Program Funding Standards and Practices.* Washington, DC: PBS, February.

Powledge, F. 1972. *Public Television: A Question of Survival.* Washington, DC: Public Affairs.

Rowland, W., Jr. 1976. "Public Involvement: The Anatomy of a Myth." In *The Future of Public Broadcasting,* ed. Douglas Cater and Michael J. Nyhan. New York: Praeger, 109–139.

Starr, J.M. 2001. *Air Wars: The Fight to Reclaim Public Broadcasting.* Philadelphia: Temple University Press.

Twentieth-Century Fund Task Force on Public Television. 1993. *Quality Time? The Report of the Twentieth-Century Fund Task Force on Public Television.* New York: Twentieth-Century Fund Press.

Weiskind, R. 1995. "PBS Isn't Elitist or Liberal, MacNeil Asserts." *Pittsburgh Post-Gazette,* March 28.

Weisman, J. 1987. "Public TV in Crisis: How to Make It Better." *TV Guide,* August 8, 26–30, 34–40.

22

The Grassroots Radio Movement in the United States

Marty Durlin and Cathy Melio

> More than audio outlets, volunteer-based community radio stations are cultural institutions in their communities, reflecting the unique concerns and passions of the people who live there. With a system based on openness and collaboration, and diverse programming produced by volunteers and funded by listeners, these stations are cornerstones of participatory democracy, offering ordinary citizens the chance to exercise First Amendment rights in a mass medium and audiences the opportunity to directly support the programming that is of interest to them.
>
> —*Mission Statement, Grassroots Radio Coalition*

Our mission statement goes to the heart of what we are. A global coalition of community broadcasters, producers, volunteers, and activists, we are unified in our commitment to the "community" in community radio, encouraging openness and accountability in governance as well as programming.

What Is Grassroots Radio?

Grassroots Radio is an offshoot of public radio, characterized by community access and volunteer involvement in every aspect of station operations. Reflecting the varied interests of their communities, grassroots radio stations have diverse formats, including eclectic music and information from a variety of sources. Some of the programming comes from independent producers around the country, via satellite or Internet. By "independent," we mean that these producers, for the most part, are not affiliated with any large distribution or production house, such as National Public Radio (NPR) or Public Radio International (PRI), and that their programs are not underwritten by corporate interests.

What sets grassroots radio apart is that *local citizens* are the programmers, producers, and hosts. The average grassroots community station will have between 40 and 100 citizens on the air each week, sharing their musical knowledge, passions, concerns, and ideas with their communities. They have been trained, often free of charge, in the art of radio production and the craft of radio journalism. The licenses for these stations, issued by the Federal Communications Commission (FCC), are noncommercial and educational—two important aspects of the overall mission of community radio.

Grassroots radio stations are more than simple audio outlets; they actually *help to create community* in their listening areas by fostering civic participation. There is magic and power in the concept of community radio. In exercising their First Amendment rights, people bring issues to our airwaves that are often misrepresented, if represented at all, by other media. Listeners can be educated, uplifted, activated, enlightened, frustrated, surprised, and empowered by our programming. Our stations become lifelines in their communities. In the Grassroots Radio Coalition, program directors work with volunteer programming committees (usually elected by volunteers) to create broadcasting schedules, with input from other community members as well. Some stations have no program directors, only program committees.

The fresh atmosphere that surrounds grassroots community stations is recognizable anywhere in the country, due largely to the variety of ordinary citizens on the radio—new voices that have often become competent as a result of the extensive training encouraged by these stations. The mission statements of grassroots stations refer to "giving voice to the voiceless," "serving those not fully served by other broadcast media," "providing a place for community dialogue," "exploring alternative issues," "promoting freedom of speech," and so forth.[1] Since the movement's beginnings in the United States half a century ago, grassroots community radio stations have been a magnet for progressive causes and organizations as well as political and artistic freedom.

While local programming is the backbone of community radio, another element that connects grassroots stations is the wide array of independently produced national programs they share, including *Alternative Radio, New Dimensions, This Way Out, Counterspin, TUC (Time of Useful Consciousness) Radio, Loafer's Glory, Democracy Now!, WINGS* (Women's International News Gathering Service), *Independent Native News,* and *Making*

Contact. Along with local public affairs programs, these shows exemplify a type of alternative programming that features voices and issues not fully heard on other broadcast media. National programs connect grassroots stations, while our local programs ground us in our own communities. Radio consultants find much to criticize about grassroots radio's "patchwork" programming, but community radio practitioners realize that diversity is a strength, not a weakness. Most people who support grassroots stations cite diversity of programming as one of the reasons they contribute financially.

Radio consultants often promulgate a myth about "the way that people use" radio—that people need to know exactly what they'll find every time they tune in to a particular station. This view is countered by one of the central tenets of grassroots radio: that it is insulting to the intelligence of local people to think that they cannot accept or appreciate a variety of programming, especially at a station owned and operated by the community. We believe in expanding our audience for the purpose of achieving program variety, not in reducing variety for the sake of expanding the audience. We also broadcast long-form discussions, interviews, and lectures that counter the "sound bite" mentality of much of today's corporate media. Our stations engage communities in dialogue about issues, local and global, and encourage thought, debate, and action.

Grassroots radio stations foster community by sponsoring events that bring community members and other nonprofit organizations together. Concerts, lectures, fairs, and book and music sales are common forms of fund-raising for grassroots stations. In Maine, WERU-FM's annual Full Circle Summer Fair and, in Tampa, WMNF's Tropical Heatwave bring thousands of people together to celebrate a sense of community and to create awareness of the stations and their diverse program schedules. In Boulder, KGNU's fund-raising lectures, featuring speakers such as Noam Chomsky and Amy Goodman, reinforce the mission of the station while also raising awareness about the importance of community support. Grassroots stations often have "community rooms" at their facilities that are used for meetings, events, and live concerts in front of studio audiences.

The principles that are most important for maintaining a community-involved grassroots station are participatory governance, with active committees involved in decision-making; community and volunteer involvement in all major decisions; openness on the air (no gag orders!); elected volunteer representatives serving on boards of directors; open access to the airwaves; the active recruitment and training of volunteers; a commitment to diversity; and consideration of those people who are underserved by other broadcast media.

Grassroots stations generally have 100 to 200 volunteers each, depending on the size of the communities they serve. These volunteers become ambassadors for community radio; indeed, the sense of local ownership in a station increases as the number of community members involved increases. This is the crux of an important issue for grassroots radio: the more people involved in your station, the better off you are. If grassroots stations are to be cornerstones of participatory democracy, they need to engage as many people as possible in their operations. Grassroots radio fosters democracy, both in its programming and its governance. Grassroots stations keep the public informed about important legislation and other issues in national, state, and local government. By doing so, they encourage people to become more active as citizens and, indeed, as community activists.

We in the grassroots radio movement need to consider the public interest and the common good in all that we do and to realize that the U.S. broadcasting system on the whole does not inevitably need to keep dumbing everything down for listeners. People are uplifted when they hear intelligent dialogue, when there is room for humor on the air, and when we help satisfy their need for art. Grassroots stations facilitate and activate culture in their communities. From live radio drama to high school jazz bands, the airwaves are open to creative expression. Unhampered by commercial interests, art can take place on grassroots radio. You'll hear a wide range of music from all parts of the world, including productions by small labels and independent artists that are not played on other radio stations. You'll hear live music and interviews with musicians regularly on grassroots radio. Many musicians who travel the country feel welcome at grassroots stations, and they appreciate the role our stations play in helping their music to be heard. Our stations will take chances with programming that other stations would never take; for example, we broadcast original comedy and satire. Our airwaves sing with poetry, drama, music, and dreams. People of all ages become involved in, and excited about, the fact that their community has its own radio station. In this sense, grassroots stations are truly alive.

Our public affairs programs often awaken people to the need to take action on issues, sometimes by starting issue-specific organizations. Our stations are advocates for other nonprofits and serve as conduits for their missions and messages. Environmental organizations, social justice groups, students, labor organizations, and many other alternative groups find that grassroots stations will give them airtime when they want it to spread the word about their actions, meetings, and events. Grassroots stations broadcast call-in programs on important topics, giving the listener a chance to be heard and enabling community dialogue about topics that deserve full discussion. The signals of some grassroots stations also cover large areas, allowing people to raise issues that effectively cross-pollinate with those offered by the citizens of other towns and counties.

Access is key in community radio, and it needs to happen in a variety of ways. People think of their grassroots stations when issues come up that need to be explored or aired, because they know that access to these stations is not only possible, but necessary. Much of the impetus for programming comes from the community through letters, e-mail, phone calls, and visits to the station. When people begin to understand how grassroots radio is different from other media, community involvement naturally increases. The fact that grassroots stations can be competitive with other radio stations that have much larger budgets speaks well of their high levels of community access and involvement. There is a wealth of knowledge, creativity, and passion in every community, and grassroots radio helps communities share these gifts in many ways.

The impact of grassroots radio stations is broad and deep, especially when you consider the number of people involved, both on the air and behind the scenes. Many people who call a community radio program or are on the air as guests will become volunteers and, before long, producers or programmers. In towns and cities that have grassroots radio, everyone knows someone who is on the radio, who has been on the radio, or who soon will be.

Individuals move in and out of grassroots radio stations with ease. A listener may become a volunteer and, later on, a board or staff member. Volunteer programmers end up working on events, writing program guides, or maintaining our buildings and grounds. When volunteers first get involved, they are usually not aware of the extent to which they may eventually participate in different levels of station operations, but time and time again, volunteers help these stations thrive by giving more of their time and talent. Many people are drawn to the stations simply to learn about broadcasting. Soon, they find themselves willingly involved in fundraising, governance, concert production, training, and many other important tasks. Volunteers serve on many different committees: programming, personnel, development, finance, engineering, public affairs, and others. The active participation of volunteers sets grassroots stations apart from other types of radio stations. The fact that these roles are so flexible and accessible demonstrates the organic nature of these organizations as well as their ability to grow, change, and flower. It also demonstrates how much choice volunteers have for involvement, depending on their own interests. Many volunteers who are involved in other organizations connect these organizations back to their stations. True ownership by the people fosters community in a very real way.

When grassroots radio stations make decisions, their governance structures provide plenty of time and space for discussion with interested members of the community. We broadcast call-in programs about important community issues and decisions, as well as station issues and decisions. Our governance structures have checks and balances built into them, to avoid some of the pitfalls that often plague other noncommercial radio stations. Grassroots stations have their problems, and the challenges are many. But if structures and systems are in place to continue an open, collaborative style of governance, positive change can and does happen.

How Grassroots Radio Came About

The grassroots radio movement in the United States grew organically from the wider community radio movement over the past ten years, as it became evident that some community stations were falling prey to the negative forces of commercialization, corporatization, and homogenization that have infiltrated so many media. Under pressure from Congress to prove that public media could compete in a commercial marketplace, the Corporation for Public Broadcasting (CPB) encouraged these trends by altering grant criteria and policies, rewarding the creation of new funding streams (e.g., more and longer underwriting announcements and entrepreneurial ventures), funding programs that would appeal to a greater segment of the American public (read "mainstreaming"), and encouraging consolidation to cut costs.

At the same time, CPB stopped providing the 5 percent credit for volunteer hours that used to count as income at volunteer-based stations, thereby giving them more access to grant money. Instead, the corporation began to use Arbitron ratings performance as one measure of whether stations should even qualify for funding. Because ratings focus mainly on a station's bottom line, CPB's policies came to threaten the very foundation upon which community radio was built: citizen access to the airwaves through noncommercial, community-owned and -operated public radio stations, powered by volunteers and funded by listeners.

By rewarding the creation of new funding sources, including more "enhanced" underwriting and other profit-making ventures, CPB shifted the burden of financial support away from listeners and federal funds and toward the commercial sector. By encouraging a particular style of focus group research, CPB encouraged the production of programs on nonoffensive topics. By encouraging consolidation in noncommercial radio, it also encouraged conglomeration—with bigger stations swallowing smaller ones and statewide networks competing with local community stations (often with nonlocal programming).

In the face of these pressures, staff members from grassroots, volunteer-powered, consensus-oriented radio stations found themselves gravitating toward each other at public radio gatherings, like the annual conference of the National Federation of Community Broadcasters (NFCB). The discussions that ensued led to the conception of two distinct models of community radio: one that seemed to emulate the NPR model (in fact, some community stations actually broadcast NPR programs) and the grassroots community model, with its commitment to volunteers, access to the airwaves, and alternative programming.

Grassroots stations such as KGNU-FM of Boulder, Colorado, and WERU-FM of East Orland, Maine, decided to support each other in a commitment to free speech radio. As managers of these stations, we decided to host the first grassroots radio conference in Boulder in 1996 and cofounded the Grassroots Radio Coalition (GRC) at that same conference. We recognized a need for grassroots staff, volunteers, producers, and community members to have forums for discussion beyond those that already existed. By sharing concerns about trends in public broadcasting, grassroots stations were able to articulate some of the challenges they faced and to acknowledge a desire to work together to deal with them.

The Healthy Station Project

Questions arose about the direction of NFCB. In the early 1990s, it began to push stations toward a model of community radio driven by audience share and homogenized programming through a CPB-funded initiative called the Healthy Station Project (HSP). WERU-FM was one of the stations tapped for the Healthy Station Project in 1993–1994. It withstood the challenges of the HSP by doing what any truly healthy community station would: bringing the topic up for discussion and debate among the entire community and holding open meetings and on-air call-in programs. WERU solicited listener input on the air by asking "What does community radio mean to *you*?" Community members wrote many eloquent letters to elaborate the things they valued about *their* radio station.

Radio consultants were brought in during the HSP, and their measurements of station "health" were truly questionable, if you take the public interest standard into consideration. The consultants criticized the eclectic programming of community stations and urged homogenization. Further, the HSP tried to dismiss the importance of volunteers by excluding them from decision-making and discounting their importance as programmers. Listeners were kept informed about the HSP, even though project staff urged WERU managers to separate "internal" from "external" concerns. The project also favored closed-door meetings that excluded volunteers and some staff members. WERU went against the grain of the HSP, exposed its weaknesses and its skewed priorities, and ended up more committed than ever to the diverse programming and the collaborative form of governance that the study's consultants had ridiculed.

NFCB never finished its implementation of the HSP at WERU. The station's listeners, volunteers, staff, and board reaffirmed their commitment to measuring success in terms of more than just dollars and ratings numbers. Any community station could garner more listeners by mainstreaming its programming, but it would then no longer be an authentic part of its community. For example, the HSP favored carriage of PRI's *World Café,* a daily music program produced at WXPN-FM in Philadelphia. WERU resisted, because it had a fine local program of eclectic music called *On the Wing,* hosted by five different volunteers each week. It had the ability to bring local information into the music program and to respond to listener input and community concerns. If all community stations carried *World Café* every day, many community voices would be displaced, changing the very nature of those stations.

As part of the HSP, David LePage of NFCB also urged community stations to hire "paid morning hosts" for the sake of "consistency." Again, grassroots stations rejected this message. Our diverse volunteer morning hosts strive for consistent programming while, at the same time, sharing their own unique knowledge and experience with listeners. Unique programming has always been a hallmark of community radio.

The Grassroots Radio Conferences

By 1996, enhanced underwriting, focus groups, and Arbitron-based programming decisions had begun to alter the landscape of community radio. The Telecommunications Act of 1996, passed with little public discourse or debate, led to greater corporate monopolization of all broadcast media. There were tremendous external pressures on our stations, including technological changes, increased competition, and shifting political winds. The push toward reducing the diversity of programming, in order to increase the number of listeners, threatened to diminish the eclectic feel of community radio. The trend toward programming that lies closer to the mainstream also threatened to water down the strong political messages and voices that were typically heard on community radio.

We hosted the first grassroots radio conference in Boulder in 1996 to provide a forum for discussion about these pressures. In the process, we hoped to save some community stations from the rush to homogenize programming and disempower their volunteers—practices that had already happened at other stations. So much is lost when a community radio station restructures itself in response to consultants who favor mainstreaming. While "community connection" cannot be measured, it is safe to say that it is not outweighed by profits of any size. If a station goes mainstream, the community loses the airwaves. We jokingly called this phenomenon "the invasion of the body snatchers," but this was really no laughing matter. We wanted to provide support and information to new stations and stations in the planning stage, so they would know that they could operate with volunteer power, collaborative governance, and diverse programming. Perhaps the grassroots stations that are just being started will provide a counterbalance to those that were lost to homogenization and greed. For some stations, the change from volunteer-produced, local programming to homogenized, satellite-fed programming increased listenership and revenue, and was hailed as a "success." Discussions at the grassroots radio conferences have led us to clarify how community radio can measure success beyond the financial bottom line. In these conferences, we have explored the importance of being noncommercial, maintaining community access, functioning as a training ground, and, in the end, creating community.

In addition to KGNU and WERU, community stations that work under the grassroots model (and have been involved in GRC since 1996) include WORT of Madison, Wisconsin, KMUD of Garberville, California, WMNF of Tampa, Florida, KCSB of Santa Barbara, California, KZMU of Moab, Utah, KUNM of Albuquerque, New Mexico, KDUR of Durango, Colorado, and others. People from these stations, plus independent producers of alternative programming, former Pacifica radio staff members and volunteers, and members of AMARC (the World Association of Community Broadcasters), formed a core group of attendees at the annual Grassroots Radio Conferences. We had 85 participants the first year, more than 100 the second year, and 130 the third year, including a tribal caucus of 20 Native American producers and managers. More than 160 people took part in GRC's fourth annual conference.

The first three grassroots radio conferences (1996–1998) were held in Boulder, Colorado, and hosted by KGNU; the fourth took place in 1999 in Bar Harbor, Maine, hosted by WERU; the fifth was hosted by WORT-FM in Madison, Wisconsin, a grassroots station that was then celebrating its twenty-fifth year on the air. These conferences fostered dialogue about grassroots issues that were often missing at NFCB conferences—issues like community involvement, access, activism, and accountability in both programming and governance. NFCB staff members have attended all of the grassroots radio conferences, and GRC has encouraged them to pay more attention to these issues. The fourth conference, in Bar Harbor, Maine, also had many participants from Canadian Community Broadcasting, thanks to AMARC's involvement.

The dialogues that have taken place at GRC conferences, in the form of regular sessions and plenary presentations, include Advocacy on Community Radio, Programming As Outreach, Community Radio on the Internet and Beyond, The Pacification of Public Radio, Managing a Volunteer-Based

Station, The Musical Mission, Local News on a Shoestring, AMARC Update, Preserving Culture, What Happens When Everything Goes Wrong: The KOOP Lesson, Training Our Youth, Micropower Radio, Grassroots Underwriting, Collaborative Decision-Making, Volunteer Committees, Communications As a Human Right, Media and Democracy, The National Radio Project, Beyond Arbitron, Beyond Pacifica, Recruiting and Training Volunteers, Environmental Programming, Activism and Community Radio, Exploring Our Missions, Grassroots Fund-Raising, Independent Producers Panel, Walking the Talk, and many more.

The Grassroots Radio Coalition supports microbroadcasters (low-power FM operators) and has enjoyed their participation at our conferences from the beginning. We see the potential for collaboration rather than competition, believing that with the corporatization of many other media, any effort to give "a few more crumbs" to the people (in terms of more space on the electromagnetic spectrum) would be a victory for all of us. As new community radio stations start up, they often find that a period of microbroadcasting is a useful first step toward creating larger, more powerful stations. Community stations also have the potential to serve as training grounds for microbroadcasters. We think it is unfortunate and inaccurate to call microbroadcasting "pirate radio" (as some mainstream broadcasters do), since these small-scale broadcasters are not stealing anything. Instead, they are simply attempting to take back some of the airwaves that rightfully belong to the public. From this standpoint, the Telecommunications Act of 1996 might more accurately be called an act of piracy.

Grassroots radio conferences continue to explore the following questions: What does "noncommercial" mean in this age of megamergers, enhanced underwriting, and increasing pressures on community stations to be "successful"? What does "success" mean in terms of grassroots broadcasting? What can we do to support each other, along with independent producers, microbroadcasters, and other alternative media outlets, as pressures from corporate media bear down upon us? How can our boards, community advisory boards, staffs, volunteers, and committees function smoothly and fairly, while also remaining accountable to our communities? What does the future hold for the Grassroots Radio Coalition?

The GRC provides an important context for networking and alliance-formation among stations, producers, staff members, and volunteers who work toward integrity in governance and programming. For us, grassroots radio is about taking back more of the airwaves for public discourse and the common good. It's about encouraging the community to be involved in station operations. It's about openness on air, freedom of speech, the discussion of important issues, the inspiration of creativity, and community activation on many levels. It's about seeking out voices that are unheard, underrepresented, oppressed, or suppressed. It is also about recognizing that art and culture are vital human needs that stimulate activism and richness of experience in a community.

Pacifica's Role in Grassroots Radio

Most of the stations involved in GRC are Pacifica radio affiliates,[2] carrying such programs as Pacifica Network News and *Democracy Now!* We have kept our listeners informed of events within the Pacifica Network and have requested that Pacifica, itself, cover events and issues that impact the network— because it is important news for our stations. During Pacifica's recent period of turmoil (see Matthew Lasar's chapter in this volume), grassroots broadcasters have watched as increasingly autocratic network managers dismissed volunteers at some of the five network-owned stations and came into conflict with unionized staff and the union itself. We watched with horror and disbelief the takeover of KPFA-FM in Berkeley, California, which culminated in the presence of armed guards at a pacifist community radio station celebrating its fiftieth anniversary.

When Pacifica switched to the Ku band (a range of frequencies used for direct broadcast satellites) for satellite distribution in 1996, affiliates were offered a three-year contract. This contract included a gag order that prohibited stations from broadcasting critical comments about Pacifica. Since KGNU and WERU do not, themselves, have gag orders, we refused to sign and negotiated a change in our contracts to eliminate the gag order. Actions by Pacifica's board and management made it increasingly difficult to collaborate with the network. The Pacifica crisis did not simply appear out of the blue in 1999; indeed, we were concerned about problems at the network at least five years earlier. We organized actions in response to the Pacifica crisis, such as "A Day Without Pacifica"—a one-day boycott of network programming in October 1999 that was observed by sixteen affiliates nationwide. We stressed the value of the programming provided by Pacifica, particularly *Democracy Now!,* yet highlighted our concerns over management's affronts to democracy and Pacifica's lack of accountability. At the 1997 grassroots radio conference in Boulder, Pacifica touted the potential of Ku band satellite distribution for enabling affiliates to distribute their own local productions and to share programs with each other. This was actually impossible at the time because of the breakdown of communication between Pacifica management and the affiliates. With the settlement of the crisis in 2002, however, this is once again a possibility.

We believe that some of the problems at Pacifica came from the same philosophical place that the misguided Healthy Station Project came from—a desire to increase audience size while sacrificing the very qualities that make community radio so rare and valuable. These qualities include access for the public, programming that is simply not heard elsewhere, and accountability in governance. We all want to have more listeners, but not at the expense of the mission of our stations.

What's Next for GRC?

The Grassroots Radio Coalition is helping to strengthen access to the airwaves by providing an opportunity for grassroots broadcasters to come together, discuss important issues, and act collectively on those issues. As people organize, grassroots community radio is a natural tool for spreading the message, as it has always been.

Grassroots community radio stations are now in a position to share information in new ways, thanks to new technologies. No matter how many streams of great music and news programs become available to the public, grassroots radio will continue to have a niche all its own, set apart by the sheer number, variety, and talent of the community volunteers who make it all happen. This type of radio is also unique because it is rooted in the community; it is radio with an open door that regularly draws people in. GRC is optimistic about its future and about the prospect of reclaiming more of the airwaves for the public.

We are excited about the Internet and other new technologies, the convergence of alternative media, microbroadcasting, and independent media centers. We now have people at our stations who are working in multiple formats—people who will, for example, use a digital video camera to shoot something for cable access TV and then bring the audio in for use in a radio news story. These kinds of interactions will happen more and more in the years to come; with that in mind, we hope to encourage collaborations across all forms of new media. Grassroots community radio stations are natural allies for microbroadcasters. The Internet is also a natural source of information and connection for grassroots broadcasters, enabling many stations to "go global." Because of Webcasting, we are able to listen to other grassroots stations from around the country. This has brought us to another level of kinship that was difficult to achieve when the only way a person could hear a particular station was to visit the area covered by its signal. Hearing other stations helps us to understand what sorts of community ties give each station its own unique character, and it also helps us to know why this sort of interaction matters.

What does the future hold for the Grassroots Radio Coalition? We will continue to explore the potential of collective action for dealing with the challenges our stations face and to share information and other resources in creative ways. GRC has provided a necessary complement to the NFCB, not to mention a challenge to its position of primacy in community radio. We are a coalition of stations that evolved organically out of a need for new approaches to noncommercial broadcasting. How can we increase involvement by all underrepresented people at GRC, at our stations, and in our programming? In the years to come, we will address the issue of diversity among GRC participants, finding ways to ensure that people who are not seated at our table will be there in the future.

We would like to see grassroots community radio flourish and thrive, creating more space for dialogue in the public's interest instead of the interests of corporations. We will continue to encourage grassroots radio stations to speak out about self-censorship in mainstream media, increasing corporate control over media, and the need for more community voices on the airwaves. People need and deserve media that tell them about everything that is going on in the real world—not just the latest trends in consumer products. Grassroots radio will continue to work in collaboration with the alternative press, cable access television, Internet media, microbroadcasters, and other nonprofit groups. We hope the number of grassroots community radio stations will increase, along with gains in microradio and other media, and that the wonderful potential of grassroots radio will be more fully realized.

Following the lead of folk singer Pete Seeger, we hope you will support community radio and remember to "make music yourselves." If you do, the twenty-first century just might be a time when new technologies are brought into the service of democratization. The airwaves are a precious natural resource, much of which has been lost to commercialism, corporate control, and censorship. The Grassroots Radio Coalition hopes to keep shining a light on these forms of corruption, not only to preserve what has been saved thus far, but also to create more public space on the airwaves—to democratize technology in small, but important ways.

Notes

1. Statements taken from various mission statements and program guides.
2. The Pacifica Network was founded after World War II by Lewis Hill, a pacifist with a strong commitment to freedom of speech. He created KPFA-FM in Berkeley, California, with a vision of building a listener-sponsored community radio station with a diverse range of voices. In the late 1990s, the network underwent a major crisis of governance, as producers from some of the five network-owned stations were fired and banned from the premises. A gag rule was imposed and several lawsuits were initiated to try to return a democratic structure to the board of directors. Pressure from these lawsuits, along with an organized campaign against what were seen as illegal board members, forced a restructuring that was finally implemented in January 2002. For more on the latest details in the Pacifica story, see Matthew Lasar's chapter in this volume.

23

Microradio

A Tool for Community Empowerment

Andrea Cano

The strength of this country lies in its democratic ideals and rich cultural diversity. While true democracy depends on access to accurate, complete, and timely information, that access is genuinely achieved only when communications media are available and responsive to the diverse cultures and characteristics of every community. At present, our democracy is being weakened by the pervasiveness of large commercial media interests whose priority is profit, not the public interest. One result of the Telecommunications Act of 1996 was an unprecedented concentration of media ownership, especially in the radio industry. Within four years of its enactment, major corporate mergers and consolidations led to the reinforcement of barriers that have kept traditionally underrepresented groups at the margins of power and influence. These groups simply lacked the basic channels of participation that one might expect in a democracy, especially in terms of information gathering and dissemination through media outlets located in their own communities.

Media activists witnessed the growing homogenization of radio programming at a time when the population of this country was actually becoming more diverse and when technical developments promised to give us new ways to deliver media content. In the wake of the 1996 act, large national radio groups supplanted local ownership and decision-making, with negative consequences for the delivery of local news and information. Thus, many stations adopted formats that were largely irrelevant to local communities and special language groups. Stations that fell prey to these trends often failed to meet the information needs of recently arrived immigrant groups, inner-city youths, senior citizens, migrant farm workers, and people in mountain and rural communities isolated by geography or topology.

To counter this drift away from locally based radio programming, the Federal Communications Commission (FCC) approved a new service in January 2000 called low-power FM radio, otherwise known as LPFM or microradio. A week later, the FCC released its Report and Order on the Creation of Low Power Radio Service, outlining the process for construction permits and licensing, along with the technical requirements for these 10- and 100-watt stations. Two months later, the commission announced five time periods, or "windows," for the filing of applications, from the end of May 2000 until the same time in 2001. Applications from eleven states or U.S. territories were to be filed in each window, with specific dates to be announced one month before the forms were due.

Eligibility and Requirements for LPFM

The FCC decided that LPFM applicants must be either not-for-profit educational organizations or other entities that proposed a noncommercial service designed to protect the safety of life, health, or property. The first category of applicants had to demonstrate an educational mission and, in order to preserve the ideal of localism, ensure that their organizational headquarters (and 75 percent of their board members) resided within a ten-mile radius of the proposed transmitter site. (Other requirements came into play for public safety radio services.) Regarding ownership, the FCC stipulated that neither the organization—nor its board members or their relatives—should hold an interest in any other television, radio, newspaper, or cable TV operation, excluding cable access channels. If the applicant was a local chapter of a national organization, it had to demonstrate a distinct local presence and mission. The FCC also posed questions about the character of the people seeking licenses in terms of prior convictions or past participation in unlicensed radio operations. Finally, applicants had to promise that they would broadcast for at least thirty-six hours per week.

In the case of competing applicants, a point system was offered whereby organizations earned credit if they could document their presence in the community for more than two years (with an address that lay within ten miles of the proposed transmitter site during that time), promise to broadcast for at least twelve hours per day, and offer at least eight hours per day of locally produced programming.[1] The commission said it would also consider the voluntary time-sharing of LPFM frequencies by applicants that had amassed identical point totals.

The Microradio Implementation Project

In response to the FCC's low-power FM initiative, the Office of Communication, Inc., of the United Church of Christ (UCC) established the Microradio

Implementation Project (MIP).[2] Funded in part by the Ford and MacArthur Foundations and the Open Society Institute, MIP assists local community and church-based organizations in developing LPFM stations, encourages grassroots support for this initiative, and provides groups that are both interested and qualified with the legal, organizational, and technical expertise they need to apply for LPFM construction permits. When permits are granted, project staff also help with the actual effort to get LPFM stations on the air, especially in the case of applicants from historically marginalized groups.

In its first six months of operation, MIP identified and began to serve nearly 300 community-based groups from Maine to California that sought to establish LPFM stations. From the time the project's Web site (www.microradio.org) was established in May 2000 until January 2002, it received more than 183,000 hits from 22,000 unique users. Two unanticipated consequences noted by project staff were the collaborative spirit of many women and men who have been at the heart of the community radio movement for years and the number of pro-LPFM voices—including representatives from community radio stations and the wider broadcasting industry—who contacted MIP directly to offer support and assistance. It soon became evident that other types of grassroots support for microradio were already in place, especially from groups engaged in public access issues, those with prior LPFM experience, so-called pirate radio operators, and those with ties to an already sympathetic academic community. However, these groups did not necessarily have alliances with national advocacy organizations, nor did they effectively spread the word about low-power FM throughout their own constituencies. Their voices may have been heard during the FCC's comment period for LPFM, but there was little in the way of an echo to their regional and local constituencies.

Internal communications at the UCC helped close the gap between theory and practice. Once this process began to unfold, the Office of Communication began to identify key contacts in potential client organizations such as national advocacy groups, faith partners, and other service organizations. In order to equip applicants with the skills needed to secure an LPFM license, it was first necessary to gauge the level of wisdom and know-how that each interested group possessed. Clearly, organizational needs and technical skills varied from group to group. This fact, juxtaposed with the style, format, and content decisions each group would soon have to make, complicated matters even further. MIP staff began piecing together information about each applicant group through phone calls, e-mail queries, mailings, and communications with other appropriate resource people.

The Effort to Educate, Advocate, and Promote

The primary goal was to educate community organizations throughout the country about the advantages of noncommercial low-power FM stations. The first task for MIP, then, was to determine which groups were interested, where they were located, and what kind of support they needed. News about "frequency saturation" in New York, Chicago, Los Angeles, and (perhaps) San Francisco initially dampened hopes for securing LPFM channels in these cities. As channel search technology was refined, however, several "niche" frequencies were found in these areas and workshops and other activities were initiated.

The FCC's sudden decision to authorize LPFM in January 2000 thrust MIP quickly into the task of serving client groups. At first, it was thought that one general window for applications from all fifty states (and several U.S. territories) would open in the late spring of 2000. By the end of February, though, it was clear that a lottery would be held and that the FCC would divide the country into clusters of states and territories. MIP assumed that the lottery would be held on the basis of geographically defined regions. By the end of March, we knew this would not be the case; in fact, each of the five applicant clusters was composed of randomly selected groups of states and territories. This posed a challenge for MIP, since we had developed initial plans for a sequence of regional workshops (the Northeast, the Southwest, etc.). Fortunately, we were able to partner with other supportive groups to make sure that the people and other resources needed for these workshops got where they needed to go, within a workable time frame.

As planning for the workshops progressed, Cheryl Leanza from the Media Access Project produced an easy-to-follow guide for the filing of construction permit applications. Nan Rubin, a consultant to the United Methodist Church Low-Power Radio Project, also produced a guidebook on the FCC's technical requirements. Soon afterward, we scheduled workshops for the first cluster of states—states in which there was greater potential for applications to succeed. MIP considered an offer by the United Methodist Church to set up national training teleconferences for applicants from states and territories whose filing windows would come later on. Michael Bracy of the Low-Power Radio Coalition in Washington, D.C. kept us informed about pro- and anti-LPFM sentiments among members of Congress, secured LPFM endorsements from key senators, and staged creative high-profile events, such as a concert and press conference featuring the popular music group, the Indigo Girls. A team of experienced women and men were contracted to run MIP's training events. Workshops and other meetings were then organized in New Orleans, Sacramento, Fresno, San Diego, and Baltimore. We also arranged workshops for the second cluster of states and territories—including Connecticut, Illinois, Kansas, Minnesota, and Puerto Rico—whose filing window would arrive in August 2000.

MIP's second goal was to build strategies that fostered widespread community support for microradio. While the FCC's vote on LPFM in mid-January was favorable, opposition by the National Association of Broadcasters (NAB) and National Public Radio (NPR) grew with a vengeance in February and March. These organizations lobbied heavily for the passage of HR 3439 and S 2068, bills that would undo the commission's decision to authorize the new service. They used scare tactics, misleading and inaccurate information, and a compact disc recording that allegedly (and fraudulently) demonstrated potential "frequency interference" by LPFM stations—all designed to win members of Congress over to their point of view. LPFM advocates responded with strategies of their own to mobilize potential applicant groups and gain more support at the grassroots level. In spite of these efforts, news about the growing level of support for LPFM was being communicated neither to elected officials nor to the press and electronic media. The silence on the issue from national television and cable news outlets was deafening. MIP dutifully mailed news advisories about local LPFM initiatives and encouraged letters to the editor, as well as actual news stories, about those same initiatives. A sprinkling of daily and community newspapers wrote about projects in their areas.

The strongest challenge for MIP was to convince potential applicants that they should continue with their planning in the midst of the political threat to eliminate low-power FM. Staff members encouraged applicants to let their congressional representatives know about their plans and about the potential benefits of LPFM to local communities. We also encouraged these people to contact various media organizations with stories about MIP and the misconceptions that were being circulated by anti-LPFM groups. In summary, we felt it was imperative to continue a program of strategic outreach to individuals and community organizations, to further empower them to explain the ways in which low-power radio could address community needs and enhance people's ability to take part in the democratic process. The MIP staff worked hard to spread the word through Web sites that were organized at the city and state levels. Unexpectedly, we began to get queries from a much broader spectrum of society. In addition to churches and other faith communities, we were contacted by municipal governments, community colleges, cable access TV projects, refugee and immigrant groups, senior citizens housing complexes, and other organizations. Also, people working for community radio stations—and even some NPR affiliates—volunteered to serve as resource people, trainers, and advocates.

Challenges and Celebrations: The Experience of Filing FCC Form 318

Though MIP worked to guide applicants through the filing process, a variety of problems and uncertainties cropped up at the local level. For some community-based organizations (CBOs), the thirty-day notice the FCC provided before the opening of a filing window was simply not enough. The timetable for the application process also conflicted with the normal meeting schedules of many nonprofit organizations; not surprisingly, their executives were unwilling to make decisions alone, especially in terms of programming, personnel, financial outlay, and long-term institutional commitments. "Put simply," said one applicant, "many groups would have to have been planning for this since about the time the FCC first started taking comments [on LPFM in 1999]. Sadly, many CBOs were not aware at that time that this resource might become available for them." Gathering documents and other paperwork often took more time than anticipated, and applicant groups sometimes agonized over whether to file separately or join the efforts of other like-minded groups.

Comments from groups that actually applied for construction permits are instructive in terms of the philosophical orientations they imply and the networks of collaboration that were developed in the name of serving the common good. Tom Hanlon of the GSRI Property Owners Association in Baton Rouge, Louisiana—a group that operates a youth mentoring project and community issues forum—feels that LPFM is "the best thing to happen to the public airwaves in several generations." His group decided to go forward with an LPFM application after realizing that the monetary investment would be relatively small. "We have worked with individuals and groups on community issues for the last five years," he said, "so we know how to make that formula work for our community." Regarding the application process, Hanlon agrees with the FCC's position that it would not "go door to door like the Census and beg for applicants." That said, he feels that some groups that might have benefited from LPFM missed out on the chance to apply in the first round. "If a community did not have an activist or an Internet connection (preferably both) and contact those that were following events on a day-to-day basis, the odds increased dramatically [that] they missed the boat. My guess . . . is that you would find a distressing lack of low income and [community-based] minority applications in the first wave. These are the communities that stand to gain the most empowerment from LPFM." Despite these problems, Hanlon likes the potential synergies that an LPFM project can offer, in terms of walking the line "between commercial and public, community based and corporate, subsidized and private, individual and government."

Because of these potential connections, he argues that LPFM stands a good chance of being effective in the long run.

Fred Pierce of the national Multi-Ethnic Families Association admits that his group was initially nervous about its application, but adds that the process went smoothly because "all the hard work had already been done a long time ago. Our organization came together in 1989, incorporated in 1991, received its 501(c)(3) status in 1994 . . . and our program included a significant educational component. Our organization has had for some years a small internal group of radio-interested people who followed the microradio movement. This meant we had up-to-date knowledge of developments at the FCC and some level of tech expertise. We knew enough to ask the right questions and get the draft [application] completed." Fred's group received help during the application process from Radio Free Berkeley, the Prometheus Radio Project, REC Networks, the Microradio Implementation Project, and the National Lawyer's Guild, among others. "The support of these groups was helpful not only directly with the FCC application," he says, "but their existence and support had the effect of lending 'legitimacy' to the entire project, making it easier to convince our board and membership to go ahead."

Doug Dessero of the La Habra Christian Church in California was initially confused about whether a church could apply for an LPFM license. "We are trying to reach out into the community and radio would be a perfect way to do this. There are many people who are shut-ins or are too sick to get to our services or a Bible study. We will be broadcasting our weekly services as well as past sermons [and] also a Bible study where people can participate through phone-in, faxes, and the web; plus live call-in shows dealing with parenting, teenagers, the loss of a loved one, advice for the elderly based on the teachings of the Bible, [and the] promotion of community events. Since it's difficult to get info on the commercial stations about small town events, LPFM would be a great vehicle."

Arthur Cribbs, senior pastor of the UCC Christian Fellowship in San Diego and former executive director of the Office of Communication, United Church of Christ, hosted one of the May 2000 LPFM workshops. He offers an eloquent statement of the philosophical foundations of the microradio movement: "Our need is very clear," said Cribbs:

> there is an almost complete absence of African, Afro-Caribbean, and African American presence on local radio. These communities represent roughly eight percent of San Diego County [and] that does not include the prominent military presence and the increased Black representation in the armed forces based here. At the same time, the current local radio programming is decidedly politically conservative-to-right-wing reactionary with a good

dose of homespun racism. Additionally, the antagonism toward the international communities, and particularly the Mexican and Latino immigrants, is vile, evil, unnecessary, and anti-human. There are too few voices of moderation or opposition on the airwaves here. Thus, there is more sufficient reason for us to be more involved in this issue of community-based radio.

When we consider the amount of commercial and banal programming that is otherwise meaningless and strewn with banter about things unimportant, along with the sensationalism that is our daily fare, we have a rather disturbing use of [a] public utility—[namely] radio stations and public airwaves. On the other hand, there seems to be very little outrage about this situation. Most of us just grin and bear it or tune out and do something else. The fact is, people are affected by this kind of programming. It is my contention that misuse, abuse, or callous use of the airwaves leads to an erosion of democracy and adversely affects the quality of community life. As a result, we continue to experience a reduction in citizen participation at all levels of political discourse and opportunity. We are either not informed or misinformed about real issues that have a direct effect on our lives.

Politics and Policy Implications

The FCC's decision to authorize LPFM marked perhaps the first time in the agency's history that it responded to the wishes of individuals and community organizations instead of corporate executives and broadcasting lobbyists. Members of Congress also began to hear from their constituents about the negative consequences of their votes for the Telecommunications Act of 1996. Communities across the nation gained a better understanding of their media environments, including the ways in which LPFM could be used for the gathering, production, and delivery of information that is highly relevant to the lives of local citizens. LPFM brought a wide variety of people together at the national, regional, and local levels to share wisdom and experience, thus creating relationships based on mutual trust and consultation.

As the year 2000 unfolded, it became clear that the anti-LPFM factions in the Senate would not bring legislation that would kill this new service to the floor for debate; instead, they would attach the measure to a year-end appropriations bill as a rider. Senator John McCain (R-AZ) led a bipartisan push to offset the anti-LPFM rider and denounced both the NAB and NPR on the Senate floor in October for their complicity in trying to kill microradio. President Bill Clinton, an LPFM supporter, first refused to sign the appropriations bill. However, it was returned to Clinton at the end of the year, once again with the anti-LPFM rider attached. He had no choice but to sign it this time, as he prepared to turn the White House over to George W. Bush. The fall 2000 presidential elections also had a strong impact on the prospects for microradio. FCC chairman William Kennard left his post by the end of the year and his successor, Michael Powell, was appointed by President Bush in early 2001. Based on his prior statements as an FCC commissioner, we deduced that Powell was not a strong advocate for LPFM.

The legislation Clinton signed into law ordered the FCC to modify its technical requirements in order to provide additional space between adjacent channels on the FM dial, a move that effectively eliminated about half of the frequencies that were first available for LPFM throughout the country. This drastically affected the prospects of the 1,200 or so applicants who had filed during the first two windows. During the second window, 474 applications were filed, and, by April 2001, the FCC had conditionally approved about 30 applicants who complied with the new technical rules. The agency dismissed about 30 more bids for an LPFM license and placed over 600 applications in a "remedial list." Applicants on this list could make technical amendments to convince the FCC that their operations would not interfere with any existing radio signals, but given the nature of the new regulations, it was unlikely that many would be able to do so. As of January 2002, the FCC had not announced another filing window for remedial applicants. Despite the commission's new technical requirements, the number of applicants in subsequent window filings was greater than anticipated—536 in the third window, 925 in the fourth, and 567 in the fifth.

By the start of 2002, the FCC had granted fewer than 200 construction permits. Only a handful of LPFM stations had made it to air and thousands of other applications awaited processing by an already overworked agency staff. One other reason for the slow rollout of LPFM has to do with a disturbing observation made by MIP and other LPFM advocates. A number of applicants seemed to ignore the FCC's stipulation that no LPFM licensee may retransmit, terrestrially or via satellite, the signal of a full-power radio station. MIP, the Center for Democratic Communications, the United Church of Christ, and the Prometheus Radio Project have begun filing petitions to deny such applications, which come primarily from religious radio networks.

The good news is that thousands of community groups—including social service agencies, schools districts, colleges and universities, and racial and ethnic communities—have entered into creative, collaborate efforts to secure LPFM frequencies. Publicity for the movement was certainly enhanced by the production of a fourteen-minute documentary titled *The People's Voice*. Narrated by Emmy Award–winning actor Peter Coyote, this video chronicles the formation of the LPFM movement as well as the persistence of church and community groups in the face of pressure from the national radio interests that tried to shut microradio down in the year 2000.[3] The video was distributed nationally by the United Church of Christ and was also screened at various national, regional, and local events. More than 500 copies were sent to LPFM applicants, media advocates, national organizations that endorsed LPFM, and members of Congress.

Conclusion

Over the past two years, we have observed and celebrated the creativity and commitment of citizens in local communities to improve their media environments and empower themselves with LPFM. Some local groups had monitored the developing microradio movement for years; others mobilized for the purpose of securing a license within a few months of learning about the movement. An incalculable amount of human and financial resources have been poured into this effort. We applaud the resilience and resourcefulness demonstrated by LPFM's national and regional partners in confronting the anti-LPFM campaign by national broadcasters. Their desire to move forward in spite of a diminished number of available frequencies is also laudable.

We now realize the extent to which the FCC's work—indeed, its existence— is bound to the workings of Congress and how lobbyists can exert undue influence on elected officials.

We have discovered that "gatekeepers" in many congressional offices have rendered some of our e-mails, letters, faxes, and other communications ineffective; certainly, we feel that not enough lawmakers have learned about our point of view on LPFM. In spite of these obstacles, we hope that members of both the House and Senate have become convinced that the views of ordinary constituents back home should be given weight in this matter, in addition to the views of national broadcasting executives and lobbyists.

While deeply disappointed by the corporate posture of NPR and certain other public radio organizations, we also know that these groups have attracted a fair amount of criticism from citizens who are sympathetic to microradio. Some organizations were criticized for gobbling up numerous translator frequencies in their regions of operation, while others were chastised for buying community radio stations in states other than the ones in which their primary stations are licensed. The response by LPFM proponents included "un-pledge drives" against these and other mainstream public radio outlets. To be fair, we must also note that managers and staff members from several NPR affiliates either have called to offer support and assistance or—in the case of stations in Albuquerque, New Mexico, and Portland, Oregon—have endorsed LPFM publicly.

We treasure the profound level of trust and confidence that has been established through the collaboration of the national LPFM partners cited earlier in this chapter. It was the pooling of wisdom, experience, and problem-solving skills during this exercise that helped this special collective to succeed. We have also expanded our hub to include an ever growing network of media activists and communications attorneys, along with radio professionals who have expertise in engineering, program production, and journalism. Finally, we are grateful for the trust and confidence that have been placed in us by the foundations that have supported our project. After two years of LPFM activity, we are confident that thousands more communities will one day be empowered by this new radio service.

Notes

1. This was delineated in FCC Form 318 for LPFM application.

2. For more information, contact the Microradio Implementation Project by mail at 633 SW Montgomery Street, Portland, Oregon 97232. The organization's Web site is available at www.microradio.org.

3. This video featured a diverse collection of interviews with Senator John McCain (R-AZ), Representative David Bonior (D-MI), former FCC chairman William Kennard, Wade Henderson of the Leadership Council for Civil Rights, and people planning an LPFM station in Yellow Springs, Ohio. Other comments come from LPFM advocates such as Andrea Cano, Microradio Implementation Project; Cheryl Leanza, Media Access Project; Pete TriDish, Prometheus Radio Project; and Wayne Henderson, Leadership Forum on Civil Rights.

About the Editors and Contributors

B. Lee Artz (Ph.D., Iowa) is an associate professor at Purdue University, Calumet. He is secretary for Harbor Country Radio, a low-power FM applicant in southwest Michigan. As director of the communication and social justice concentration at Loyola University, he was a chief architect in the restructuring of Loyola's WLUW radio format from pop music to community broadcasting. In the 1990s, Artz was producer for *Strategies for Change* on Pacifica Radio's KPFA and national coordinator for a live international satellite broadcast of the Nicaraguan elections. His books include *Cultural Hegemony in the United States* (Sage, 2000), *Communication and Democratic Society* (Thomson Learning, 2001), and *Globalization and Corporate Media Hegemony* (forthcoming, 2002).

Robert K. Avery (Ph.D., Pennsylvania State) is professor of communication at the University of Utah. His research interests include telecommunications policy, communication history, and interactive media. A former public television administrator, Professor Avery has served as chair of the National Association of Educational Broadcasters. He is author or coauthor of numerous articles and other publications on the subject of public broadcasting, most recently *A History of Public Broadcasting* (Current, 2002). He is also founding editor of *Critical Studies in Mass Communication.*

Ira Basen (M.A., Wisconsin) is executive producer of *Workology*, a weekly CBC radio series on the world of work. His job at CBC focuses on new ways of telling stories and reaching audiences—while remaining true to the values of the organization. Basen was formerly executive producer of *This Morning* on

CBC Radio One. His academic specialty is American history and he teaches a course at the University of Toronto called "Spin: PR, Journalism and the Search for Truth." Basen is now writing a book about public relations and the media.

Andrea Cano is director of the Microradio Implementation Project in Portland, Oregon. She has twenty-five years of experience in the development of social communications projects and was the first director of the California Chicano News Media Association. She also served as the communications officer for the Geneva-based World Council of Churches and as the consultant for communications for the Latin American Council of Churches in Quito, Ecuador. A native of Southern California, Cano attended California State University at Fullerton and worked as a newspaper and television reporter in Los Angeles.

Judi Puritz Cook (Ph.D., Temple) is assistant professor in the Communications Department at Salem State College. Her current research involves a comparison between the underwriting spots on *PBS Kids* and the commercials on "commercial" children's programming. She published an article titled "Consumer Culture and Television Home Shopping Programming: An Examination of the Sales Discourse" in the Fall 2000 issue of *Mass Communication and Society.*

Barry Dornfeld (Ph.D., Pennsylvania) is director and associate professor in the Communication Program at the University of the Arts in Philadelphia. Dornfeld is a media researcher, organizational consultant, and documentary filmmaker, and his research interests include media organizations, media reception, and cultural performance. He is the author of *Producing Public Television, Producing Public Culture* (Princeton University Press, 1998), an ethnography of a PBS documentary series.

Marty Durlin has been station manager at KGNU-FM in Boulder, Colorado, for the past thirteen years. She began her career in public radio in the early 1970s in Denver and has also worked in commercial radio and as a newspaper journalist and editor. Durlin served on the board of the National Federation of Community Broadcasters for four years and is cofounder (with Cathy Melio) of the Grassroots Radio Coalition. She has developed principles of effective management for volunteer-based radio stations, a topic she has lectured on at numerous conferences and workshops around the country.

Lyombe S. Eko (Ph.D., Southern Illinois) is assistant professor in the Department of Communication and Journalism at the University of Maine. His areas of research and teaching interest include comparative mass media law and policy, visual communication, and telecommunication via the Internet. Prior to his academic career, Eko was a journalist and producer at the African Broadcasting Union (URTNA) in Nairobi, Kenya, and at the Cameroon Radio and Television Corporation. He has produced several video documentaries on African topics and now manages a digital mass media lab at the University of Maine.

DeeDee Halleck is a media activist and cofounder of Paper Tiger Television and the Deep Dish Satellite Network, the first grassroots community television network. She is professor emerita in the Department of Communication at the University of California at San Diego. Her film *Mural on Our Street* was nominated for an Academy Award in 1965. A past winner of Guggenheim and Rockefeller Media Fellowships, Halleck has also written widely about independent media. She is director of development for the television version of *Democracy Now!*, a well-known Pacifica radio program.

William Hoynes (Ph.D., Boston College) is associate professor and chair of the Sociology Department at Vassar College, where he teaches courses on media, culture, and social theory. He is author or coauthor of several books about the U.S. media industry, including *Public Television for Sale: Media, the Market, and the Public Sphere* (Westview Press, 1994) and (with David Croteau) *The Business of Media: Corporate Media and the Public Interest* (Pine Forge Press, 2001).

Mary E. Hurley (M.A., University of the Pacific) is lecturer in the Department of Communication at Humboldt State University at Arcata, California. Her research interests include radio and television history, aesthetics and programming, classic Hollywood films, and mediated religious rhetoric.

Matthew Lasar (Ph.D., Claremont Graduate School) served through the 1980s as a staff volunteer for the news department of listener-supported radio station KPFA in Berkeley. In 1999, Temple University Press published his dissertation as *Pacifica Radio: The Rise of an Alternative Network*. Lasar has written articles about alternative media and free speech debates for the *Journal of Policy History*, the *Journal of Radio Studies*, *Pacific Historical Review*, and *Current* magazine. He is now working on a second volume on the history of Pacifica Radio.

Michael P. McCauley (Ph.D., Wisconsin) is assistant professor of communication and journalism at the University of Maine. A former radio journalist, he has written articles and book chapters about the history, politics, and philosophy of public broadcasting, the U.S. radio industry's transition to digital technologies, and the role of women in America's early history of broadcasting. McCauley is an Advisory Board member for the Broadcast Pioneers Library of American Broadcasting and serves as an editorial board member for *SIMILE* (Studies in Media and Information Literacy Education). His history of National Public Radio is scheduled for publication in 2003 by Columbia University Press.

Robert W. McChesney (Ph.D., Washington) is associate professor at the Institute for Communications Research of the University of Illinois at Urbana-Champaign. His research focuses on the impact of the globalization and consolidation of mass media on democracy and public life. McChesney has written seven books and more than 100 journal articles and book chapters. His most recent books include *Rich Media, Poor Democracy* (University of Illinois Press, 1999), *Capitalism and the Information Age* (Monthly Review Press, 1998), and *The Global Media* (coauthored with Edward Herman for Cassell, 1997).

Cathy Melio cofounded the Grassroots Radio Coalition (with Marty Durlin) in 1996. She is a media activist, artist, and radio producer who served as general manager of community radio station WERU-FM in Maine from 1995 to 1999. She hosts *Off the Cuff*, a weekly program on WERU, and teaches communication courses at Unity College, Unity, Maine.

Vincent Mosco (Ph.D., Harvard) is professor of communication at Carleton University in Ottawa. A research affiliate with the Harvard University Program on Information Resources Policy, he is also the author of numerous books on the sociological dimensions of mass media, telecommunications, computers, and information technology. His most recent book is *Continental Order? Integrating North America for Cybercapitalism*, edited with Dan Schiller (Rowman and Littlefield, 2001).

Eric E. Peterson (Ph.D., Southern Illinois) is associate professor in the Department of Communication and Journalism at the University of Maine. He has published essays on media consumption in *Critical Studies in Mass Communication* and *American Behavioral Scientist*, on communication diversity in *Communication Education* and *Women and Language*, and on narrative performance in *Narrative Inquiry* and *Text and Performance Quarterly*. His current research focuses on storytelling and narrative in Weblogs and e-zines.

Steve Pierce holds a doctorate in Science and Technology Studies from Rensselaer Polytechnic Institute in Troy, New York. His dissertation research focused on the social and technical infrastructure of community media. Pierce is actively involved in a number of community-based telecommunications projects in the New York Capital District, including the development of the Hudson Mohawk Independent Media Center and negotiations over a cable-based community media and technology center in Troy. He previously lived in New York City, where he worked as executive director of Deep Dish TV and assistant manager for operations at Pacifica radio station WBAI.

Gary P. Poon is the founding principal of DTVision, a consulting firm that advises public broadcasting organizations, commercial companies, and private philanthropic foundations on digital strategies and public service media. Poon was formerly executive director of the Digital Strategic Planning Office and an attorney at PBS. In addition to providing strategic advice to clients, Mr. Poon is also a writer and a frequent guest lecturer at the University of Maryland Business School. The views expressed in his chapter are his own and do not necessarily reflect the opinions of any of his clients.

Vanda Rideout (Ph.D., Carleton) is an assistant professor in the Department of Sociology at the University of New Brunswick, Fredericton. Her research interests include media and communication policy and the impact of information and communication technologies on society. Her recent publications include *Continentalising Canadian Telecommunications: The Politics of Regulatory Reform* (McGill-Queens University Press, forthcoming, 2003); "Public Access to the Internet and the Canadian Digital Divide," *Canadian Journal of Information and Library Sciences* (2000); and (with Andrew Reddick) "A Multi Media Policy for Canada and the United States: Industrial Development as Public Policy," in V. Mosco and D. Schiller, eds., *Continental Order? Integrating North America for Cybercapitalism* (Rowman and Littlefield, 2001).

Amit M. Schejter (Ph.D., Rutgers) is vice president for regulatory affairs at Cellcom Israel Ltd. Prior to that he was an assistant professor at Tel Aviv University's Communication Department and director of legal affairs and international relations for the Israel Broadcasting Authority. His research and teaching interests include mass communication and communications law and policy.

Dan Schiller (Ph.D., Pennsylvania) is a professor in the Institute of Communications Research at the University of Illinois at Urbana-Champaign. He also holds a joint appointment in the Graduate School of Library and Information Science. Schiller's research focuses on the history and political economy of communication. He is the author of *Digital Capitalism: Net-*

working the Global Market System (MIT Press, 1999) and *Theorizing Communication: A History* (Oxford University Press, 1996) and is coeditor (with Vincent Mosco) of *Continental Order? Integrating North America for Cybercapitalism* (Rowman and Littlefield, 2001).

Leslie Regan Shade (Ph.D., McGill) is an assistant professor in the Department of Communication at the University of Ottawa, where she teaches classes on the social, ethical, and policy aspects of media, including new media. Her recent publications include *Gender and Community in the Social Construction of the Internet* (Peter Lang, 2002). She is also coeditor (with Marita Moll) of *E-Commerce vs. E-Commons: Communications in the Public Interest* (Canadian Centre for Policy Alternatives, 2001); (with Sherry Ferguson) of *Civic Discourse and Cultural Politics in Canada: A Cacophony of Voices* (Ablex, 2002); and (with Paul Attallah) of *Mediascapes: New Patterns in Canadian Communication* (Nelson Canada, 2002).

Sandra Smeltzer is a doctoral candidate in communications at Carleton University. Her academic interests include international communications, communications as a social force, and the political economy of new information and communication technologies. She has conducted extensive research in East Africa and Southeast Asia and has an academic background in both anthropology and communications. She has worked for the Department of Canadian Heritage on social and cultural issues dealing with new technologies. Previously, she has lectured at the University of Ottawa and Carleton University and has published in the areas of the privatization of public institutions, Canadian cultural policy, and the economic benefits of cultural expositions.

Jerold M. Starr (Ph.D., Brandeis) is professor of sociology at West Virginia University and executive director of Citizens for Independent Public Broadcasting (www.cipbonline.org), a national membership organization promoting noncommercial educational broadcasting in the public interest. His latest book, *Air Wars: The Fight to Reclaim Public Broadcasting*, was published by Beacon Press (2000) and reissued in paperback by Temple University Press (2001).

Alan G. Stavitsky (Ph.D., Ohio State) is associate dean of the School of Journalism and Communication at the University of Oregon. He teaches and conducts research in the areas of public broadcasting and electronic journalism. Professor Stavitsky is a former broadcast journalist and a frequent consultant in the public radio industry. He is the author of *Independence and Integrity: A Guidebook for Public Radio Journalism* (National Public Radio, 1995).

Index